# Transsexualism and Sex Reassignment

# Transsexualism and Sex Reassignment

### edited by

### *William A. W. Walters*
### *Michael W. Ross*

OXFORD UNIVERSITY PRESS
Oxford New York Toronto
Delhi Bombay Calcutta Madras Karachi
Singapore Hong Kong Tokyo
Nairobi Dar es Salaam Cape Town
Melbourne Auckland
and associates in
Beirut Berlin Ibadan Nicosia

National Library of Australia
Cataloguing-in-Publication data:

Transsexualism and sex reassignment.
Bibliography.
Includes index.
ISBN 0 19 554462 5.

1. Sex change. 2. Transsexuals. I. Walters, William
A. W., 1933–  .  II. Ross, Michael W., 1951–  .

305.3

Edited by Wendy Laffer
Cover designed by Deborah Savin
Typeset by Syarikat Seng Teik Sdn. Bhd., Kuala Lumpur, Malaysia.
Printed by Singapore National Printers
Published by Oxford University Press, 7 Bowen Crescent, Melbourne
OXFORD is a trademark of Oxford University Press

# Contents

# Contributors

**Dr Murray Barson,** MBBS, BMedSci, General Practitioner

**Dr Herbert Bower,** MD, DPM, FRCPsych, FRANZCP, Consultant Psychiatrist at the Melbourne Clinic, the Queen Victoria Medical Centre, and at the Mount Royal Hospital

**Mr Don Burnard,** BA(Hons), TPTC, MAPsS, Clinical Psychologist in Dept of Family Psychiatry, Queen Victoria Medical Centre

**Mr Simon Ceber,** MBBS, FRACS, Assistant Plastic Surgeon, Queen Victoria Medical Centre and Prince Henry's Hospital

**Sister Lorraine Clarke,** SRN, SCM, Queen Victoria Medical Centre

**Ms Georgia Dacakis,** BAppSc, Lecturer, School of Communication Disorders, Lincoln Institute

**Dame Joyce Daws,** DBE, MBBS, FRCS, FRACS, Surgeon, Queen Victoria Medical Centre

**Mr Douglas Graham,** Q.C., LL.B(Hons), Barrister at Law

**Mrs Sue Harding,** DipSocStud, AUA, Social Worker, Commonwealth Rehabilitation Service

**Dr Trudy Kennedy,** MBBS, MRANZCP, DPM, Consultant Psychiatrist to the Queen Victoria Medical Centre

**Ms Lena McEwan,** MBBS, FRCS, FRACS, Plastic Surgeon, Queen Victoria Medical Centre

**Ms Jennifer M. Oates,** MAppSc, MAPsS, Lecturer, School of Communication Disorders, Lincoln Institute

**Ms Donna Riseley,** BA, MSW, DipClinPsych, Student Counsellor, Flinders University

**Dr Michael W. Ross,** BS(Med), MA, PhD, MAPsS, MNZPsS, MBPsS, Senior Demonstrator in Psychiatry, Flinders University Medical School

**Mr Murray Stapleton,** FRACS, Plastic Surgeon, Queen Victoria Medical Centre

**Professor A. W. Steinbeck,** MD, BS, PhD, FRCP, FRACP, Associate Professor of Medicine, University of New South Wales

**Sister Margaret Stubbings,** SRN, Queen Victoria Medical Centre

**Professor William A. W. Walters,** MBBS, PhD, FRCOG, FRACOG, Associate Professor, Dept of Obstetrics & Gynaecology, Monash University

**Ms Elizabeth Wells**

# Acknowledgements

The editors wish to acknowledge the advice and support given by individuals with whom and organizations with which they have been associated in providing total health care for people with gender dysphoria: the Queen Victoria Medical Centre and Monash University, Melbourne; the Flinders Medical Centre and Flinders University, Adelaide; Professors Carl Wood, Ross Kalucy, Richard Ball, Shan Ratnam and Tony Taylor; Drs Jillian Need, Graham Sinclair, Hunter Fry, John Grigor, Ron Barr, Neil Buhrich, John Clayer, Cornelius Greenway, Malcolm Holmes, Harry Imber, James Quinn and Anthony Zorbas; Ms Gwen Graves; Mr Derek Darby; Mr David Lee; Sisters Moira Schwartz and Margaret Havard; the Commonwealth Rehabilitation Service and the Lincoln Institute, Melbourne, and the Victorian Transsexual Coalition.

In the provision of total health care, the contribution made by hospital chaplains is gratefully acknowledged, in particular that of Sister Hilda Ross, of the Community of the Holy Name, and the Reverend Father Gonzales Muñoz at the Queen Victoria Medical Centre, Melbourne.

This book would not have reached the publisher without the expert and dedicated secretarial assistance of Christine Simpson and Janine Judd.

Finally, our thanks are due to Louise Sweetland of Oxford University Press, Melbourne, who brought our efforts and those of the authors to fruition.

*William A. W. Walters*
*Michael W. Ross*

# Preface

During the mid-1970s a situation arose in Australia where it was impossible for transsexuals to obtain sex reassignment surgery anywhere in the country. In the preceding five to ten years a few operations had been performed in Sydney and Melbourne but thereafter, for various reasons, surgical treatment of transsexuals ceased in both cities. Subsequently a few transsexuals were referred to the Queen Victoria Medical Centre, Melbourne, a teaching hospital that had not previously been involved in the care of such patients. In due course, Professor William Walters was asked to establish a gender identity clinic in the hospital with a view to helping transsexuals and others with gender disturbances, and an interdisciplinary team of ten specialists in the medical and paramedical fields was formed. Since the clinic was established in 1976, just over a hundred male-to-female complete gender reassignment procedures and seventeen female-to-male partial gender reassignment procedures have been carried out.

Recently the climate of opinion within the medical and nursing professions and in society at large has changed. As a result, transsexuals are no longer regarded as freaks or perverts but as people with genuine problems deserving of compassion, understanding, and appropriate medical and social management.

This book is the result of the experience of the editors and contributors, who thought that it might be beneficial to make that experience available to other health-care professionals, lawyers, clergy, the police, teachers at secondary and tertiary institutions, interested lay people, and to transsexuals themselves, as well as their relatives and friends. It should also be helpful in the education of students of medical, nursing, and other paramedical sciences, of law, pastoral theology, psychology, sociology, the police force, and schoolteaching. While several aspects of the book relate primarily to Australian conditions, the major part is relevant to transsexualism in all parts of the world.

No claim is made for this book being comprehensive. Rather it is a general overview of transsexualism, which we hope will contribute to a better understanding of this problem in society.

# 1   Gender Identity
## Male, female or a third gender
### Michael W. Ross

Transsexualism is generally understood by the public and by the professions to be a state in which an individual who is biologically and unambiguously a member of one sex is convinced, and has been convinced since childhood, that he or she is in fact a member of the opposite sex. Characteristic also, as a rule, are disgust with the genitals and a desire for genital reassignment. Frequently, such individuals have lived for some time as members of the opposite sex, and, apart from their genitals, the majority are indistinguishable from other members of the sex to which they have assigned themselves.

## Transsexualism as a symptom of gender dysphoria

Recently, the mental health profession has come to regard transsexualism as a symptom of an underlying disorder, rather than as the disorder itself. The underlying disorder is generally gender dysphoria, or a disturbance of gender identity: gender dysphoria is commonly regarded as being primary (present constantly from childhood and to a considerable degree) or secondary (being intermittent or of low strength, and exacerbated by some problem later in life). In many cases of secondary dysphoria, there has been some degree of gender disturbance or dissatisfaction throughout life, but problems such as the break-up of relationships, ageing, or inability to function in the appropriate masculine or feminine role, have brought it to the fore. Unfortunately, many who present for treatment with gender dysphoria have diagnosed their symptom of transsexualism as being the disorder itself, and request gender reassignment surgery as the 'cure'. It is necessary, however, for the professional to set aside this self-diagnosis and prescription for treatment, and to determine a diagnosis from a careful history and from other appropriate investigations. For this reason, we use the term 'transsexualism', in this book, to refer to the presenting symptom (the belief that one is, or should be, a member of the opposite biological sex), and use 'gender dysphoria' to describe the underlying disorder. From this it will be clear that transsexualism may present on occasions where there is no clearcut gender dysphoria.

## History

Transsexualism, as we know it today, has a long and distinguished history extending as far back as the time of the Assyrian King Sardanapalus, who is reported to have dressed in female attire and to have spun with his wives. In the modern sense, perhaps the first clearly documented cases of gender reassignment surgery were those of Lili Elbe (Dresden 1930) and Christine Jorgensen (Copenhagen 1951).[1] The term 'transsexual' was not in common usage until the publication of Benjamin's book, *The Transsexual Phenomenon*, in 1966.[2] More recently, a wealth of papers on the subject has provided a much clearer picture of transsexualism and of its bases for classification. However, in order to understand gender dysphoria and other possible factors influencing the occurrence of transsexualism, it is necessary to examine in some detail the components of sexual identity, both biological and psychological.

## Biological and psychological components of sexual identity

It is commonly believed that individuals are either male or female, both biologically and psychologically. However, it has become increasingly apparent that in some areas, notably biological, there are gradations between the two extremes, and that in other areas,

**Table 1.1 Components of sexual identity**

Psychological

Gender identity (sense of being male or female)
Social sex role (masculinity or femininity)
Public sex role (living or dressing as male or female)
Sexual orientation (homosexual, heterosexual, asexual)
Sex of rearing (brought up as male or female)

Biological

Genetic (presence or absence of Y chromosome)
Gonadal (histological structure of ovary or testis)
Hormonal function (circulating hormones, end-organ sensitivity)
Internal genital morphology (presence or absence of male or female internal structures)
External genital morphology (presence or absence of male or female external genitalia)
Secondary sexual characteristics (body hair, breasts, fat distribution)

including psychological, male and female characteristics may both be present, with one not being the converse of the other. Table 1.1 enumerates the various components of sexual identity: in some individuals these may vary independently, although in the vast majority there is no incongruence. Since transsexualism is defined in terms of the psychological state being incongruent with the biological sex, which is almost always without abnormality, we will discuss psychological aspects of sexuality first, and biological aspects later in this chapter.

## Psychological aspects of sexual identity

### Gender identity
Gender identity is the sense of being a male or female, and is the primary area in which transsexuals are dysphoric. It may vary independently of the other four areas of psychological sexual identity, but in cases of primary gender dysphoria there tend to be abnormalities in all areas of psychological sexual identity. The wish to be a member of the opposite sex is accompanied by the wish to have the genitals ablated or transformed into facsimiles of those of the opposite sex, and the wish to live both publicly and privately as a member of that sex.

### Social sex role
Social sex role refers to what is commonly known as masculinity or femininity, and as such is culturally determined: what is regarded as masculine in one culture may not be in another. Recent evidence has demonstrated that masculinity and femininity, as measured in Western cultures, are not the poles of a single continuum: presence of femininity does not imply a reciprocal lack of masculinity.[3] An individual can possess high levels of both masculinity *and* femininity (androgyny), high levels of one and low of the other (masculine or feminine sex-typed), or low levels of both (undifferentiated state). In some situations, it has been argued, individuals who do not fit into the stereotyped male or female role feel that, because their social sex role in inappropriate, they must therefore be transsexual.[4] Such individuals are often in flight from the aggressive masculine role if male, or the submissive feminine role if female. Certainly more transsexuals present in countries where sex roles are more rigid than in those where they are less so.[5] Whilst most transsexuals with gender dysphoria do adopt the social sex role typical of the opposite sex, deviant social sex role need not be associated with gender dysphoria.

## Public sex role

Public sex role covers cross-dressing in the outer clothes of the opposite sex and attempting to pass as a member of that sex. Most individuals with primary and long-term gender dysphoria will report this occurring, and note that there is a strong sense of relief and comfort whilst cross-dressed. However, this must be distinguished from transvestism, in which cross-dressing is intermittent, there is no conviction of belonging to the opposite sex, and there is often sexual arousal. In general most medical teams will not carry out gender reassignment unless the patient has lived publicly as a member of the opposite sex for a period of time, usually about two years.

## Sexual orientation

Perhaps one of the most common stereotypes of the transsexual is that of the individual who wants to have sex with members of the same sex: that is, homosexuality and transsexualism are confused. In fact, there is a great deal of evidence to suggest that transsexualism may occur in heterosexual, homosexual, bisexual or asexual individuals. For example, Bentler reports that of his group of male-to-female transsexuals, approximately one-third were heterosexual (and therefore, post-operatively, would be lesbian); one-third were homosexual (and therefore, post-operatively, would be heterosexual); and one-third were asexual, and would remain that way post-operatively.[6] While we are aware of changes in sexual orientation following gender reassignment, they are uncommon. Thus it can be seen that sexual orientation and gender dysphoria are functionally independent of one another. Nevertheless, it is not uncommon for individuals who are homosexual to request gender reassignment. Such individuals usually have disturbances of social sex role also and are unable to accept their homosexuality, reasoning that their same-sex partner choice will become acceptable to society only if they themselves change sex and legitimize such a relationship as 'heterosexual'. Fortunately, as homosexuality becomes more widely accepted, such cases become more infrequent.

At this point, mention should also be made of genital dysphoria, which is usually synonymous with gender dysphoria. Very occasionally, however, individuals may present as patients who dislike their genitals intensely and wish to have them ablated without wanting to change sex; conversely, the wish to live as a member of the opposite sex, while retaining the genitals unmodified, may occur. In the former situation, gender dysphoria is not an appropriate diagnosis; in the latter, the diagnosis is probably mimicry of femininity, and gender reassignment is unwarranted. Issues of diagnosis, however, are dealt with fully in chapter 4.

## Sex of rearing

Finally, in some situations individuals may have been brought up as members of the opposite sex for a period of time, due either to being assigned to the wrong sex at birth, or to one parent, usually the mother, bringing up the boy as a girl or vice versa. While this is most uncommon, cases have been reported. More commonly, some parents or caretakers may encourage children to cross-dress or to behave in ways more typical of the opposite sex.

## Summary

It can be seen that the psychological components of sexual identity are frequently independent of one another, and that disturbances of some or all may lead to individuals presenting as transsexuals (that is, with the symptom of wishing to change their sex) without necessarily being primarily gender dysphoric: in such cases, gender dysphoria may be secondary to other disorders of sexual identity. Similarly, it must be emphasized that the view occasionally expressed of transsexuals being a 'third sex' assumes that transsexualism is a single and consistent phenomenon and not a symptom which may have a number of causes.

# Biological components of sexual identity

The very nature of both the biological and psychological components of sexual identity is such that they may be dichotomous (as in the case of internal genital morphology which is either male or female) or continual (as in the case of hormonal function). As a consequence, it is difficult to see primary gender dysphoria as anything other than a psychological disturbance.

It is of particular interest that, of the many transsexuals presenting for treatment, primary gender dysphoria is not the most common diagnosis, nor gender reassignment the most common treatment. Lothstein points out that they are a diverse group[7], and Lothstein and Levine suggest that up to 70 per cent of their transsexual patients, following long-term psychotherapy, do not want gender reassignment surgery.[8] Similarly, Morgan has commented that of presenting transsexuals 10 per cent will have a major mental illness, 30 per cent will be homophobic (anti-homosexual) homosexuals, and 20–25 per cent will be sexually inadequate individuals with ambiguous gender identity.[9] The remaining 35–40 per cent will probably be individuals with primary gender dysphoria, for whom gender reassignment surgery may be the treatment of choice.

From the point of view of transsexuals themselves, however,

gender reassignment surgery is seen as the only answer to their problems and many firmly hold the belief that their symptoms and condition are biologically determined. Such a belief allows them to avoid attributing any responsibility for their condition to themselves or to others close to them and, more importantly, presents the condition as immutable and unmodifiable: 'biology is destiny'. It is therefore important to look at biological components of sexual identity with regard to transsexualism and gender dysphoria, and to query the existence of a biological basis for the psychological components of sexual identity.

## Genetics

Many individuals assume that the genetic component of the body, as reflected in analysis of body cell chromosomes, defines whether it is male or female. Generally, the presence or absence of a Y chromosome will determine whether the individual is male or female, but this is not always the case. There may be individuals who are genetically male, possessing 46 chromosomes in each body cell of which one sex chromosome is an X chromosome and the other a Y chromosome, yet who have a female body and are physically indistinguishable from females to the casual observer. Conversely individuals who are genetically female, possessing 46 chromosomes in each body cell of which both sex chromosomes are X chromosomes, may subsequently develop as males. This may occur as a result of a number of disorders described below under hormonal function. Clearly the genetic programme may be overridden by other factors, and it is as inappropriate to define an individual by his/her chromosomal constitution as by his/her physical appearance: neither is definitive. This is particularly obvious in cases of genetic mosaics, where some cells in an individual's body may have X and Y chromosomes and others two X chromosomes but no Y chromosome.

## Gonadal structure

In cases where there may be a mosaic of male and female genetic types, the actual structure of the cells in the gonads (testes or ovaries) is the defining principle. In some situations, testes or ovaries may be present as gross structures, but on microscopic examination it may be found that they are not composed of appropriate cell-types and thus may not function as gonads. If there are no gonadal structures appropriate at a microscopic level to define the individual as unequivocally male or female, the biological definition of gender is difficult.

## Hormonal function

In those situations in which an individual may be genetically male or female but where some abnormality altered the hormonal system during development so that the genotypic expression was blocked, the individual may have a body develop which is typical of the opposite gender. One example of this is congenital adrenal hyperplasia, a condition in which the adrenal glands secrete excess androgens which produce a male body and genitals in a genetic female. In genetic males, a disorder known as testicular femininization may produce an apparent female: this may occur because the target organs are insensitive to androgens. Thus, levels of hormones circulating during early physical development and the response of the target organs to such hormonal stimulation may both determine the final outcome. Where genetic and hormonal factors are at variance, it is often the hormonal variables that determine the final physical development, at least in terms of the foetus.

## Internal genital morphology

In some cases, the internal organs may be absent, as in the case where Turner's syndrome (the absence of one X chromosome in the female) exists. The presence of appropriate internal genital structures is not critical in terms of definition of gender, but may be a useful adjunct to other biological variables.

## External genital morphology

The structure of the genital organs (penis and scrotum in males; vagina, clitoris and labia in females) is commonly used to determine the sex of the infant at birth. As noted in the discussion of hormonal function, however, this may depend more on the hormonal status of the developing foetus than on its genetic constitution. In cases where the genital organs are ambiguous, the individual's chromosomal status is generally used to assess the appropriate gender. However, if the genital organs appear unambiguous, the individual is usually reared according to genital sex, irrespective of chromosomal status.

## Secondary sexual characteristics

The secondary sexual characteristics include the extent and distribution of body hair, distribution of body fat, presence of breasts, nipple size and pigmentation, and depth of voice. These characteristics, unlike the morphology of the genital organs, may be influenced by hormone administration after birth. In transsexuals, depending on when hormones have been administered, body shape may be altered to some degree. The longer after puberty hormones are first administered, however, the smaller the effect as a rule.

## Conclusion

Thus, a number of potentially independent and variable measures may be used to determine the sex of an individual. Where genetic constitution and external genital organs are incongruous, for whatever reason, it is usual to rear such individuals as members of the sex appropriate for their bodies rather than for their genetic constitution. However, almost without exception, transsexuals are biologically normal members of their sex; if they are biologically abnormal, a diagnosis other than primary gender dysphoria would be indicated. Symptoms of transsexualism are characteristically psychological in nature rather than biological, but it is important to realize that biological contributions may be as inconsistent as psychological ones to the components of sexual identity.

# 2   The View from Within

## What it feels like to be a transsexual

### Elizabeth Wells

In William Golding's novel *Free Fall*, a young man asks the girl he is in love with, 'What is it like to be you?' At least one psychiatrist has quoted the passage to illustrate the normal curiosity we all have about what it must be like to be someone else. Far more significant for me was the girl's reply: 'Just ordinary'. I remember when I read it, thinking how wonderful it would be to feel like that—whole, integrated, all-of-a-piece, ordinary. And to be able to take it for granted! It was almost too much for me to comprehend, since all my life I had felt myself to be very un-ordinary. Unlike the girl in Golding's novel (and, it seemed to me, the rest of the world), I was at total odds with my body, a person divided. To all appearances I was male. But I knew I was female.

That was a long time ago, when I was living in what might be called my first stage. I often wish there were three terms for 'transsexual', one for each of the three stages: 'needing to cross over', 'crossing over', and 'having crossed over'. I think many fulfilled transsexuals see it like that. Certainly each stage has its own problems, and makes different demands upon us. For me, the worst time was that long, hopeless, pre-surgery, pre-transformation period of my life. To try to describe how I felt then is a little like trying to describe a new colour that nobody else can see. There never was a blinding flash of light when I suddenly realized what my problem was. Recognition of it seemed to come gradually over several years—from about age four to about age seven. I remember once wondering if all small boys felt the same way, but it soon became plain to me that they didn't. I seemed to be the only one, so I said nothing.

In those early years, my days were well filled with the business of eating, sleeping, going to school, drawing, dreaming. Probably the full significance of my problem had still to dawn on me, since I was still able, to some extent, to put it to one side. It would only get in the way when I wanted to do something that 'boys didn't do'—though there seemed to be a growing number of those. Later it became more persistent, and there were times when it was actually frightening. Those moments are the most difficult of all to describe. They would occur anywhere—at home, at school, or while I was playing. Suddenly the strangest feeling would engulf me like a wave.

If I were walking along, the intensity of it would stop me in my tracks. It wasn't pain, or nausea, or giddiness, but an overwhelming sensation of uncleanness, of not belonging—to anything or anyone, family, friends, the planet, or even myself. There seemed to me *space* between me and the body I stood in, like a skeleton in a suit of armour lined with something unpleasant. I didn't fit. It was awful. Mercifully it would last only a minute or two and then fade. Afterwards, if anyone asked I would just say I'd felt a bit sick. It didn't seem to cause anyone any concern, though for a while it was happening almost daily. I never told anyone about it because I knew by then what was wrong.

I can't speak for all transsexuals on every aspect of the condition, but I believe every transsexual knows only too well the feeling I experienced during those awful moments of seeming to hang in space: 'I am in the wrong body.' For that is the feeling. To someone who has known only the harmony of body and inner identity— 'ordinariness'—the idea is absurd. All those years ago it was even more absurd. If I'd revealed to anyone what my feelings really were, they would have told me to face the facts—I was a boy. My face, my body, my name, my birth certificate, all proclaimed my sex as male. How could I, in the face of such proof, deny it and insist that in fact I was female? But I was: and it was more than just a wish or a preference—I *knew* it. Though if anyone had believed me, what could have been done about it? Transsexualism had not been heard of then. Even sex was a forbidden word. I never told my mother, to whom I was able to tell most things. Telling my father was out of the question—for me he was someone to avoid. I had to keep the secret to myself. I suppose I thought my dilemma might be resolved somehow one day, or possibly fade away.

My three years in the army were pretty uncomfortable. The policy was to make me tough, masculine, and aggressive—the exact opposite of what I wanted to be. I did my best, having no choice in the matter, and with luck and sheer willpower managed to keep up with the rest. I liked many of my companions, and constantly envied their unconscious 'wholeness'. Apparently I projected a suitable image, because I seemed to be accepted as one of them. To all appearances I *was* one of them. But in fact I was separate, apart, 'a spy in the enemy camp', as someone has put it. I knew I didn't belong. A few times I invited a girl to the movies or to a party. It was partly to keep up appearances, I suppose, and perhaps also a half-hearted attempt to go through the motions in the hope that I might learn to prefer the male role. And also because I *liked* women; I liked their company, the way they saw things. I felt they were more honest than men, and with a more finely tuned perception. They very quickly sensed that I was not one of the mainstream males, and no doubt made the obvious assumption. But I wasn't homosexual, either. I had nothing against homosexuality—it just wasn't for me.

Out of the army, I threw myself into all kinds of strenuous activities—deep-sea fishing, mining, sawmilling, truck-driving. I hardly knew why; I certainly wasn't built for them. I suppose I was trying to force myself into masculinity, seeing no other course of action open to me. But apart from travelling the world and meeting a lot of people, my efforts were exhausting and futile, and brought me no nearer to a solution. Indeed, I seemed to be worse off than before, with my frustration greater than ever. The problem came between me and everything. If I tried to study or concentrate, it loomed in front of me. I found myself asking angrily over and over, 'Why me? Why me?' Somehow I contained it. No one, not even my closest friends, ever guessed my problem, or suspected that I had one, so successfully and desperately did I hide it. I often think about all those unknown transsexuals, millions throughout history, who must have lived with the same secret anguish.

As the years went by my distress continued to worsen. The bouts of depression I had managed to hide became periods of black despair, sometimes lasting for days at a time. I would withdraw into myself and sit drinking, filled with self-hate. Twice I came very close to suicide, which I thought would provide a quick and glorious release. Finally I could bear it no longer. I told my doctor. He was genuinely surprised, having known me for years as 'a calm, well-balanced person', and listened with much patience and sympathy while I poured it all out. I felt as if I'd been holding my breath all my life, and at last had been able to let go of it.

The first specialist I saw wanted to give me aversion therapy. But it seemed to me to be based on a false assumption: that the *real* me was my body, the visible part of me. I couldn't see it that way. My body was indeed only a *part* of me—it wasn't me. As far as I was concerned the real me (to which all other aspects of me, I felt, should be subordinate) was inside, unseen, unseeable—which made the nature of its identity harder to establish than the sex of my body, I admit, but *I* knew what it was. If that were to be bullied into submission there'd be nothing of me left. So I refused the offer. The next specialist actually appeared to believe me. The relief was enormous. At last I felt there was some hope of resolving my predicament. A feeling of optimism (a new experience) began to stir within me. I was about to enter a new phase.

My thoughts now turned to the question of surgery. In order to be accepted by a public hospital for the operation I wanted (I couldn't afford to pay for it to be done privately) I had to satisfy a medical team as to my suitability on a number of counts: was I emotionally stable? I assumed I was. If this meant could I control my emotions, then I was a 'Rock of Gibraltar'. Was I aware of the irreversibility of the operation? I was—I'd done everything I could to live as a man, and hated it. Why would I ever want to return to all that misery? Could I live and work as a woman? I was sure that I could, but I had yet to find out. I was self-employed in a field where one's gender was irrelevant. This was fortunate, because I don't think I would have found the courage to make the change in the 'spotlight', on 'centre stage', as some of my friends have done. I needed to learn 'the part' first, to disappear into the 'wings' and, after a decent interval, emerge as a 'woman'.

One day I took off my men's clothes for the last time. I remember thinking how symbolic the act was of all I was casting off. And in my new role I took a small apartment in a district where I was unknown. I was painfully conscious of my appearance. I didn't expect to challenge Raquel Welch, but would I *pass*? After all, I had lived in a fairly male body for most of my life, and had worked hard to make all my movements and gestures appear as confidently masculine as I could. These were habits I would now have to unlearn. The first time I actually walked down the street in my new clothes I was half-expecting lightning to strike me, and people to stare in horror and point at me with loathing. But nothing happened—no one even noticed me. The physical shortcomings that had handicapped me so much as a man—slender frame, narrow shoulders, small hands and feet—were now happily working in my favour. It was wonderful. But the most surprising thing was that even after a lifetime of living as a man, I didn't feel the least awkward or out of place. My clothes didn't feel strange or unfamiliar. They felt *right*. In fact, the whole feeling was so much one of rightness that I forgot all about the historic significance of the occasion, and found myself looking into a delicatessen shop and wondering if I needed more bread.

Another aspect of my change also brought a pleasant surprise. All my life I had trained myself not to say anything too spontaneously in case I inadvertently revealed my secret in some way—perhaps by an unmasculine phrase or observation that might be considered 'suspect'. Now I found that I needed to stop censoring whatever I wanted to say. I just let the phrases come out, and they sounded fine.

I think I learned a lot about myself in that first year or so of living as a woman. So also, I assume, did the medical people. In their meticulous search for some measurable mental or physical clue, I was x-rayed, blood-tested, personality-tested, photographed and electroencephalographed. I don't know if they found anything untoward. During it all I would find myself speculating about the experts who conducted all the tests so inscrutably. Did they have any feelings about transsexuality one way or the other? Was I just one more patient to fit in before lunch? Or another pervert wasting their valuable time and equipment? Surely they'd heard some of the things that had been said about us—'They only want the operation so they can become prostitutes', 'misguided homosexuals', 'unreliable, unco-operative, and ungrateful'.

Aware that this attitude was not uncommon, I wasn't surprised that one or two of my friends, on learning of my change, regarded it with suspicion and distaste. None of my women friends was the least put out by it. I got the impression they somehow rather approved of it, and were perhaps even a little flattered. It was only a few males who seemed to find it hard to accept me (though most did, with a heart-warming readiness). I tried to imagine their feelings. Did they feel threatened by the idea of it? Perhaps betrayed by my sudden and unaccountable action? What I was forgetting was that I had spent a lifetime thinking about it—for them it was totally unexpected. I was a 'turncoat' whom they needed time to reclassify and even, perhaps, to forgive. I did all I could to soften their ordeal of 're-meeting' me. I felt the need to reassure them that I wasn't a danger to their children or planning to overthrow society. So, with each of them, after the first hesitant greeting (there was usually a good deal of apprehension on both sides) I would try to be as matter-of-fact about it all as I could, and act as if nothing much had changed—at least, not for the worse. There had simply been a correction, necessary but essentially harmless. Most of them were marvellous, and clearly relieved to find me quite presentable and not at all like Dracula's mother, with 'the person inside' whom they had known before still there. But of course 'the person inside' didn't need changing. Even so, I didn't fully realize how incomprehensible it must have been to them until I read a book by a female-to-male transsexual. While being wholly sympathetic, I found I just couldn't *imagine* why the writer would want such a change (from female to male). And I began to appreciate how generously my friends, and especially my male friends, had accepted the revised me.

After I was notified that I had been accepted for surgery and was on the long waiting list, I spent a further two years in my state of sexual limbo. It was a condition not without its hazards. I worried about what would happen if I were in an accident, or suddenly taken ill. Would I be put in the men's ward? What if I were arrested (though chronically law-abiding, I occasionally needed to enter a ladies toilet, thereby technically breaking the law)—with whom would I share a cell? During this period I was asked by a close female friend who was aware of my previous indifference towards sex-as-an-activity: 'Since you seem to be living so successfully as a woman already, do you think the operation will make very much difference to you?' The only way I could get across to her how I felt was to ask her: 'Suppose you, a happy and secure female, woke up tomorrow to discover you had male genitals . . . what would *your* reaction be?' True I'd had little interest in sex before, for obvious reasons. But now, my steadily-growing confidence in my new role, and a brief encounter of the romantic kind, allowed me to hope that I might one day experience a relationship that was more than just friendship. Surgery would enable me to respond as a woman as well as to live as one. But it was even more than that: I was still incomplete, unresolved. While my face and figure had subtly changed through hormone therapy, there remained one part of me that was not me. I was still in the wrong body.

I began the business of redocumenting myself under my new name—bank account, electoral roll, driving licence, taxation department, medical insurance. Each confrontation had its hurdles, and often its funny side too. With each step I felt I was consolidating my new life, like furnishing an empty house one piece at a time. My days settled into a routine. I would work until five or six in the afternoon, and then go for a walk in the park and look at the sky and the boats and the 'normal' people, all innocently aware of their good fortune. Though I was certain that all would be well in the end, the months of waiting were punctuated by periods of intense depression. I felt old and foolish. The years had sped by while I'd wasted my life in hating myself and struggling to keep up appearances. Had I left it all too late? Was I a washout anyway? Then some compliment or little act of kindness would lift me out of depression and remind me of how lucky I was and how far I'd come. I would just have to hang on and try to think positively. The great day was getting closer. When it arrived at last, I felt perfectly calm, filled with the happiness of certainty. I felt no doubts, no regrets, no hesitation. This was it, the final step in my transformation, the miracle I wanted more than anything in the world.

A miracle it was indeed! When I came out of the anaesthetic I felt thirsty, groggy, and simply wonderful. I was through the looking-glass, in a magic place. Everything seemed to be charged with some cosmic significance, to take on a special meaning. The ward was paradise and every nurse an angel. What had been a perfectly unremarkable tree in the courtyard outside had become an enchanted tree. I suddenly saw through Monet's eyes—beds, windows, chairs, even shadows that glowed with colour. The grey building opposite was a palace, its dilapidated chimneys a sultan's turrets. I sat spellbound, propped up on my pillows like a tipsy Miss Havisham, exuding goodwill. I'm sure all those infinitely kind nurses decided I was quite dotty, and I probably was. One of them found me in tears one morning and did her best to comfort me. It was several minutes before I could explain that I was crying for joy. I don't know if all transsexuals feel their final release as intensely as I did. For me those two weeks were the happiest of my life. Over the following few months my euphoria subsided to a manageable level, though the feeling of being reborn persisted. The world looked so much better now, and was filled with all kinds of possibilities. I discovered that I could think more clearly and work far more productively.

Sometimes I look back at that 'other person' I used to be, and it seems to me that the real tragedy of the problem was that it had stifled so much of my potential. So ever-present was it over the years that it had claimed all my attention. I was almost totally self-centred because of it, impatient with other people's problems (they looked so trivial compared with mine), bitter about my own, and cynical and negative. So much time and effort had been wasted. In many ways I had never grown up. It's a wonder I had any friends at all. Yet I still have most of them. And I've made a lot of new ones, people who have never known me as anyone but the person they see now. Some know about me, and some don't. If they guess (I always assume they do), they apparently decide that it doesn't matter, for which I am thankful.

I've been told that I'm a more mellow human being than I was. I hope it means nicer—I always felt there was so *much* room for improvement. I think if I'd had the change earlier in life, at an age of greater emotional resilience, I'd have been able to un-cramp more of myself. As it is, a lot of the previous me remains. I still tend to look on, rather than join in—though now with a more concerned and empathetic eye, a warmer regard. I respond to things far more emotionally that I used to. Babies and small children I find especially poignant. I smile at strangers, and keep wanting to give things to people. At moments of over-enthusiasm I suppose I can be a 'bit of a pain in the neck' to some people. Still, I'm not as unreliable as I was, or as unco-operative. And I *am* grateful—to all those whose patience, skill, and goodwill have helped to give me a second chance. Life looks pretty good to me now, and I suspect the best may be to come yet. You never know, one morning I may wake up feeling 'just ordinary'.

# 3  Causes of Gender Dysphoria
## How does transsexualism develop and why?
### Michael W. Ross

While the most common history given by the gender dysphoric patient is one of wishing to be a member of the opposite sex to that assigned them at birth and of this wish being consistent and persistent over a long period of time, there may be number of reasons for this situation. Just as we can distinguish primary and secondary gender dysphorias, so we can distinguish a number of postulated or potential reasons for the wish to be a member of the opposite sex. It is a grave mistake to assume that because the symptom presenting to the medical practitioner is the same (that of wanting to change sex), there is a similar cause for each case. Just as the causes of the symptom of chest pain may range from a coronary attack to hiatus hernia, so the causes of the symptom of transsexualism may be many and varied. While it is convenient to look for these in the areas of biology, family, psychology and social conditions, it is most likely that there will be significant interactions between several of such variables, and that it will not be possible, even in the individual case, to point to a single clear cause. In fact, research attempts to elucidate the causes of transsexualism in the past invariably have led to inconclusive results largely because it was assumed that there was a single cause for a single symptom. It may well be that there are different types of gender dysphoria, some with biological contributors, some with familial contributors, and some with primarily psychological or social contributors. Until a study and interpretation of types of gender dysphoria can be developed which differentiates subtypes on the basis of variations in presentation and psychodynamics (the underlying causes for psychological symptoms) and which is able to differentiate subtypes empirically in terms of causation, little progress is likely to be made. Nevertheless, in the fairly extensive literature already extant on transsexualism, there is a body of data which provides a number of indications as to what some of the precipitating factors may be. As has been said, while it is possible that an interaction of co-factors may occur, it is probably conceptually easier to examine possible causes in terms of the biology, family, social environment and psychological structure of the gender dysphoric individual.

# Biological factors

This area has been exhaustively examined over the past three decades during which the growth of the clinical phenomenon of transsexualism and that of laboratory science in the areas of endocrinology and genetics have paralleled each other.

## Genetic influences

Generally, genetic studies of transsexuals have proved negative in terms of abnormal chromosomal constitution (karyotype) although cases of Klinefelter's syndrome (47, XXY) and XYY karyotype have been reported, as have cases of XX–XY mosaicism. Chromosomal abnormalities, however, are the exception rather than the rule, and appear to occur in transsexual populations with about the same frequency as in the general population. So far there is no evidence for a genetic explanation of transsexualism.

## Hormonal influences

More attention has been paid to possible endocrinological explanations of transsexualism. In a series of elegant and perceptive reviews of the hormonal bases of both gender identity and sexual orientation, Meyer-Bahlburg has examined the available evidence.[1] He notes that most endocrinological researchers have put forward the same theories to explain both homosexuality and transsexualism, ignoring the evidence which demonstrates that these are two distinct conditions without any necessary connection. In terms of theories which suggest that there are differences in circulating hormones in transsexuals, there is no evidence of lowered testosterone in transsexual or homosexual men. Nor have differences been demonstrated in testosterone as a function of degree of femininity in homosexuals, or in levels of oestrogen. Data on females are less consistent but there is no clear evidence of abnormalities of circulating hormones in homosexuals or transsexuals.

With regard to rat models of sexual development, several theorists, such as Dörner,[2] have suggested that some areas of the central nervous system (particularly the medial preoptic and anterior hypothalamic regions in males, and the ventro-medial hypothalamus in females) may be differentially stimulated by prenatal or perinatal hormones and predisposed to develop in the direction typical of the opposite sex. However, Meyer-Bahlburg points out that, for humans, the model predicts that prenatal androgen deficiency in males will lead to feminine behaviour with normal plasma testosterone levels in adulthood.[3] This is consistent with sexual behaviour found in the rat model, but clearly in adults humans sexual behaviour and gender identity are quite different concepts. In the case of the female rat model, the theory does not even fit the rat data, since in female rats same-gender sexual behaviour will occur only after gonadectomy and androgen administration in adulthood. In addition, hormone administration alters the genitals in rats but does not do so in humans. As Meyer-Bahlburg emphasizes, not only does the theory not fit the known facts about rats in some cases, but it is also impossible to generalize large sections of it from rats to humans because of differences between the two species.

There is, however, in humans, much more direct evidence which disproves the prenatal hormonal theories of gender dysphoria and homosexuality. In endocrine syndromes with prenatal hormone abnormalities, such as congenital adrenal hyperplasia (a condition in which excess androgens are produced) in women (regardless of whether there was early or late treatment), there was no predominance of homosexuality or gender dysphoria.[4] Similarly, in follow-up studies of women exposed to excess androgen *in utero*, there has been no evidence of gender dysphoria or homosexuality.[5] There has been a great deal of publicity given to Dörner's suggestion that in males, an oestrogen surge in response to luteinizing hormone (LH) priming (typical in females) is evidence that the central nervous system has been organized in a typically female pattern by prenatal hormonal abnormalities. Yet not only have his results suggesting that this occurs in male homosexuals not been replicated, but two studies have demonstrated that in males with androgen insensitivity syndrome (testicular feminization), whose hypothalami are androgen-insensitive, this does not affect hypothalamic development and the LH response is not female-like but male-like (that is, oestrogen is suppressed rather than increased).[6] Such patients have a female identity and female heterosexual orientation but male LH dynamics. It must therefore be concluded that there is as yet no evidence to support the theory of abnormalities in central nervous system development as a result of prenatal or perinatal hormone abnormalities.

Similarly, it has been argued that a report by Imperato-McGinley *et al.*, which described the transformation of males with 5-α reductase deficiency who were raised as 'females', developed male sexual characteristics at puberty, and subsequently shifted to the male role, supports the argument that hormones play a part in gender identity.[7] Unfortunately, as Meyer-Bahlburg[8] and others have pointed out, not only was this phenomenon known and such individuals referred to by a special term in the Dominican Republic, where the data were gathered, but the change could also be better explained by the cognitive dissonance theory, and by examination of the differential status of males and females in the Dominican Republic. In addition, Meyer-Bahlburg notes that were the changes based on hormonal, that is, brain-activating mechanisms, they would not have covered a ten-year range. He concludes that all the evidence in this situation demonstrates that the changes in gender identity and social sex roles which Imperato-McGinley *et al.* report are based on the effects of hormones on the body (and particularly genital development), on self-perception, and not on directly hormone-mediated changes in the central nervous system. In summary, there is no evidence to date that endocrinological factors feature among the causes of gender dysphoria or of homosexuality.

## Theories of brain dysfunction

There has been some parallel theorizing which suggests that there may be higher incidence of gross brain dysfunction in transsexuals. As far back as 1965, Wålinder reported that over one-third of transvestites had abnormal electroencephalograms (EEGs), of which half were focused on the temporal lobes.[9] Similarly, Hoenig and Kenna found EEG abnormalities in 48 per cent of transsexuals, with a further 24 per cent of subjects showing evidence of borderline EEG abnormalities.[10]

It is difficult to interpret these findings: Alanko and Achté note that there was no evidence of transsexualism in Finnish brain-injured war veterans, despite the fact that over 41 per cent were epileptic and over 8 per cent psychotic.[11] Some more general evidence which suggests that there is no consistent biological basis for gender dysphoria is provided by Ross *et al.*, who found that there were marked variations in the incidence of transsexualism across similar Western cultures:[12] were there a biological basis, rates would be expected to be fairly similar between like societies. While at present there is no evidence to suggest a biological basis for gender dysphoria, it is premature to rule out completely either a biological–environmental interaction or the fact that there may be some cases or subgroups of transsexuals with biological involvement. Such speculation, while not supported by present theories and data, may receive support from techniques, analyses and theories yet to be developed. On the other hand, the insistence by some individuals, both transsexuals and medical scientists, that gender dysphoria is biologically determined is an entirely different matter. Such a belief on the part of transsexuals themselves is often an indication that they do not want to question the origins of their condition or explore its causes and development: such individuals are often unwilling to accept any responsibility for their gender dysphoria and will not entertain any attempts to change it. Professionals who believe that gender disorders are biologically determined may also be attempting to justify the continuation of gender reassignment surgery without too close an examination of the bases of gender dysphoria in particular patients. It is important to separate belief and fact in such cases, and to recognize the difference between individuals having a need to believe in biological determinism, on the one hand, and the scientific support for theories of biological causation on the other. Of course, the same applies to beliefs in environmental causation. Given the controversy aroused by debate on the issue of the causes of transsexualism in the past decade, making this distinction may help avoid unproductive dispute and help us recognize that the concept of causation may subsume a number of personal meanings for individuals, not just the impersonal findings from the examination of scientific data.

## Familial theories

While there is little if any evidence to support a biological basis for gender dysphoria, there is some evidence to support the argument that, in some cases of transsexualism, there is a degree of family pathology. Such pathologies include findings that there is decreased masculinity in boys with absent fathers,[13] although other researchers have reported no differences between homosexual and transsexual men in terms of the unreplaced loss of mother or father before the age of thirteen years.[14] On the other hand. Halle *et al.* reported that one-third of their transsexual subjects were from families reared by maternal grandmothers who often encouraged cross-dressing.[15] The familial pattern noted by Buhrich and McConaghy included the fact that the mothers of male transsexuals and transvestites wanted a daughter more often than did other mothers, and while there was no evidence of an abnormal relationship with the mother, there was a trend for fathers to lack interest in their children.[16] More specifically, Uddenberg *et al.* found that half of their male-to-female patients had warm and close contact with the mother and poor contract with the father throughout childhood, adolescence and adulthood: however, it is difficult to determine whether this is a cause or effect of femininity in their sons.[17]

The major difficulty in looking for consistencies in the parental rearing patterns experienced by transsexuals is the fact that transsexuals are grouped on the basis of their symptoms rather than on the basis of any common causes for the symptoms. In some cases, it has been assumed that a high level of femininity in boys is sufficient to diagnose subsequent gender dysphoria, although Green has noted that while feminine boys prefer to be like their mothers, most of them, on follow-up, turn out to be homosexual rather than transsexual.[18] Of interest in this context, however, is the finding by Hellman *et al.* that the parents of transsexuals tend to be more religious and more homophobic than the parents of homosexuals, and that transsexual characteristics increase at intermediate rather than high levels of femininity.[19] These findings also suggest that it is unlikely to be of much benefit to look at heterogeneous groups of transsexuals, but that it is important to distinguish gender dysphorics in terms of differing psychodynamics which may produce transsexual symptoms but which may be diametrically opposed in terms of causation. For this reason, it is probably better to look at the causes of transsexualism in terms of the differing psychodynamics of parental relationships rather than to look for constants in such relationships.

## Psychodynamics of gender dysphorias

The fact that a large number (up to 70 per cent)[20] of individuals who present for gender reassignment may be able to give up their request for surgical procedures and come to terms with their gender dysphoria, strongly suggests that the disorder is not biologically determined and that psychodynamic considerations in many cases may determine the request for surgery. Familial data are not consistent, although they do suggest that the psychodynamics of gender dysphorias are related to parental rearing practices in childhood. Lebovitz, for example, found that age of onset was the best predictor of transsexualism; three of six boys with early onset of symptoms (less than six years old) became transsexuals, one a transvestite, and two homosexual, and the vast majority of his sample (fourteen of sixteen) saw their fathers as negative.[21] This does suggest that attention should be paid to the very early psychodynamics of upbringing, although this is the very area which patients are least likely to be able to remember.

Generally, there are two psychodynamic formulations of the aetiology of gender dysphorias. Green[22] and Stoller[23] have suggested that the essential psychodynamic processes producing gender identity conflicts in boys include excessive identification with their mothers as a result of their inability to separate from their mothers' bodies. They suggest that while the normal processes of child development include the infant moving farther and farther away from mother as it gains autonomy, in the case of gender dysphorics the mother is unable to permit such freedom and treats the infant as if it were part of her own body. This failure to separate, according to both Stoller and Green, is often brought about by the mother keeping the infant close to her body far more often than in normal Western mother–infant relationships. On the other hand, there are societies, including some North American Indian ones, in which mothers keep the child close to the body for a number of years and yet there does not appear to be a greater incidence of gender dysphoria in such cultures. In terms of early childhood psycho-dynamics, Lothstein has delineated a number of scenarios which may lead to gender dysphorias: it is particularly important to note that he suggests that seemingly opposite results can come from similar situations, and similar results from apparently dissimilar situations, rather than that there is a universal dynamic.[24] In this regard, he has probably come closer than previous researchers to describing a varied set of conditions which may lead to a similar state of gender dysphoria. Lothstein argues that the mother's contribution to her son's gender dysphoria is profound, whether she is too distant or too close, too engulfing or too aggressive. If there are extremes of maternal reaction, the patient who is gender dysphoric will yearn to reunite (if mother is too aggressive) or feel ambivalently fused (if she is too engulfing). Female-to-male patients, as well, usually see mother as a bad object or at least very ambivalently.

There are a number of ways elucidated by Lothstein in which the transsexogenic (transsexual-creating) mother may create gender dysphoria in her offspring. First, following the scheme put forward by Stoller and by Green, the transsexual's mother will allow her child to separate from her, but in non-gender-related ways, since she will be unable to tolerate her son's masculine identity and will see it as a threat to her own identity. Thus, Lothstein argues, the projection of the mother's pathological internal conflicts on to the child may lead to gender identity disturbance. Second, he notes, gender dysphoria may arise from the loss of close objects and from separations: where the individual is socially isolated and has limited socialization, there may be an attempt to reunite with the lost object by taking on its characteristics. Third, for some individuals, male-ness may be synonymous with aggression: taking a female identity may be a way of controlling anger and destructive drives, and receiving love as a female which was unacceptable as a male. In the case of the female-to-male patient, the female role may be associated with passivity and helplessness. Fourth, there may be rebirth fan-tasies associated with the idea that death or loss may be cheated and that the mother may be kept alive by accepting a female role. Fifth, there may be either gender envy of the opposite sex or, alternatively, bodily disgust with the male body. Such individuals can be distinguished because those with gender envy are indifferent to their genitals, whereas those with bodily disgust actively dread them. Finally, gender dysphoria may be an attempt to ward off decompensation and psychological breakdown which occurs from a lack of core gender identity and defective self-identity: opposite-sex gender identity thus serves as a protective shield. Levine notes in a case history that, in some instances, the frantic search for meaningful identities may encompass gender identity if there have been early disturbances in significant relationships.[25] It can thus be seen that there are a number of possible psychodynamic routes to gender dysphoria, and that they need not necessarily occur in childhood.

Secondary gender dysphoria is the term given to those cases in which the transsexualism is secondary to some other disorder. It occurs later in life than early childhood and may often involve psychodynamic or psychopathological antecedents. For example, Morgan reports that about 10 per cent of those requesting gender reassignment will have a diagnosable major mental illness, including delusions, 30 per cent will be homophobic homosexuals, and some 20–25 per cent will be sexually ambiguous, inadequate personalities who need changes in their life and life structures.[26] Morgan goes on to ask whether inadequacy with a vagina is superior to inadequacy with a penis, and notes that in all these cases the diagnosis is a pejorative one, and that, with the increasing medicalization of transsexualism, we may simply be acceding to a less pejorative diagnosis in some cases where we should have the courage to make a more accurate but less socially acceptable one such as homosexuality or personality disorder. In a similar vein, Prince has commented that transsexualism should be seen as a communicable disease.[27] Her suggestion that gender reassignment surgery is often grasped as the answer to problems which appear around the same time as contact with or publicity about transsexual surgery is a perceptive one, and clinicians who note an increase in referrals to gender clinics following publicity about gender reassignment surgery would tend to agree. Secondary gender dysphoria is distinguishable aetiologically by the fact that there will have been mild to moderate gender identity problems in childhood and adolescence, but that there will be a clear set of precipitating factors, such as more recent object losses or separations, stresses, or identity crises such as imprisonment, break-up of relationships, parental death, job loss or ageing.

Ageing serves as a good illustration of a precipitating factor in secondary gender dysphorias. Steiner et al. characterize the middle-aged transsexual (aged 40–65 years) as attempting to escape from the pressures of the mid-life crisis, depressed, and approaching what they term the 'male menopause'.[28] Such individuals are often also trying to escape from the difficulties of a long-standing transvestite existence. Lothstein, while commenting specifically on the older transsexual, makes a number of points which have application for cases of late-onset gender dysphoria (after about the age of twenty years).[29] He notes that an ageing body may also denote a worthless self, a need for a lover to counter loneliness (especially in males who see the masculine role as unable to accommodate accepting love), withdrawal from objects, displacement of anxieties to the body, and last chances to resolve pre-existing gender conflicts. While such individuals often provide a history of difficulty in establishing a gender role appropriate to their biological sex, they often also display heightened anxiety about a masculine identity and take refuge in being passive and feminine. Wålinder and colleagues have also noted, in this regard, that the later the age of presentation the more negative the prognosis.[30]

Thus a number of possible and probable causes of gender dysphoria can be identified. Where there is early onset (before the age of six years) and where strong and consistent gender dysphoria is probably due to parental pathology and failure to differentiate from the mother in the case of males, such cases will usually present early and be diagnosed as primary gender dysphoria. Where the onset of gender dysphoria is post-pubertal and there are clear social or psychodynamic precipitating factors, or where there is a history of moderate gender dysphoria and identity crises or other apparent stresses such as ageing, the gender dysphoria is likely to be secondary to these and gender reassignment is not the treatment of choice.

At this point, some mention must be made of social factors contributing to gender dysphoria. In most Western societies, homosexuality is stigmatized. Ross *et al.* have suggested that, in some cases, transsexuals are homosexual males who rationalize their preference for a male partner into the socially acceptable form of a heterosexual relationship by altering their gender.[31] There is a reasonable amount of evidence to support this: Lothstein has noted that society accepts a transsexual adaptation while it does not usually accept a homosexual one:[32] similarly, Bentler notes that his 'homosexual–transsexual' group have increased sex with males after changing role, suggesting that it may be an adaptation to stigma and homosexuality.[33] Using a similar set of putative dynamics, McCauley and Erhardt note that most transsexuals have exceedingly rigid views on gender roles, and it follows from this that in societies with rigid gender roles, transsexualism may also be less stigmatized than 'feminine' males or 'masculine' females.[34] This suggestion was tested by Ross *et al.*, who found that in a more gender-role-rigid and anti-homosexual society there were three times more consultations by individuals who labelled themselves as 'transsexual' than in a comparable society which was less so.[35] Of interest also is the finding by Hoenig and Kenna that most transsexuals are from the lower socio-economic levels: in working-class environments, gender roles do tend to be much more rigid and well defined.[36] It thus becomes clear that the social environment must also be considered as a dynamic, as well as sociological variables such as class and education. It can thus be seen to be futile to attempt to look for a 'cause' of gender dysphoria, as there are a number of separate contributory psychodynamic factors. Furthermore, these may also interact with social characteristics of the environment, psychological characteristics of the individual, and stresses such as object losses and ageing to produce the individuals who label themselves as transsexuals.

## Conclusion

It appears fairly clear from evidence to date that there are no known biological causes of gender dysphoria: it is, however, impossible to rule out a biological basis for transsexualism being discovered as further research and refinements of research techniques continue. Present evidence strongly suggests that the great majority of gender dysphorics, including by definition all cases of secondary gender dysphoria, result from varying disorders of parental rearing patterns, psychopathology and psychological disturbances or lack of ego development, social and environmental factors, object losses or separations, general stressors, or lack of core gender identity. The difficulty in establishing causes of transsexualism has centred around the fact that it was considered a unitary syndrome with unitary aetiology. Now that we are able to consider it as a symptom and recognize that there are a number of psychodynamics, some not mutually exclusive, which produce the symptoms of gender dysphoria, it is possible to advance our understanding of transsexualism by postulating several different categories in terms of different causes. In order to do this it is necessary to take detailed histories and make testable psychodynamic formulations: not until we are able to differentiate subgroups of gender dysphorics on the basis of their psychodynamics will we be able to do more than guess at the causes of transsexual symptoms and delineate the gender dysphoria syndromes.

# 4  Gender Identity Disorder of Childhood

## Diagnostic and treatment issues

*Donna Riseley*

Adults with gender dysphorias frequently report experiencing transsexual feelings, cross-dressing and participation in cross-gender behaviours from an early age.[1] This early history coupled with the immense difficulties experienced by these people in adult life has led to an interest in the treatment of children presenting with gender identity difficulties.[2] The understanding of the nature, causation and treatment of such difficulties is, however, still in its infancy. This may be a function of the relatively low estimated incidence of both the adult and child disorders. Estimates of the prevalence of transsexualism vary from 1:37 000 (Sweden) to 1:24 000 (Australia) for biological males in the general population. For biological females the estimates vary from 1:103 000 (Sweden) to 1:150 000 (Australia).[3] The prevalence of childhood disorder is more difficult to estimate. Zuger estimated an approximate incidence of one in twenty boys in a population referred for psychiatric evaluation.[4] There is less information available concerning the incidence and nature of gender disorders in girls.[5] The present chapter reflects this disparity: of necessity this discussion is preoccupied with the problems of male children.

Green has compared matched samples of 110 feminine boys and masculine boys (Table 4.1).[6] Feminine boys were found to participate significantly less in rough-and-tumble play, to cross-dress more frequently and to express the wish more often that they had been born a girl. These children had a greater interest in play-acting and more frequently played feminine roles. They were also more isolated from their peer group. A similar study compared matched samples of ninety-nine feminine and masculine girls.[7] The masculine girls were found to play significantly more sports and to play more frequently with boys, and were more isolated from their peer group. They played more with trucks and guns, and often stated they wanted to be boys. In contrast to the boys, there were no significant differences in their interest in play-acting: however, when they did so they more often played male roles. All these cross-gender children appeared to be biologically normal.[8]

How important are these variables in determining gender difficulties? Are all such children inevitably destined for adult gender difficulties? And, if so, which features are critical in discriminating 'at risk' children from those who are not? What are the treatment implications once such a diagnosis is made? Should such children be treated? And, if so, with what goals in mind? Is it possible to prevent the onset of adult transsexualism by intervening in childhood? Do these children have other difficulties which need to be considered? These questions remain unsatisfactorily answered, and are the subject of this chapter.

## Diagnostic issues

Discussions concerning the relative importance of various aspects of these children's presentation recognise that, as in adults, gender identity difficulties have a heterogeneous quality.[9] Nevertheless, there exists a belief that a more 'severe', 'primary' or 'pure' childhood syndrome can be differentiated.[10] Children so diagnosed are judged likely to develop adult transsexualism. There is incomplete agreement concerning the nature of the criteria which differentiate this more 'severe' or 'pure' disorder, if, indeed, there is simply one 'severe', 'pure' syndrome. As clinical assessment leading to diagnosis is never based on the simple addition of diagnostic criteria, it is important to note also areas of substantial agreement. The *Diagnostic and Statistical Manual of Mental Disorders* (3rd edition) (DSM-III) diagnostic criteria for boys and girls include the following aspects:

1. The stated desire to be or belief that he/she is a member of the opposite sex.
2. A repudiation of male/female anatomic structures.
3. Preoccupation with female stereotypic activities (e.g. cross-dressing or a compelling desire to participate in female games). This criterion is not included in those for the diagnosis of gender identity disorder of girls.
4. The onset of the disturbance before puberty.[11]

Prior to the development of these criteria, Stoller described the syndrome 'male childhood transsexualism' in terms of a child's belief that he is (or stated desire that he be) a girl, of his 'feminine' behaviours (e.g. cross-dressing from an early age), of his preference for girl playmates and games, and of his 'feminine' gestures and mannerisms.[12] The boy gives the appearance of being 'perfectly' feminine.[13]

Stoller's diagnostic criteria for male childhood transsexualism included a particular family dynamic (seen also as aetiological),

**Table 4.1    Summary of cases treated using behaviour modification procedures**

| Case no. | Age began/duration | Nature of Procedures | Outcome | Follow-up |
|---|---|---|---|---|
| **1** Carl (Rekers, Lovaas & Low, 1974) | 8.8/ 15 mth period | 1. Modification of:<br>a) feminine gesture, mannerisms, speech<br>b) play-acting feminine role<br>c) feminine play with sister<br>d) masculine play<br>e) masculine play with brother<br>2. Treated in:<br>a) clinic—therapist schedule D.R.O.<br>b) home—mother trained in token economy<br>c) school—response cost procedure used by teacher | 1. Masculine speech appeared under influence of D.R.O. schedule but had to be treated in each setting.<br>2. Response cost procedure suppressed feminine gestures, speech play, but did not produce major increases in masculine behaviours<br>3. Treatment at school did not generalize across classrooms (i.e. stimulus specific)<br>4. After 15 months' independent evaluation of case using interviews and psychometrics. No evidence of feminine behaviour or cross-gender identification but observed Carl's 'need for reassurance and support' when<br>5. Feminine behaviour when Carl anxious | 1 year follow-up age 12 years<br>1. No evidence of feminine behaviour<br>2. Normal peer relationships<br>3. Not competitive or aggressive<br>4. Improved emotional stability |
| **2** Kraig (Rekers & Lovaas, 1974) | 4.11/ 10 mth period | 1. Modified behaviours as above. Also generally undesired behaviour<br>2. Treated in:<br>a) clinic—mother D.R.O. schedule<br>b) home—token reinforcement | 1. Increase in masculine and decrease in feminine behaviours with some generalization related to mother's presence<br>2. Reduced feminine behaviour at home<br>3. Improved sibling relationships | 26 months later effects still present (still treated during that time) |

| Case | Age | Treatment | Results | Follow-up |
|---|---|---|---|---|
| **3 Bobby** (Rekers, Yates, Willis, Rosen & Taubman, 1976) | 8 | 1. Modification of:<br>  a) play behaviours<br>  b) cross-gender mannerisms<br>2. Treated in:<br>  a) clinic using mother D.R.O. schedule<br>  b) home setting | Mother successfully increased masculine and reduced feminine behaviour. This generalized in father's presence in clinic playroom. Inadequate data on home and setting due to withdrawal from treatment | 25 months after termination of treatment<br>1. Psychometrics<br>2. Observation at home and school revealed:<br>  a) no effeminate behaviour<br>  b) better interpersonal relations especially with father<br>3. Mildly effeminate with no cross-gender behaviour but not 'stereotypic' male |
| **4 Paul** (Rekers, Willis, Yates, Rosen & Low, 1977) | 8 | 1. Modification of behaviour as above.<br>2. Treated in:<br>  a) Paul trained to self-observe (video-tape); trained to identify feminine behaviour; trained (modelling) in masculine behaviour<br>  b) home (response cost)<br>  c) shaped athletic skills<br>  d) other behaviour modified | 1. Suppression of play with girls, doll play<br>2. Voice inflection and mannerisms modified<br>3. Shaped male behaviour; increased frequency of play with peers<br>4. Frequency of tantrums and encopretic episodes decreased | 2 years' follow-up<br>1. 'Usually' male<br>2. Occasional cross-gender/behaviour<br>3. Decreased anxiety level<br>4. Decrease in femininity |
| **5 Brian** (Rekers, 1977) | 6,7/6 mth period | 1. Modified behaviours as above<br>2. Treatment:<br>  a) social reinforcement (uncle and aunt at home)<br>  b) used self-monitoring procedure combined with behavioural cueing<br>  c) self-reinforcement procedure | 1. Increased male and decreased female behaviour<br>2. Exclusive male play<br>3. Minimal stimulus generalization | 12 months' psychometrics<br>1. quiet<br>2. friendly<br>3. non-feminine (treatment prematurely terminated) |

namely, a psychologically bisexual mother who is 'empty' and depressed: she cannot allow her son to separate from a state of 'blissful symbiosis' with her. Hence, the non-conflictual development of a feminine gender identity early in life by a learning process seen to be similar to, but not identical with, imprinting. The father is emotionally distant and unable to interrupt this symbiosis.[14] Although his criteria for assessment of female transsexualism in childhood were less well developed and cautious, they were seen also in terms of a specific family dynamic, namely, a feminine mother who is affectively removed from the child at birth (e.g. by depression) and a masculine father who is unable to support his wife in her depression or his daughter in her femininity, and who sends his daughter into the breach to support mother. The clinical presentation of the girl as cross-dressing, preferring male playmates, and stating a desire to be a boy was also viewed as diagnostic of childhood gender disturbance.[15] On the other hand, Zucker sees inclusion of family dynamics as inappropriate 'because it would seem that information regarding such dynamics would be irrelevant if male childhood transsexualism were in fact a syndrome'.[16] (When using the DSM-III classification, such family dynamics would be recorded on a separate axis and would not be considered primary to the diagnosis.)

How important are family factors? Several studies have compared retrospectively the family backgrounds of adult males who present with gender difficulties. Freund *et al.* found no significant difference between homosexual and transsexual men's relationships with or loss of father or mother.[17] However, they found that there was a significant difference in these variables between homosexual and heterosexual subjects. Homosexual subjects indicated that they had a significantly poorer father/son relationship and that they were closer to the mother. Buhrich and McConaghy found that transvestite, transsexual and homosexual subjects tended to report less positive feelings towards and involvement with their fathers.[18] However, this family pattern did not provide a basis on which to distinguish between these three groups. Pauly reviewed the family histories of eighty female adult transsexuals and found limited support for Stoller's family dynamic; there was, however, no control group in this study.[19] Green studied the family relationships of feminine boys along several dimensions, including father/son separations, marital role division, and parental emotional closeness.[20] He found that 20 per cent of the boys were living without a father or substitute at the age of four. Rekers *et al.*, on the other hand, studied forty-six male children referred to the University College of Los Angeles Child Gender Clinic and found that 67 per cent of the biological fathers were physically absent from home.[21] Of those biological or substitute fathers who were present, 60 per cent were described as psychologically absent. The study concluded that the more severely gender-disturbed a boy was, the higher the probability of the father being absent.

Green's study, mentioned above, compared the role division between parents of feminine and masculine boys. This revealed significant differences only in how the fathers viewed themselves, the fathers of feminine boys seeing themselves as the overall boss whereas the fathers of masculine boys saw both parents as sharing this role. Twice as many mothers of feminine boys felt very close to their sons compared with fathers who felt moderately close. More feminine boys (75 per cent) preferred their mother to their father. Masculine boys' preferences for parents were more varied (e.g. some preferring both parents, some preferring one parent). In their study mentioned above, Rekers *et al.* demonstrated that in families with a gender-disturbed boy, work was more likely to be divided into 'mother's' and 'father's' tasks. Twenty-eight boys were administered the Bene-Anthony Family Relation Test. When compared with a normal group they were found to experience significantly more negative feelings towards their fathers and mothers. However, they perceived more positive feelings coming from their mothers than did the normal group.

Both studies provide some support for Stoller's suggested family dynamic, but in his study, Green concluded that no consistent pattern of causation for extensive boyhood femininity could be found. Stoller appeared to use these family dynamics to differentially diagnose feminine boys who present with cross-gender behaviour and 'true' transsexual children. However, when he described Nikki, an 'extremely feminine boy' who did not exactly fit his own family dynamic criterion, he concluded that, although this boy 'is not dynamically and aetiologically similar (to other male transsexual boys) there are enough similarities to conclude that he resembles them more than he does a masculine boy'. He then introduced another diagnostic criterion which he saw as more central to the diagnosis, namely, 'the crucial measure, for me, will be whether he enjoys using his penis for sexual pleasure'.[22] Thus Stoller introduced both the notion of a continuum in the assessment of these children and another factor which seems closely related to the second criterion listed in the DSM-III, that is, the persistent repudiation of male/female anatomic structures.

This appears to agree with Zucker's belief that the second DSM-III criterion is essential in the diagnosis of both boys and girls and appears to reflect the underlying dislike of their male or female anatomy which these children experience.[23] Is this the childhood precursor of the adult gender dysphoria which some authors believe underlies the presenting symptoms of adult transsexualism? Is this anatomic dysphoria primary or secondary to the desire to be a member of the opposite sex, or do these two feelings co-exist? And is this related to or the same as the own-sex aversion referred to in Goldman and Goldman's cross-cultural study of the sexual thinking of children?[24] They demonstrated that in a population of normal children 5 per cent of the boys and 9.5 per cent of the girls expressed an aversion to their own sex. This aversion appeared to peak in early adolescence: the highest percentages of boys in any one age group were 30 per cent of Australian and 20 per cent of North American thirteen-year-olds. This stated own-sex aversion was virtually non-existent in Sweden. The percentage of other sex aversion statements was also seen to vary across cultures with Swedish boys expressing fewer negative statements and their expression ceasing at an earlier age than in Australia and North America. Interestingly, Ross has also noted that male homosexuals in Australia identified much more strongly as feminine than matched Swedish homosexuals.[25]

Newman has divided the behaviour of feminine boys into two categories.[26] The first category consists of four behaviours: preferring cross-gender clothing, stating preferences to be a girl or to grow up to be a woman, play-acting female roles in games and imitating in an exaggerated way a woman's gestures, mannerisms and speech. The second category consists of six behaviours: avoiding rough competitive games, disliking trucks or other mechanical toys, preferring artistic or sedentary pastimes, liking girls as playmates and reporting being teased by other boys. The presence of first category behaviours is seen to be diagnostic of gender pathology whereas that of second category behaviours alone is not. This division is based on his observation that 'these first category behaviours are those which if carried into adult life, would make up the picture of adult transsexualism'. Certainly an adult presenting with these symptoms would be likely to earn such a diagnosis.[27] (Whether such children do grow up to be adult transsexuals is yet to be discussed.) Noteworthy in this differential classification of behaviours is the distinction drawn between 'exaggerated effeminate' behaviours, seen as diagnostic of more severe disorders, and 'gracefulness in bodily movements and gestures'. This observation contrasts with Stoller's view of the quality of the feminine behaviours of these boys.

Thus, Stoller draws a distinction between the 'feminine behaviour' of male transsexuals and the 'effeminate behaviour' of effeminate homosexuals; the latter contains more elements of mimicry of feminine behaviour. This distinction is based on his view that the dynamics underlying these qualitatively different behaviours and the syndromes of which they are a part are different. Stoller does not see transsexualism as a product of conflict, repression and defence but believes homosexual effeminacy to be so. In other words, the degree of mimicry or imitation of feminine behaviour reflects some degree of conflict and anxiety, and therefore is indicative of less severe pathology.[28]

Westfall *et al.* found the degree of effeminate behaviour of adult male homosexuals and heterosexuals to vary according to social context.[29] For homosexuals, effeminacy scores (based on a rating scale)[30] increased in an anxiety-provoking situation, but for heterosexuals these scores decreased. In the homosexual group, effeminate behaviour was used also to signal sexual availability. As yet, boys' feminine/effeminate behaviour is not well understood. Bates *et al.* saw the existence of precocious, feminine mannerisms as an important clinical problem.[31] Rekers also drew attention to the sex-role inflexibility and stereotypic extremes in gender behaviour of these children, maintaining that 'many individuals . . . would be very concerned if a young girl swished into a room and demonstrated the kind of profound feminine identification described by Rekers and Lovaas in the boys they treated'.[32] Bates *et al.* also suggested that, a general lack of social skills accompanied this precocity. It is this lack which they believe contributes to the social rejection and isolation these boys experience, especially in later years.

In a study designed to develop a Gender Behaviour Inventory for Boys, Bates, Bentler and Thompson found significant mean differences between a clinical sample of gender problem referrals and normal controls.[33] The discriminating factors were:

Factor 1. (Termed feminine behaviour), which included many items indicating precocious feminine behaviour (e.g. he prefers the company of adult women), mimicry of adult female behaviour (e.g. he 'swishes' and swings his hips when he walks; he imitates females; he uses feminine gestures with his hands when talking), as well as behaviours associated more with normal female children (he plays house; he plays with dolls; he plays with girls). *All* these behaviours were found to be unusual among normal boys.

Factor 2. An extraversion factor dealing with outgoing physically active, 'masculine' orientation.

Factor 3. A measurement of general behavioural disturbance in children.

Thus these boys were more effeminate, less outgoing, and more behaviourally disturbed than normal boys.

Rosen, Rekers and Friar described two closely related but distinct syndromes: cross-gender identification and gender behaviour disturbance.[34] The term cross-gender identification (the more severe disorder) is characterized by the boy's stated preference to be, or belief that he is, a girl (or will grow up to be a woman) accompanied by cross-dressing and extreme, stereotypic feminine behaviours. They noted that a boy may learn to suppress cross-gender behaviours as he grows older to avoid social ridicule and ostracism. Zucker has also noted the importance of developmental changes in the manifestation of symptoms.[35] In a series of thirty children referred to a gender identity clinic, the eighteen children meeting DSM-III criteria were significantly younger than those who did not (mean age 6.8 years compared to 9.3 years). Some of the older children would have met these criteria when younger. This 'burning out' of some symptoms has been noted also by Zuger.[36] Similarly, Rosen *et al.* noted that older boys tend to inhibit behaviour such as femine play if they are able. However, feminine mannerisms and gestures were seen to be more difficult to suppress, although the boys tended to learn that it is socially unacceptable to state a preference to be a girl. For boys between nine and twelve years the feminine play and cross-dressing are less conspicuous than their mannerisms. These authors have also shown that sex-type play varies according to the social situation (e.g. sex of observer).

Developmental changes were also observed in all children's perceptions of sexual differences. The Goldman study found that overt recognition of real sexual differences, although present, was slow in developing.[37] In early years, the major differences between mothers and fathers were perceived by children in terms of physical characteristics (height, weight, hair, clothing), roles and abilities. It was not until the children were about nine years old that overt sexual differences were regularly voiced. As puberty approaches, when children presumably become aware of sexual taboos, discussion showing their awareness of anatomical differences decreases. However, as a caution against taking this observation too seriously, Thompson and Bentler asked groups of male and female adults and children if they could be the opposite-sexed parent.[38] About 15 per cent of all the adults and about 13 per cent of all the children gave an affirmative response. One of the study's conclusions was that it was unwise to use a child's belief in the possibility of sex-role change as an exclusive method of identification of child gender difficulties! Interestingly, Zucker, in his previously mentioned study, has criticized Stoller's apparent inconsistency in connection with the relative importance of a child's stated belief that he *is* rather than his stated desire *to be* a girl.[39] This is because Stoller does not always appear to see the stated belief as important in the diagnosis of 'pure' transsexualism. Rather he seems to believe that a child's strong belief as opposed to a desire to be a girl is simply indicative of the intensity or degree of femininity in the child. The DSM-III does not make this distinction.

What are the implications of this for gender-disturbed children? Perhaps these children notice anatomical differences but may not necessarily realize until about nine years of age that such differences are fixed and permanent. Is this the beginning of the time when they realize the implications of their anatomical sex for their future adult status? Does the impact of cultures which more rigidly stereotype sexual differences begin to affect these children's feelings of same-sex aversion which are more frequently observed in Australia and North America than in Sweden?

Given these developmental differences, it is not surprising that Rosen *et al.*, in their study mentioned above, suggested a complex assessment procedure when seeing these children that takes into account six factors:

1. Identity statements.
   The statement of the child wanting or believing himself to be a girl is diagnostic for a young child. However, for a child over eight the absence of these statements is not conclusive. For this reason the use of a series of projective tests is seen as a useful diagnostic aid.
2. Cross-dressing.
   Cross-gender identification syndrome is diagnosed by higher frequency and intensity of cross-dressing and by age of onset. The earlier in life the cross-dressing begins and the more frequently it occurs, the more severe the disorder is seen to be.
3. Cross-gender play behaviour.
   The authors see this factor in two aspects. The child may express an actual dislike or abhorrence for male games (e.g. rough-and-tumble play) while playing feminine-type games. They consider it important that the child's play behaviour be observed while he is alone (using a one-way screen), and believe that play behaviour when alone is of crucial diagnostic importance.
4. Parent-child relationships.
   The authors appear to agree that the existence of a family dynamic such as Stoller described is a critical factor in the diagnosis of cross-gender identification.
5. Parental attitudes towards cross-gender behaviours.
   The parents apparently fail to notice that these children are

behaving atypically until someone outside the family points this out (e.g. kindergarten or school teacher).

6. Physical appearance.

The boys appear, on clinical observation, to be 'attractive' in appearance. However, Stoller saw the boys he identified as sometimes very attractive, and sometimes simply believed by the mother to be outstandingly attractive.

Rosen *et al.* also noted the importance of secondary adjustment difficulties which these boys suffer in later years due to social isolation and ostracism. They used a five-part rating scale to diagnose the severity of this disorder ranging from profound cross-gender identification to normal gender identification. The term 'gender behaviour disturbance' is used to describe a less severe problem in which the boys do not express a desire to be a girl but behave in a feminine (but less extreme) manner. Here too the authors used a five-part rating scale in diagnosing this separate (but related) disorder, ranging from extreme to no gender behaviour disturbance.

In this two-syndrome classification, the stated belief that he is, or desires to be, a girl, coupled with the severity, frequency, and early onset of feminine sex-type behaviours, and effeminate/feminine gestures and mannerisms, are the differentially diagnostic symptoms. The anatomical dysphoria does not appear to be relevant to this schema. The *quality* of the feminine or effeminate behaviours does not seem important so much as their *frequency*, although the intensity and stereotypic quality is observed.

There appears to be some agreement that there are children who exhibit cross-gender behaviours and who may also experience frequent transsexual feelings. However, evidence suggests that the expression of some of these behaviours (e.g. degree of effeminacy, cross-gender play behaviours and statements of transsexual wish) may vary according to the social situation, developmental stage and culture. Thus, to distinguish one 'pure' childhood syndrome on the basis of these variables, is difficult. Some of these boys have been observed to lack pleasure in their penis, or to experience pain with erections, to prefer to sit down when urinating and to express desires to have the penis removed. Are all these experiences the expression of growing anatomical dysphoria? Does this dysphoria become more intense once the child enters the so-called latency period? Does this contribute to their social isolation, especially in more sex-role rigid cultures?

Because of these many unknowns, the assessment of such children obviously needs to allow space and time to understand not only the complexity of their outer worlds but, most importantly, the individual meaning of their inner worlds.

## Treatment issues

The problems in treating these children are many and complex. Winkler raises the question of therapist allegiance.[40] Is it to the patient, the parents or to society? This is always a difficult question to answer when working with any children. Rekers et al. quite clearly wish to work in the best interests of the child and his family. However, Winkler criticizes the grounds on which Rekers and Lovaas make their treatment decisions.[41] Their rationale for intervention is, primarily, the high risk of adult gender difficulties such as transsexualism, homosexuality and transvestism. Is there clear evidence available to predict such an outcome?

While many adult transsexuals retrospectively report gender disturbance in childhood, conflicting reports can also be found. Person and Ovesey described an adult syndrome called 'primary transsexuality'.[42] In a series of ten adults fitting this picture nine showed no evidence of effeminacy in childhood and were never referred to as 'sissies' . . . all participated in rough-and-tumble play when required but 'with an inner sense of abhorrence'. They did not engage in girls' activities or play with girls any more than did normal boys.[43] In most gender identity clinics such a history would not be likely to enhance these persons' chances of surgery. Do effeminate boys become transsexual? Zuger, in his previously mentioned study, reported twenty cases of 'effeminate' boys ranging in age from 4 years 3 months to 16 years. In addition, he reported a follow-up of the same boys after ten years (average age at follow-up twenty-two years).[44] Of the sixteen with whom he still had contact, the later sexual orientation was one heterosexual, one probably heterosexual, eight homosexual, two probably homosexual, one transsexual, one transvestite and two uncertain. The feminine-type behaviour of these boys outlined in tabular form by Zuger indicates that they are similar to the feminine boys described by Green in Sexual Identity Conflict in Children and Adults. However, these boys all received one consultation at least and fifteen received some form of psychotherapy or follow-up interview in their early contact with Zuger.

Lebovitz followed up ten male patients selected from the files of the Child Psychiatry Division of the University of Minnesota Hospital.[45] The main criterion for inclusion was that the presenting problems were described as 'feminine behaviour'. The average age of the group at follow-up was twenty-one years. The subjects were separated into two groups based on age of onset of symptoms. For eight subjects, the feminine behaviour started at or before six years of age. When the groups were taken together, three subjects were found to fit the transsexual syndrome (one had Klinefelter's syndrome), two acknowledged homosexuality and one appeared to be a transvestite and was married. A fifth subject had stated a desire to be rid of his male genitals. One subject had psychotic episodes (it is unclear which one). This report is unsatisfactory and does not allow any conclusion to be drawn about the future outcome of children who present with gender difficulties. Until Green's longitudinal studies[46] have been completed it is difficult to know what the *future* will be for these children. Nevertheless, it is clear that only a minority of feminine boys become transsexual: more become homosexual.

Can childhood gender dysphorias be treated? Barlow *et al.* reported the behavioural treatment of a transsexual seventeen-year-old boy.[47] Feminine behaviour, statements of transsexual desire and patterns of sexual arousal were modified, although these classes of behaviour were seen to be relatively independent of one another. These changes were maintained at one year follow-up (heterosexual arousal was measured at about 55 per cent and homosexual at about 15 per cent) The boy had a girlfriend but was not apparently engaging in intercourse. Similarly, Davenport and Harrison claim to have changed the gender identity of a fourteen-year-old female transsexual following two years of individual psychotherapy (with a male therapist) and in-patient milieu therapy.[48] This appears to have consisted of staff differentially reinforcing *desirable* feminine as against *undesirable* masculine behaviours. The girl was followed up until nineteen years of age. Her behavioural changes had been maintained. She was not apparently sexually active but alluded to her interest in boys.

A second rationale for intervention is the social isolation and consequent unhappiness which these children suffer. Rekers *et al.* sees this social isolation as a direct result of cross-gender behaviours, such as play behaviour and feminine and/or effeminate mannerisms (remembering that the latter appear more resistant to 'spontaneous' suppression as the child grows older).[49] However, Bates *et al.* attribute this social isolation directly to a general lack of social skills.[50] Data already presented in this chapter suggest the possibility that increasing anatomical gender dysphoria and cultural factors may also contribute. It is the belief that these cross-gender behaviours and mannerisms lead to harmful consequences that provides the rationale for their removal by behaviour modification.

In this area Winkler has been critical of the work of Rekers and Lovaas. Winkler, in his study cited above, maintains that the modification of feminine sex-typed behaviours is harmful to the child because it encourages the adoption of rigid male sex-typed behaviours.

The polarization of the debate along these lines is unfortunate. It tends to obscure an area of general agreement, that is, that rigid sex-role behaviour is not good for anyone and that these children need to develop more flexible patterns of behaviour.[51] Rekers *et al.* believe this is possible through the modification of cross-gender behaviours; Bates *et al.* suggest it is achieved by learning a broader range of social skills.[52] Green, Stoller and Newman[53] and other more dynamically oriented therapists see the additional importance of individual psychotherapy, which is more likely to allow space for exploration of the child's inner world.

How effective are these treatments? Table 4.2 summarizes five boys using behaviour modification techniques.[54] These procedures focus on the training of parent(s) or guardian(s) in the differential reinforcement of masculine versus feminine behaviour. They were found to be effective in doing so, although a lack of generalization across settings necessitated specific training in clinic, home and school. The development of self-monitoring and self-regulation in the last two cases has been suggested as a way around this difficulty. However, in case 4 (Paul), it was found that external reinforcement procedures were needed to increase specific male behaviours in addition to the self-monitoring and the modelling procedures provided by the therapist. These children (except for case 3) appeared to have other behaviour difficulties (e.g. tantrums, non-compliance with parental requests, involuntary passage of faeces, anxiety and lack of social skills). It seems that some of these difficulties were also treated and improvements noted at follow-up.

Attempts to model or increase more stereotypic male behaviours (e.g. athletic behaviours) did not seem very successful (especially case 1) except in the case of Paul (case 4). Longer-term follow-up (ranging from twelve to twenty-six months) showed a persistence in the reduction of feminine play behaviour, mannerisms, and speech, as well as an improvement in measures of overall social functioning. However, most of the cases were described in terms such as 'by no means would Bobby be considered a super-active, stereotypic masculine boy' and 'However, Carl's preferences are for activities which are relatively less competitive, less physically demanding, and more passive in nature'.

Rosen, Rekers, and Brigham examined the effects of the behavioural treatment of twenty-two gender dysphoric boys.[55] This analysis showed no evidence of an enhancement of masculinizing behaviour or a reduction in feminizing behaviour. A comparison of the scores of ten treated and four untreated gender dysphoric boys and eight normals was made using the Bem Sex-role Test. The authors concluded that behavioural treatments operate 'to enhance the broader spectrum of behaviours accessible to the youngster; to enhance supporting masculine behaviours, while maintaining the co-existing feminine behaviour'. Although this view does not reflect the procedures actually used in the cases cited above (feminine behaviours were actively discouraged) it does appear to reflect actual outcomes.

The treatment rationale outlined by Bates *et al.* reflects a move towards positive enhancement of general social skills.[56] Treatment goals were defined as:

1. To increase the target child's repertoire of masculine behaviours.
2. To increase the child's social skills and peer interactions.
3. To improve family relationships, particularly the relationship between the target child and his father . . . to decrease their effeminate mannerisms and play interests . . . was *not* the focus of . . . interventions.

Sixteen 'feminine' boys were treated in such a programme which included:

1. Individual play sessions in which masculine behaviour was reinforced but feminine behaviour was not.
2. Sessions in which parents were instructed in the use of a token economy and other behavioural techniques to use in the home setting (to encourage masculine versus feminine behaviours).
3. The boys being assigned to an age-specific group (9–11 years; 12–13 years; 5–8 years). Two male co-therapists encouraged and modelled good social interaction skills as well as masculine behaviour.
4. Supportive parents groups being provided. These were led by both a male and a female therapist.

Unfortunately there was no control group for this study so firm scientific conclusions as to effectiveness cannot be drawn. Questionnaires were sent eighteen months after the end of the treatment and were returned by two-thirds of those treated. They reported moderate gains in overall social functioning, moderate increases in masculinity, no gains in school performance and that they were doing well in social interaction with peers and family.

Green, Newman and Stoller reported the treatment of five boys who were seen individually by a male therapist.[57] The therapy was a combination of psychodynamically oriented psychotherapy coupled with role modelling of appropriate male behaviour and direct information giving (e.g. the irreversibility of anatomic gender). Parent(s) were seen and instructed on how to encourage masculine behaviours and discourage feminine ones (along general behavioural lines).

The length of therapy was over some years (four years and more in some cases). At follow-up, from one to two years, there appeared to be a range of changes, from a reduction in cross-gender behaviours and statements of choice to be a girl to improved relationships with the father (Table 4.2). In these case presentations, it is difficult to know whether therapeutic intervention was responsible directly for the changes, as these behaviours have been demonstrated to change sometimes with maturation. However, such intervention allows space and time for the child to explore the meaning of his beliefs, wishes and behaviours. The effects of such therapy are quite difficult to measure.

The use of explaining that anatomic gender is irreversible is noteworthy. This information may complement an already growing awareness in the child or correct a misunderstanding. Davenport *et al.*, in their study previously cited, found such discussions became central in the therapy.[58] They found their patient (at 14.5 years) naïve about the sex-change operation and surprised that it could not make her a real potent male. In this era of re-assignment surgery and widespread publicity, it may be crucial for these children to have an opportunity to openly discuss the meanings and realities of such surgery. Again, as Green implies, the knowledge of the existence of 'sex change' operations may create an additional conflict as the impossible becomes remotely possible.[59]

Metcalf and Williams reported a case study of a six-year-old boy whom they describe as meeting Stoller's criteria for diagnosis of male childhood transsexuality.[60] The child was seen in individual psychotherapy (following Green's and Stoller's model) and the mother was also engaged in psychotherapy. The parents were instructed in behavioural procedures for use in the home and also participated in marital therapy. In this case, the follow-up (eighteen months later) revealed behavioural change that was situation-specific (e.g. in the family home rather than in the grandparents' home). For their part, Pruett and Dahl reported the analytic treatment of three boys (4 years 10 months, 3 years 9 months, and 5 years 10 months), with moderate reduction in desired masculine behaviour but with ample time and space for exploration of their inner worlds.[61]

Both these studies lack controls, so conclusions of efficacy can only be limited. However, it seems that behavioural techniques are effective in reducing cross-gender behaviours. In their study mentioned on page 39, Rekers *et al.* clearly demonstrated that the behavioural programme needs to be more intensive than that attempted in these other studies. Again, the time given for the child and parents to explore themselves is difficult to evaluate. Similarly, Higham outlined a 'rehabilitation intervention programme' designed to offer a wide range of alternative 'sex-role and erotic-role behaviour experimentation and differentiation' rather than to encourage one sex-typed behavioural repertoire over another.[62] There is no information on outcome accompanying this report so the impact of such a programme cannot as yet be evaluated.

While treatment of these children is possible, it is still unclear exactly what is being treated. Behaviour modification procedures effectively modify various cross-gender behaviours. However, the long-term effects of such procedures are as yet unknown. Although there is a suggestion that specific modification of patterns of sexual arousal has some impact in adolescents there is no evidence to support the view that modification of cross-gender behaviours in childhood will result in later changes in sexual orientation. More-

**Table 4.2   Summary of cases treated by Green, Newman and Stoller, 1972**

| Case no. | Age | Treatment and length of follow-up | Outcome at follow-up |
|---|---|---|---|
| 1 | 5 | 1. Individual therapy<br>2. Mother only seen<br>4 years | Repression of active transsexual wish<br>Dislikes sports and playing with boys |
| 2 | 6 | 1. Individual therapy<br>2. Parental therapy<br>2–4 years | 'Masculine' boy at 2–4 years follow-up |
| 3 | 6 | 1. Individual therapy<br>2. Parental therapy<br>4 years | Occasionally cross-dresses<br>No statement of desire to be a girl<br>Effeminate mannerisms<br>Fearful of boys<br>Distant to father<br>Hostile to mother |
| 4 | ? | 1. Individual therapy including role modelling<br>2. Parental therapy<br>3 years | Improved father–son relation<br>No cross-dressing<br>Plays with boys<br>No longer teased<br>Occasional feminine gestures<br>Likes silk 'masculine' robes |
| 5 | 12 | 1. Individual therapy<br>2. Direct training in masculine behaviours<br>1 year | Improved body posture and male identity |

over, the effects of psychotherapy for these children are not well documented. Measures of behavioural changes which these studies cite probably provide more information about the impact of the behavioural programmes used than about other aspects of the intervention. (This may well include changes in statements of transsexual wishes.) Perhaps some measure of changes in anatomic dysphoria would provide more meaningful information. Similarly long-term effects of these treatments are unknown.

The impact of behavioural changes and psychotherapy on these children's isolation in the long-term is also unclear. However, short-term improvements may well affect these children by providing opportunities for increased peer interaction, especially during the so-called latency developmental period.

The present chapter has provided evidence to suggest that cultural and social factors may interact to produce greater anatomic dysphoria leading to greater degrees of isolation for those children living in societies where sex roles are more rigidly stereotyped. (Interestingly, these children have also been observed to come from families which are more likely to rigidly define family tasks according to gender.)

Rigid sex-role stereotyping is not good for anyone, least of all for any of our children; it may well be that gender dysphoric children to some degree represent part of the cost society pays for its present gender organization.

For this reason, intervention which allows sufficient time and space for the child to explore the individual meaning of his/her inner and outer worlds is seen as vital.

# 5 Diagnosis and Differential Diagnosis

## Homosexual, transvestite or transsexual

### Herbert Bower

The accepted definition of transsexualism already incorporates a number of diagnostic criteria. It is described as a gender disorder in which the belief is firmly held that the real sexual identity is the opposite to that represented by the sexual anatomy of the individual. This conviction is coupled with the desire to live as a person of the chosen sex, to be fully accepted as such by society and to have sexual organs reassigned by surgery. However, to arrive at a satisfactory diagnostic formulation, we must explore all dimensions of the disorder, going back to birth and early development and then following the natural history into adulthood.

## Male-to-female transsexualism

### Typical case history

Pregnancy and birth are generally unremarkable, and chromosomally as well as hormonally the baby presents as a normal male with corresponding sexual anatomy. Approximately a quarter of all male-to-female transsexuals are from families with only one child, yet the symbiotic relationship between mother and child stressed by Stoller is rare.[1] One has the impression that a number of male transsexuals were attractive as children. The family structure and, with it, the child-rearing process deviate from the norm in at least three-quarters of all patients. The father is either absent, a remote figure or in retrospect perceived as stern, cold or even threatening and cruel: the relationship with the mother is often described as close and affectionate, even over-permissive. Rarely is any attempt made, however, to rear the child as one of the opposite sex.

Between the ages of six and ten years, and without any apparent precipating factor, the boy expresses doubt about his sex role and frankly wishes to be a girl. In some subjects, the doubt is expressed in statements such as, 'I thought I would eventually develop into a girl' or 'I hoped I would grow breasts'. During this phase, the child begins to cross-dress, using either mother's or sister's clothes. Sometimes this is seen as part of a game and with the parents' amused consent, while at other times it is done secretly. In both situations the subject always derives a great deal of pleasure from it.

Girls' toys such as dolls are preferred to toy guns and cars, and a female role is adopted during play activities. At school the child is often identified as 'different', and, consequently, teasing, the use of nicknames and even physical assaults are not uncommon. The boy prefers the company of girls, avoids contacts sports, at times prefers swimming or ice-skating, but usually dislikes any sporting activities. While school adjustment is often described as poor by most transsexuals, scholastic achievements are usually in the average range.

Puberty tends to be reached somewhat late at age fifteen or sixteen and the emergence of secondary sex characteristics is unwelcome. Girls offer no erotic attraction. Auto-erotic activities are infrequent and accompanied by fantasies of being changed into a girl and penetrated by a male. Mutual masturbation seems to be uncommon and seduction by an older male rare. Cross-dressing continues in this phase and is done secretly and less frequently. Gradually, the embryonic transsexual begins to dislike his sexual organs and avoids touching them.

In late adolescence the subject is usually a lonely individual, fully aware of being different from his peer group. Often he sees himself as a homosexual, increasingly attracted to males of his own age group, and at times becoming involved in sexual acts as a passive partner. Parents are by now aware of his gender identity problem and vigorous attempts are made to 'masculinize' the boy through sport or choice of occupation. Education is in most cases below the higher school certificate level.

In early adulthood the male transsexual may already have come to terms with his sexual orientation and may perhaps have read some literature about his condition in popular magazines or have met other transsexuals. The wish for sex reassignment begins to crystallize. Although he may have had several sexual experiences with males, usually homosexuals, ideally he would prefer a hetero-sexual male partner. His attitude to anal intercourse varies; it is sometimes enjoyed as an expression of femininity but often rejected for moral and aesthetic reasons or simply described as unpleasant and painful.

Cross-dressing becomes more elaborate. Cosmetics, underwear and distinctly female clothes are acquired and the patient feels 'comfortable' or even elated when dressed as a woman. Sexual arousal is generally absent, although some report initial arousal and even masturbatory activity in adolescence. While many transsexuals pursue an unwavering course towards complete femininity, in some a final attempt is made to return to the original gender. Sexual intercourse with females is attempted and may even be physiologically successful but is depicted as unexciting, unpleasant, and definitely inferior in quality to intercourse with males. Nevertheless, a number of transsexuals marry in their early twenties and half of them produce children. During this 'return to normal' phase, often 'super-masculine' occupations and hobbies are chosen (e.g. an Army career, buck-jumping, motor-cycle racing, etc.).

Some years later, nearly all the rebels have joined the mainstream of transsexuals, and in the late twenties the majority of them live permanently as women, having approached doctors and demanded hormone administration and surgical sex reassignment. By now, they either live alone or have found a sexual companion who is male and, in their opinion, definitely heterosexual. They have a variety of occupations; few are self-employed and hardly any are in the professions. A minority work as female impersonators, dancers, or 'strippers' and a few have briefly experimented with prostitution. About half of them drink and smoke, some to excess, but they rarely take other drugs.

About one-fifth of all transsexuals have had brief psychiatric breakdowns, usually depressive in type. Suicidal attempts are uncommon and self-castration is very rare, although threats to carry out either or both are made at times. A number of transsexuals have already had plastic surgery—usually breast augmentation operations or facial cosmetic surgery. Their social adjustment is often reasonable. In some cases parents or friends take an accepting attitude. If transsexuals are attractive enough, they are not recognized as disguised males in their work sphere. Nevertheless, the wish for surgery remains intense and the treatment phase is beset with difficulties.

During their long waiting period prior to surgery, many 'act out', with suicidal gestures, aggressive behaviour and approaches to other gender clinics under false names. Their conduct invites a clinical appraisal of 'maladjustment' and a prolongation of the waiting period, which in turn elicits further behaviour disturbances. The vicious circle is finally broken by psychotherapy and eventual surgery or, rarely, by rejecting the patient as a candidate for sex reassignment. The average waiting period from first medical contact to reassignment surgery is five years and by this time, patients are usually in their early thirties.

# Differential diagnosis

While the main clinical theme of transsexualism has been described above, it must be remembered that it is a theme with many variations. When taking a case history of a patient applying for sex reassignment surgery, one must be aware of the extensive knowledge which some transsexuals have acquired through contact with fellow-sufferers and the reading of magazines and books (even special texts on transsexualism). Consequently, statements in the history must be treated with some circumspection. Before a firm diagnosis of transsexualism can be made, schizophrenia, transvestism and homosexuality must be excluded. A fourth disorder, temporal lobe epilepsy, which a number of authors associate with transsexualism and other sexual abnormalities, also deserves consideration.

## Schizophrenia

Of these disorders, schizophrenia in particular is a complex and challenging problem. To be sure, the florid schizophrenic, who is hallucinating, thought-disordered and exhibiting bizarre behaviour, presents a totally different clinical picture from transsexualism. Occasionally, however, one sees patients with a blurred presentation; gender-identity doubts interwine with schizophrenic body-image disturbances, while the transsexual preoccupation with self-mutilation acquires a psychotic flavour. In such cases a precise diagnosis is difficult.

Schizophrenics not infrequently present themselves to gender clinics for surgical reassignment. Hoenig and Kenna, in a series of seventy-two transsexuals, found a 2.8 per cent incidence of schizophrenia in male and a 5.5 per cent incidence in female patients.[2] Wålinder's figures are similar, giving a 4.9 per cent incidence of schizophrenia in his transsexual patients.[3]

How often does transsexual symptomatology emerge during the course of schizophrenia, and does it differ from primary or classic transsexualism? Although problems of sexual identity in schizophrenic patients are occasionally encountered by clinical psychiatrists, an amazing lack of precise information about it exists in current textbooks of psychiatry. Older publications consider ideas of changing sex and doubts about sexual identity to be almost characteristic of schizophrenia, without providing further data on this subject.

More recently, a number of authors have studied sexual identity abnormalities in schizophrenics without special reference to transsexualism. In 1962 Planarsky and Johnston investigated 150 male schizophrenics and found confusion of sexual identity in 15 per cent of subjects, while in 4.7 per cent definite delusions of sexual change were present.[4]

Gittleson and Levine's paper in 1966 on subjective ideas of sexual change in male schizophrenics revealed both genital hallucinations and delusion of sex change in 30 per cent and 25 per cent respectively of seventy-five subjects.[5] Such symptoms were absent in forty-five control subjects. In 1967 Gittleson and Dawson-Butterworth reported a survey of fifty-seven female schizophrenics and seventy-nine controls.[6] Again, genital hallucinations were found in 36 per cent, ideas of change in genital size and shape in 24 per cent, and delusions of changing sex in 25 per cent patients. While in schizophrenia, symptoms of genital change generally occur in a setting of acute psychosis, there are, nevertheless, startling resemblances to the transsexual syndrome, in which an overvalued idea, namely the belief in possessing a gender identity opposite to the one indicated by the genital organs, is held with almost delusional strength. A comparison between dysmorphophobia, believed to be a schizophrenic precursor, and the transsexual experience comes to mind: in the former, the patient holds the belief that an organ or part of his body is deformed, unacceptable, and must be altered at all costs. It is furthermore of some significance that self-castration occurs almost exclusively in schizophrenics and transsexuals. It is more often carried out by the former while usually only contemplated or used as a threat by the latter.

In 1963 Blacker and Wong reported four cases of auto-castration in detail.[7] Case histories undoubtedly pointed to a schizophrenic illness. However, there existed common denominators with transsexualism in the history, such as absent father-figures, sexual confusion of long duration and eventually strong feminine identification, as well as depressive reactions, all relieved by auto-castration. A common and ominous symptom in all patients was attempted mutilation of sexual organs in early childhood.

Finally, we must consider the possibility that transsexualism is nothing more than one aspect of schizophrenia. A number of authors, including Binder[8] and Baastrup[9], espouse this view. Baastrup calls transsexualism an attenuated form of schizophrenia, and Pauly, in his early papers, used the term 'paranoic transsexuals' when describing transsexualism.[10]

## Transvestism

Apart from schizophrenia, transvestism is probably the most common disorder seen in non-transsexual patients who apply for surgical sex reassignment. One may define the transvestite, who incidentally is always a male, as a person who obtains sexual gratification from cross-dressing, which is thus fetishistic in its dimension. He does not detest his sexual organs nor does he wish them to be removed. He may be heterosexually orientated and the cross-dressing either heightens his sexual experience or enables him to achieve arousal and orgasm. Most authors agree that early childhood experiences, while varied in pattern, do not include a symbiotic mother–child relationship, held by Stoller to be invariably present in male-to-female transsexuals. Father-figures, however, are often seen as aggressive and threatening or are absent. The classic transvestite is not effeminate as a child and one has an impression of the core gender identity being essentially male. Cross-dressing activity is almost invariably accompanied by masturbation or heterosexual intercourse. Transvestites are often married and not infrequently aggressive, positive and competitive individuals who are at times depressed and sometimes heavy drinkers. It is as if the act of cross-dressing represents an act of projection of a female image which is split off from the patient's personality and utilized in sexual gratification.

Due to the ageing process, a previously active transvestite may at times experience failure of sexual arousal through cross-dressing and eventually contemplate a female existence and even self-castration. He therefore seeks surgical sex reassignment almost as a protective device. At other times, a severe and often non-sexual stress may precipitate the wish for permanent feminity and sex reassignment. In some patients, however, the clinical picture is not clear-cut. Fetishistic arousal may occur in true transsexuals but may cease as the years go by, and wearing of female garments is then accompanied by a feeling of joy or satisfaction devoid of any sexual element. Probably the most significant point in the differential diagnosis between transsexualism and transvestitism is the relative asexuality, social isolation and intense preoccupation with surgical alteration of genital organs in true transsexuals.

## Homosexuality

Finally, something should be said about the passive homosexual, who rarely, and then half-heartedly, approaches a gender-disorder clinic for surgery. Person and Oversey recognize two sub-groups, the effeminate homosexual and the aggressive 'drag-queen'.[11,12] In the former, the authors note effeminacy during childhood and fantasies of being a girl, but no real belief in femininity. Core gender identity is described as male, cross-dressing occurs largely for narcissistic gratification, and personality is passively hysterical. In the case of

the 'drag-queen', the entire picture is one of aggressive and histrionic behaviour, often accompanied by drug dependency and prostitution. A demand for surgery often follows a breakdown in a
homosexual relationship.

It is not uncommon for a middle-aged homosexual, who may be
married and may not even be active sexually, to suddenly decide to
choose female gender identity and surgery in order to spend the
remaining years of his life as a dependent and secure female. Meyer
refers to such a person as the stigmatized homosexual, consciously
rejecting his homosexuality as socially unacceptable and, in Meyer's
words, 'seeking medical rationalization for his homosexuality
through surgery'.[13]

## Female-to-male transsexualism

The definition given earlier in this chapter applies equally to the
gender disorder occurring in the biological female, the clinical
picture being essentially a mirror image of male-to-female transsexualism. Therefore, only relevant differences will be discussed
here.

## Typical case history

The precise prevalence rate of this condition is unknown, the incidence being much lower than in the male. Deviations from normal
child-rearing patterns occur but are ill-defined and aetiologically of
doubtful significance. Anatomically, chromosomally, and in terms
of hormone levels, patients present as normal females. Cross-
dressing is again a feature of the disorder but, for obvious reasons,
it is less clearly defined and usually accepted by family and society.
'Tomboy' behaviour invites respect rather than ridicule from peer
groups. The stable personality structure that is almost invariably
seen in the adult female transsexual probably stems from a relatively
smooth passage through childhood and adolescence. This is in
marked contrast to the unhappy school period, merciless teasing and
often physical violence to which the male transsexual is exposed at
a similar period of his life.

The onset of menstruation is a traumatic experience. By this time,
gender doubts have crystallized and girls are seen as sexual targets.
In early adulthood the subject enters into 'lesbian' relationships but
male core-gender identity is evident and, in many instances, the
subject attracts a female partner who is clearly heterosexual. Relationships are stable and mutually satisfying. Occasionally, sexual

intercourse and penetration by a male partner takes place but is not enjoyed, and marriage is a rare event. Psychiatric illnesses, particularly the depressive reactions that are so common in male transsexuals during the long waiting period before surgery, hardly ever occur. Testosterone administration sometimes produces dramatic changes in muscle mass, hirsutism, voice, and sexual drive. Lack of menstruation follows and is accepted with alacrity. Most patients are resigned to the fact that surgery is usually limited to mastectomy and hysterectomy, and because the former removes an obvious anatomical and symbolic feature of femininity, it provides great relief. Techniques combining penile reconstruction and erectile mechanisms are at present under investigation and may eventually provide the female-to-male transsexual with a cosmetically acceptable phallus that will allow coition.

## Differential diagnosis

In the differential diagnosis, transvestism, a not uncommon sexual disturbance in the male, need not be considered here. There are no female transvestites. Women may dress in male attire in order to look attractive, unusual, or for practical reasons, but they experience no sexual arousal and the compulsive and fetishistic element is absent.

Schizophrenia and homosexuality may present differential diagnostic problems. The female schizophrenic who approaches a gender dysphoria clinic for surgical sex reassignment presents with the clinical features of the disorder. By contrast, female homosexuals hardly ever desire surgery.

## Conclusion

Whether male or female the transsexual patient's foremost request is for surgical reassignment of his or her genital organs and most clinical teams specializing in the treatment of gender disorders agree that, at present, this procedure alone offers the best hope for bringing permanent relief. Sex reassignment surgery produces irreversible anatomical changes which are of great therapeutic benefit to carefully selected patients. However, it can be utterly disastrous if the diagnostic evaluation has been incorrect. It is this element of risk that invests the diagnosis and differential diagnosis of transsexualism with special importance.

# 6  Psychosocial Aspects and Psychological Testing

## What can psychological testing reveal?

### Don Burnard and Michael W. Ross

## I  Psychosocial aspects of transsexualism

While it is fair to say that there is little consensus and few data on the causes of transsexualism, most work has been on biological and psychological factors, such as parental rearing patterns and psychopathology. Nevertheless, investigation of social factors which appear to have a bearing on transsexualism may also contribute to our understanding of the phenomenon, and of some of the factors which may influence presentation as a transsexual. In addition, it is necessary to have some idea of the epidemiology of transsexualism, and particularly of its prevalence and incidence.

The earliest epidemiological reports on transsexualism came from Scandinavia and the United Kingdom. In 1968 Wålinder reported that the prevalence in Sweden was one per 54 000 of population, with a sex ratio of 2.5 males-to-females to 1 female-to-male.[1] Subsequently, in 1971, he reported an incidence (new cases per year) of 0.23 per 100 000 of the population over fifteen years, with the sex ratio approaching 1:1.[2] In the United Kingdom Hoenig and Kenna found figures surprisingly similar to those of Wålinder, with a prevalence of one per 53 000 of population, giving a rate of 1.9 per 100 000 of population over fifteen years of age.[3] The sex ratio was higher than that in Sweden, however, with a 3.3:1 ratio in favour of male-to-female subjects. Their data also demonstrated that both male and female transsexuals were much more likely to come from working-class backgrounds; a finding which has been consistently noted in subsequent studies. In addition, they noted that transsexualism was much more common in cities than in rural areas; they accounted for this by establishing that transsexuals tend to congregate in cities. A high incidence of prolonged unemployment amongst transsexuals was also apparent in their data. More recent studies in the United States and Britain have suggested that the ratio in favour of male-to-female transsexuals, previously estimated at around 1:6 has come down to 1:4.[4]

A thorough study to investigate the prevalence and sex ratio of transsexualism and factors which may influence this was made by

Ross *et al.*[5] They compared prevalence figures for Sweden and Australia in 1978, with the hypothesis that if transsexualism was biologically based, one would expect to find roughly the same prevalence and sex ratio across a number of countries. Sweden and Australia were chosen because they are democratic countries of about the same population and level of industrial development and affluence. Results from complete information from Sweden and incomplete (and therefore understated) returns from Australia, showed that the Swedish prevalence was stable at 0.23 per 100 000 of population over fifteen years of age, compared with over three times that figure in Australia (0.74 per 100 000). Similarly, the sex ratio for Sweden was still 1:1, while in Australia there were seven male-to-female transsexuals to every one female-to-male. These findings were interpreted as suggesting that the prevalence of transsexualism is a function of the sex-role rigidity of the society in which the individual is reared and of its degree of anti-homosexuality. Swedish society is both less sex-role rigid and much less anti-homosexual than that of Australia. It could be argued that in a more sex-role rigid society, more individuals would be likely not to fit into the more stereotyped roles and thus assume that, if they did not fit the role of one sex, they must belong to the other; similarly, in a more anti-homosexual society, more homosexuals would be likely to attempt to legitimize their same-sex object preference by attempting to change sex.

The data on differences in sex ratio are more difficult to interpret, but they suggest that where there is less sex-role equality, it may be more acceptable for males to go 'down' in status by becoming women than the reverse. Recent data from Czechoslovakia, however, has suggested that in eastern European countries, the ratio is uneven and in favour of female-to-male transsexuals, which is not in line with a sex-role inequality hypothesis. Clearly, social or societal explanations are no more enlightening than biological or psychological ones, although the link between sex-role rigidity and prevalence seems confirmed, particularly as it is supported by the preponderance of working-class subjects (sex-roles being much more strongly stereotyped in working-class families than in middle-class ones).

Transsexualism is not, however, limited to Western societies. Several cases have been reported in Vietnam,[6] and it is probably as common in Singapore as in Western countries,[7] although with a great preponderance of Chinese and few Malays or Indians. In the Middle East, Wikan has reported on a class of individuals in Oman who dress as women and yet have some of the rights of men.[8] Whether this is transsexualism as it is understood in Western society, or a form of institutionalized homosexuality consequent upon disapproval of male–male relations in Arab society, is uncertain. Certainly there is no gender reassignment surgery involved, and use of male genital organs is appropriate, which would tend to suggest that this is a local response to sexual stigmatization rather than transsexualism. Religious variables may also influence presentation: Hellman *et al.* found that, amongst Roman Catholics, later adolescent concerns over homosexuality that are religiously derived, may lead to transsexualism.[9] Other clinicians have noted the apparent over-representation of Catholics in transsexual samples, but little evidence has been provided that Catholicism is a contributing factor any more than any other strongly-held religious view. Nevertheless, religion must be considered a further social variable which may have an influence, either direct or, more probably, indirect, on the development of transsexualism.

These societal data suggest that there is an interaction between social and psychological factors amongst the variables influencing the presentation, if not the causation, of transsexualism. It has already been noted in chapter 1 that a number of researchers have suggested that around one-third of candidates for gender reassignment may be homophobic effeminate homosexuals, and clearly the societal reaction to homosexuality will have some influence on whether effeminate male homosexuals or masculine lesbians internalize homophobia. Morgan has suggested that in such circumstances, transsexualism is a socially neutral diagnosis which disappears after surgery,[10] which Roback *et al.* have also noted the number of individuals who present as transsexuals and have borderline personalities with homophobia.[11] On the other hand, while this applies to perhaps one-third of transsexuals, it does little to cast any light on those people who clearly have primary gender dysphoria. To attempt to find social mechanisms which can account alone for cases of transsexualism is to ignore the fact that it is not a unitary entity and may have its origin in many factors. For this reason, it is important to gain some insight into the psyche of transsexuals and, more particularly, of those individuals who are likely to benefit from gender reassignment surgery. Psychological testing may reveal the intra-psychic influences on the development of transsexualism, as well as indicate the stability or otherwise of the subject, and his or her ability to cope with gender reassignment, if indicated, or, alternatively, with psychotherapy.

# II Psychological testing of transsexuals and its efficacy

The importance of psychological testing of transsexuals lies in the need to establish quickly and objectively those psychological factors which correlate with either positive or negative likely outcomes of sex reassignment. Sometimes, when there is clear evidence that the subject is a transsexual, there may be personality factors which weigh against successful sex reassignment. Psychological tests provide some objective data to underpin the more subjective criteria and psychodynamic material obtained by examining the mental state of the patient. They lend valuable support to the clinical diagnosis of transsexualism and help in the clinical management of the patient. When psychiatric assessment and test results are in agreement, the decision to commence hormone therapy is made easier. When there is no such agreement, further psychiatric investigation is indicated before recommending that the patient commence hormone therapy and live in the female role.

Wålinder *et al.* found that psychosis, mental retardation and unstable personality were definite contra-indications for sex reassignment.[12] Projective tests, such as the Rorschach and Thematic Apperception Test (TAT), are sensitive in identifying and predicting psychotic reactions. They can bypass defensive processes and yield evidence of such basic material as thought disorder, poor grasp of reality, and unrealistic expectations. The Wechsler Adult Intelligence Scale (WAIS) measures intellectual capacity, specific cognitive and practical skills, and formal thought disorder. It can indicate cognitive deficits and is also effective in determining a subject's levels of motivation, tolerance and basic thinking. The Minnesota Multiphasic Personality Inventory (MMPI) provides an extensive personality profile and indicates the degree of stability or instability in the organization of the subject's personality.

What is the psychopathology of the transsexual? There is no unanimity amongst authors. Many, such as Stafford-Clark[13], see transsexualism as a delusion of psychotic proportions requiring psychiatric treatment. Sex reassignment surgery is seen by this group as complicity with the psychosis and therefore both inappropriate and ineffective. Yet in the 1930s a science student who constantly spoke about his desire to be a space traveller might well have been diagnosed as a crazy dreamer, perhaps schizophrenic. Others, like McKee,[14] see transsexualism as a rare quirk of nature which produces a perfectly normal man or woman in the anatomical body of the opposite sex. Any psychopathology is a reaction to this state and is relieved by gender reassignment. Among those with various intermediate views, Meyer sees transsexualism as a defensive manoeuvre to resolve very early conflict which threatens the subject's identity.[15] Thus transsexualism represents a severe personality disorder of the borderline type. Stoller sees male transsexualism as an identity *per se*, not the surface manifestation of an interminable unconscious struggle to preserve identity.[16]

Hoenig and Kenna's study of fifty-four transsexuals supports the view that there is a substantial group of transsexuals with no formal psychiatric disorder: 1.8 per cent were diagnosed as schizophrenic, while 9.3 per cent suffered from affective psychosis.[17] Neurosis and personality disorders were more common (37 per cent). An early study by Hoenig in 1970 had reported that psychiatric disorders accompanied transsexualism in 70 per cent of the cases studied,[18] yet other researchers, such as Wålinder,[19] reported no evidence of psychosis in a study of forty-three transsexuals. Roback *et al.* compared the self-concept and psychological adjustment of homosexuals with those of transsexuals and, although they found the homosexuals to be more self-accepting and better adjusted than the transsexuals seeking sex reassignment, they found that the majority of transsexuals (64 per cent) showed no evidence of psychopathology.[20] Meerloo's view that transsexuals show gross reality disturbance may be the result of generalizing from a sub-sample of the total group.[21] Stoller found that a core group of transsexual males, characterized by a persistent pseudo-feminine narcissism, had stable ego strengths and an intact sense of reality.[22] On the other hand, Pauly, reviewing one hundred transsexuals, found that 20 per cent had sufficient psychopathology to require hospitalization.[23]

Perhaps these diverse findings can be reconciled on the basis that all transsexuals undergo crises which may temporarily stretch their defences to near or actual breaking-point. Jan Morris, the well-known English writer formerly known as James Morris, describes how, in her mid-thirties, her self-repugnance had not only intensified but had focused on her physique.[24] She was plunged into periods of despair, suffered distortions of vision and speech, experienced anxieties that developed into a mild paranoia and recognized that she was becoming obsessive. Jan Morris is now living a happy productive life following reassignment surgery. One wonders what psychological tests would have shown had she been tested during her periods of despair.

Derogatis and fellow researchers compared thirty-one transsexuals with fifty-seven heterosexual males, and established a characteristic symptom profile.[25] The transsexuals were more sensitive, more depressed, and more anxious. They had a marked sense of alienation from other people which caused them considerable psychological distress. Symptoms of hostility were mostly absent, reflecting passivity and lack of aggression.

Person and Ovesey attribute the chronic unhappiness of male-to-female transsexuals to several factors.[26] Firstly, the wish to be not only feminine but female becomes an overvalued idea. Added to this is the reality of a body type that is incompatible with male genitalia. Furthermore, there is society's moral condemnation of homosexuality. These factors, however, are by no means universally true. Society's attitude to homosexuality is changing, and some transsexuals have a body type consistent with their given sex. Finally, there is often no evidence of a transformation in the thinking of the transsexual; rather there has been a life-long conviction of gender dysphoria which has resisted all efforts to dislodge it.

What psychological tests have proved most useful with transsexuals? Many researchers, such as Althof *et al.*,[27] recognize the MMPI as having shown the most promise as a clinical instrument for identifying and predicting gender dysphoria. They reviewed the results of the large number of published studies based on the MMPI and the most common finding was an elevation on Scale 5, the femininity scale. However, a Melbourne study comparing profiles of 100 successful candidates for sex reassignment with twenty-five unsuccessful ones, found that both groups had the same significant elevation on Scale 5. The problem of so many false positives related to Scale 5 led Althof *et al.*, in the above study, to develop a gender dysphoria MMPI scale (GD). However, the unpublished Melbourne study by Burnard has found the same problem with this scale.[28] Here the Australian Sex-Role Scale (A.S.-R.S.) developed by Antill was used,[29] and although it did not support the hypothesis that the A.S.-R.S. would distinguish true transsexuals from unsuitable candidates for sex reassignment, the scale did prove valuable in providing useful objective data to support the sometimes more subjective clinical diagnosis. The A.S.-R.S. provides evidence that male-to-female transsexuals adopt a unidimensional stereotyped sex-role identity rather than an androgynous (combination of male and female) one. This is consistent with their conscious efforts to affirm the feminine core-identity which their biological sexual endowment denies them.

The A.S.-R.S. has also been useful in comparing the way transsexuals define their sex-role identity before and after reassignment surgery. Post-operatively, they define their sex-role characteristics less in relation to social desirability than before surgery. Positive feminine characteristics are less emphasized by fully reassigned transsexuals who are also more likely to admit to negative feminine characteristics. This is consistent with the report of Derogatis *et al.* who found that those male transsexuals who make a sound adjustment post-operatively as females, adjust their gender role behaviour from that of more extreme femininity pre-operatively to that more in accord with heterosexual females.[30] These phenomena may provide important prognostic indicators for the success of surgical gender reassignment.

The most common clinical correlations on MMPI testing reported by Althof *et al.* were the Scale 5 (femininity) with Scale 4 immaturity and impulsiveness), and Scale 5 with Scale 8 (confused, schizoid and bizarre thinking). Finney *et al.* made a computer analysis of the MMPI profiles of twenty transsexuals and found that 65 per cent of the sample showed evidence of hysterical personality.[31] This finding was consistent with the high incidence of hysterical personality reported by Stoller.[32] Certainly the transsexuals' own reports on their sexual history is often incomplete, fragmented and vague, reflecting the mechanisms of repression, selective forgetting and inattention to detail in the hysterical personality.

Lothstein, in his study of ten ageing transsexuals (average age fifty-two years), found that psychological testing helped to determine the extent and severity of the patients' pathology, when results on the MMPI validity scales were within normal limits.[33] The MMPI mean profile indicated marked depression, Scale 2 ranking first or second in 75 per cent of results from biological males. Although the average WAIS score was 117 (range 89–141) the pattern of sub-test scores for the group suggested major ego defects in attention, concentration and judgement. The Rorschach results indicated thought disorder and poor reality testing in six of the ten patients. Eight of them showed evidence of non-specific ego weaknesses. Thresholds for frustration and anxiety were found to be low and there was an inability to delay impulses. Lothstein concluded that his ageing male transsexual patients were depressed, isolated, withdrawn, schizoid individuals with profound dependency conflicts. Furthermore, they were immature, narcissistic, egocentric and potentially 'explosive', while their attempts to obtain reassignment surgery were demanding, manipulative, controlling, coercive, and paranoid. Immediate gratification was their goal. Female transsexuals, on the other hand, show less serious psychopathology as both Stoller and Wålinder and Thuwe reported in 1975.[34] However, it must be admitted that Lothstein's subjects could hardly be called a typical sample of transsexuals as nine of the ten studied had serious physical health problems.

A Singapore study of fifty-six male transsexuals by Tsoi *et al.* revealed the outstanding result on the MMPI to be a highly significant peak on the femininity scale.[35] The results on the schizophrenia and the depression scales were also outside the upper limit of the normal range. The authors see these profiles as reflecting the confused and bizarre life style of the subjects. Significantly, 82 per cent of them were prostitutes and atypical of transsexuals in other parts of the world.

Langevin *et al.*, in a study of 107 subjects, found that the MMPI differentiated male transsexuals living as males, male transsexuals living as females, heterosexual patients, homosexual controls, and heterosexual controls on all except the mania and lie scales.[36] The first group showed the most pathology. These workers concluded that femininity was a key factor in male transsexualism.

The Melbourne study by Burnard, comparing the MMPI profiles of seventy-five successful candidates for gender reassignment with those of twenty unsuccessful candidates, shows that the mean profiles of the two groups are significantly different.[37] It suggests that the candidates rejected for reassignment by the Queen Victoria Medical Centre's medical team tend to be those who show evidence of somatic delusions and psychotic depression. The mean profile of the successful candidates shows only one very significant peak on Scale 5 (femininity), a fairly significant peak on Scale 4 (measuring the degree to which aggressive and sexual impulses are acted out and degree of social conformity), slightly significant peaks on Scale 3 (measuring hysteria, and repression) and on Scale 8, (measuring schizoid thinking, feelings of being different, or hostility or withdrawal involving fantasy). The remainder of the profile is within the normal range for a general population. While these findings do not support the view that transsexuals have severe psychopathology, they suggest that personality disorders are more likely to be associated with transsexualism. As a person's sexual identity is an integral part of his or her personality, transsexuals would be expected to suffer some personality disorder. However, it is possible that the mean profile may be hiding gross abnormalities of personality. Moreover, there was evidence of a tendency for the subjects to fake a good result either consciously or unconsciously. Indeed, subjects with personality disorders are well known to be capable of faking a good result. The importance of a long, supervised waiting period of at least two years before surgical intervention is emphasized; subjects with personality disorders are less likely to persevere. Moreover, it is more difficult for a deception to be maintained for two years than for a much shorter time.

The MMPI has also been used as a single measure to contrast patients' pre- and post-reassignment scores. Althof *et al.* reported that treatment lowers patients' scores on MMPI clinical scales.[38] However, the lack of unanimity in the MMPI results in different studies and the sometimes contradictory findings emphasize the need for a careful elucidation of terms. Sorensen and Hertoft argue for the need to differentiate various groups whose common feature is a request for gender reassignment surgery.[39] They propose a clinical schematic outline to help differentiate such groups.

MacKenzie makes an even more trenchant criticism of the present definition of transsexualism.[40] He emphasizes the dilemma of defining a clinical syndrome on the basis of treatment-seeking behaviour. He believes that it is crucial to develop more rigorous definitions so that an increasing amount of data from various centres throughout the world can be accumulated and compared. Furthermore, Lindgren and Pauly argue for the use of standard psychological tests that will facilitate the comparison of results from any one gender identity clinic with comparable data from other clinics.[41] Such tests would enable researchers and clinicians to understand and describe transsexualism in objective and quantifiable terms. These workers developed a body-image scale to quantify the way in which the transsexual perceives his or her body and how he or she feels about it.

A complementary tactic requires that researchers using better tests attempt to standardize the samples on which they use these tests. There is little point in comparing test results of ageing transsexuals with those of transsexuals who are forced to survive by prostitution. Likewise, there is limited value in comparing candidates requesting sex reassignment surgery in the absence of prior assessment with those who have been carefully screened and have completed a waiting period of two years, living in the gender role appropriate to their desired sex. A comparison of MMPI profiles would be more productive if it was made between carefully matched groups of subjects.

A second important issue is the need to improve the measurement of femininity and masculinity. If femininity is the key factor in male transsexualism, as many researchers have found, then it is important to develop more sophisticated and subtle measures of femininity. Scale 5 of the MMPI is a unidimensional scale which assumes that male and female characteristics are mutually exclusive. It measures stereotyped feminine interests and traits. Sandra Bem, as long ago as 1974, established that individuals in whom masculine and feminine characteristics were blended into a single personality were psychologically healthier than those who adopted a more stereotyped sex-role identity.[42] Bem in England and Antill in Australia have developed more sophisticated measures of femininity, and Freund *et al.* have developed a Feminine Gender Identity Scale by assembling a nucleus of feminine gender identity items of high clinical validity to which they have added items strongly correlated with this nucleus.[43] The new scale strongly discriminates between heterosexual and transsexual males without any overlap. At the same time one-third of the androphilic males do not show any higher degree of feminine gender identity than do heterosexual control subjects and only a few have high scores similar to those of transsexual subjects. These results indicate that sex object preference and gender identity are to some extent independent.

# The need for a standardized battery of tests

Althof *et al.* have emphasized that no single measure or standardized battery of tests has ever been consistently employed with various groups of transsexuals.[44]

At the Queen Victoria Medical Centre, Melbourne, 220 male-to-female transsexuals have been psychologically tested as part of the process of assessment for sex reassignment. One hundred and twenty-five of these patients have completed the following battery of tests: Rorschach; Thematic Apperception Test (TAT); and Minnesota Multiphasic Personality Inventory (MMPI). The last ninety-five subjects in this group completed two additional psychological tests, the Wechsler Adult Intelligence Scale (WAIS) and the Australian Sex-Role Scale (A.S.-R.S.).

Psychological testing cannot establish a diagnosis of transsexualism. What it does best is screen for psychosis and gross personality disturbance, and provide, in the case of candidates who are suitable for reassignment, more information about the person and his or her problem

Projective tests, such as the Rorschach and TAT, provide data for a dynamic description of intrapsychic processes. When used together with the WAIS, they help to establish the integrity of the subject's sense of reality, the degree of development of cognitive functions, the degree of affect (emotional state) control, the nature of psychic defences, ego strengths, the nature of relationships with other people, and ability to control impulses and drives. The battery of tests should include those of both structured and unstructured type. Some subjects do very well on structured tests but poorly on unstructured tests. Projective tests, especially the Rorschach, are useful in detecting diffuse sexuality and sex-role diffusion which may be masked by claims of gender dysphoria. The full description of ego strengths is made possible by combining the WAIS, which indicates verbal I.Q., performance I.Q., and specific cognitive deficits, with projective tests, which measure the degree to which imagination and affect are constricted or uncontrolled.

On the battery of tests used in Melbourne, some subjects have shown evidence of paranoid thinking, severe personality disorder, and low intelligence. The last rules out the subject's ability to make an informed decision and is therefore a contra-indication to gender reassignment. Candidates recommended for reassignment have shown evidence of a feminine identity together with the lack of a masculine identity. The evidence, combined with a two-year waiting period in which the candidate shows a capacity to live and work in the desired sex role as a woman, provides objective data to justify surgical intervention.

The Melbourne study has provided evidence of the existence of a group of transsexuals whose members could be described as narcissistic, with a stable need for a role in which they will be nurtured. These patients try very hard to make a good impression and present themselves as warm and empathizing. Yet their TAT stories lack sincerity, are often idyllic and sometimes superficial and histrionic as are those of hysterics. A striking feature of this group's TAT stories is that their characters are given names and their stories titles. Often subsidiary characters in their stories serve the needs of the main character with whom the patient identifies. In the Rorschach test a preoccupation with clothing, jewellery and external appearances is often revealed. Little sensitivity as measured by a lack of texture responses is not uncommon. Subjects are crassly manipulative in the test situation and show a low anxiety tolerance as measured by facetiousness and/or evasiveness. There is often evidence of strong sensual impulses and poor controls. On the MMPI profile there is a tendency for peaks to occur on Scale 4 (narcissism) as well as on Scale 5 (femininity). The existence of this group is not surprising. Perhaps a person needs to be narcissistic to undergo a body transformation, especially one involving the removal of genital organs and the construction of genitalia that mimic those of the sex appropriate to the desired gender. The Melbourne study results are consistent with those from earlier published studies of male transsexuals living as women reported by Langevin *et al.*[45] The chief inadequacies of the Melbourne battery of tests are the absence of a body-image scale and a test to compare the transsexuals' perception of their real and ideal selves. The importance of the body-image scale lies partly in its ability to detect those subjects who will never be happy with the outcome of surgery.

## Conclusions

The insistence on psychological testing of all candidates for gender reassignment and the adoption of a standard battery of tests, has enhanced the criteria for selection of suitable candidates. It has also contributed to a more thorough detection of psychotic subjects and those with severe personality disorders who lack a stable identity, and has provided objective data to formulate new and test existing theories of the causation of gender dysphoria. Furthermore, psychological testing has led to the initiation of research which has contributed to an understanding of how transsexuals modify their sex-role identity after surgery. Finally, such testing has provided evidence that transsexuals cannot be regarded as a homogenous group. In fact three core groups have been identified. Subjects in the first group show manifestations of hysteria, as reported by Althof and colleagues,[46] those in the second group show signs of narcissism, as reported by Sorensen and Burnard,[47] while those in the third group lack sufficient ego strengths and show psychotic traits. For this third group, somatic delusions are part of a fantasy withdrawal which is used as a defence against depression.

# 7  Endocrine Aspects
## Hormones and their role
### A. W. Steinbeck

## Introduction

The state of transsexualism is defined on page 1 of this book. Transsexual persons who consult an endocrinologist do so for a number of reasons, some of which reflect their interests. They may be referred for assessment, therapeutic advice, support, and counselling. Some seek help to obtain reassignment surgery or therapeutic advice after its completion. Patients often have companions who need to be involved or supported. Not all transsexual persons seek complete sex reassignment and some look for counter-measures in treatment.

It is a truism that generalizations are unwise and, unless those seeking advice are representative of all levels of society, errors of detail are likely. The following comments relate to widely differing members of society, having widely different professional and vocational qualifications. Perhaps, because of different societal attitudes, those with sexual dysphorias have come forward among those with gender dysphorias. Among the transsexuals seeking endocrinological advice, the least common is probably the true transsexual, someone who from earliest childhood and its vaguest memories has regarded himself or herself as a person of the opposite sex. Such people have played out this gender role in the family unit without semblance of psychological stress. For them, some unexplained or accidental developmental process has produced an opposite physical and sexual appearance to that appropriate to what they perceive as their real sex. They are incarcerated within transsexual bodies. Some will have theories as to why this has occurred and the concepts largely depend upon educational sophistication, especially a knowledge of biology. Most, however, remain in a state of confusion over the reasons for their condition. For some, the normality of chromosomal appearances is disturbing. Their gender role, though performed in society with at times amazing aptitude, cannot be fully played out, no matter what their longings, aspirations, strivings, and care. The material existence of a sexually opposite body, which may lead to hatred and revulsion for a penis or a similar reaction to breasts, precludes their perceived rightful role and behaviour. They are adamant that they have the evidence to substantiate their claims that their minds, their personalities, and they themselves react according to their true sex. They have conflicts within themselves and with much of society, excluding their own group, when they act out their rightful gender role. They do not believe that their body cells correspond with their true sex, and indeed such a belief, and others like it suggesting that alternative internal sex organs may be found, would seem to imply psychotic thinking. Some are fully aware of this reality.

The true transsexual seems qualitatively different from a person who has been brought up by a coterie of the opposite sex or by members of the family who have imposed a transsexual role upon him or her. The male child brought up by a grandmother and unmarried aunts after the death of parents, and the young female child brought up by a father and his male friends may finally behave, and only feel comfortable when behaving, in a role opposite to that of their biological sex. Such people appear to have a different quality to their behaviour and responses to endocrine therapy compared with true transsexuals.

As has been said, true transsexuals seem to be encountered less commonly than other persons who exhibit some transsexual behaviour. The incidence of true transsexualism may well depend upon diagnostic criteria, the clinic's reputation and policies, and the esteem in which the clinicians are held within the transsexual community. Centres helping subjects to obtain reassignment surgery appear to receive more initial requests than individual clinicians, and those who make such requests are not members of a homogeneous group. Some who have had reassignment surgery have appeared to trained observers to be homosexual persons with strongly developed cross-dressing activities. They claim to have always played a passive role in their thinking, sexual activity, and play and to have derived satisfaction and stimulation from such involvement. Others in this group may have wished for homosexual involvement, but their sexual expression was confined to cross-dressing with fantasies because of business or marriage commitments; for some, marriage seems to have been possible for a while because of sexual fantasies. A number of these people seem to suffer from guilt feelings, self-criticism, and a sense of existential anxiety because of the 'wrongness' that has been thrust upon them by natural and creative forces. Some have a recurring wish to be members of the opposite sex, while looking for an opportune time to realize this in practice. The subsequent comfort and solace that comes to some after reassignment surgery would seem to confirm the validity of the treatment for gaining better self-acceptance and social ease for members of this group.

There is yet another group which seems to be almost asexual.

Members of this group are quite confident that they are other than they appear physically, and are quite unwilling to be involved in any sexual activity that is not congruous with their hidden sexuality. This seems to be true more of male than of female transsexuals, the latter often being less sexually active than the males. Persons in this group are often retiring, apprehensive, and may communicate poorly but they may well suffer acutely from the indignity of their lot in life. A number of them, however, seem to be able to retain equanimity while looking for a solution. Surgical reassignment has helped some in this group but has complicated life for others. Yet others in the group have rejected surgery because the effects would mean explanations to their family, friends and colleagues at work. Indeed, some have given themselves more actively to their work to suppress their longing for a change of sex. There are also those who display great passivity in all forms of behaviour, with little sexual activity, who seem to become involved in a quiet homosexual lifestyle and who seek solace in an altered body. There is yet another smaller group of transsexuals, who should be styled iatrogenic (engendered by doctors) transsexuals, where a categorization appears to have been imposed upon them. Sometimes this appears to have been inadvertent, but at other times more directive in an attempt to explain symptoms of distress not always related directly to sexual activity. For instance, some males have identified strongly with a female relative, especially a deceased mother, while others have simply been distressed about sexual intercourse, with distaste or some other explanation being given for this.

The most difficult of all transsexual persons to classify are those who have been fertile in marriage and seemingly without problems in the early years of their lives. Some have even fostered liaisons outside marriage. For example, a female may claim that the one and only child she has borne resulted from enforced sexual intercourse either before or early in marriage. A marriage of long duration would seem to compound the problems. None the less, anamnesis (the faculty of recalling to mind) for some would seem to reveal hidden distress, agitation, and subsequent cross-dressing or dysphoria. The children of transsexual parents may see the parent in the opposite sex role, whilst others are ambivalent about accepting him or her in this role. Some who have separated or divorced may continue a relationship with their children that does not deny paternity or maternity, and this produces conflicting expressions. Reassignment surgery for members of this group seems to allow greater self-acceptance and contentment with life.

Finally there is a small group of male transsexuals who have had reassignment surgery but disdain being referred to as transsexuals. Characteristically, they work in the entertainment world. Surgery has allowed them to be excellent female impersonators. Generally they appear to be completely professional and dedicated, while their sexual activity is often quite limited. Some members of this group do not even regard themselves as women.

It is very difficult for observers to decide the extent of unhappiness that people feel when they believe themselves to be incarcerated in a body that does not express their true personality. Some of these people have accepted the situation and lived with it, accepting also the challenge to succeed as they are. Some have sought an incongruous or ambiguous development towards that of the opposite sex, breast development in particular providing them with some comfort.

## Endocrinological features

The gender dysphorias form such a variable group that it would be unlikely to find common endocrinological features characterizing either the males or females in the group. Furthermore, syndromes of discrepant sexual behaviour cannot be systematically related to discrepancies of hormonal function, despite the fact that there have been efforts to correlate homosexuality, transvestism, and trans-sexualism with sex steroid hormone levels in the blood. Some publications have suggested that homosexual men have a positive oestrogen feed-back effect upon pituitary luteinizing hormone (LH) in contradistinction to heterosexual and bisexual men.[1] In one study homosexual men were found to have lower biologically-active plasma testosterone levels and plasma follicular-stimulating hormone (FSH) levels than normal heterosexual men.[2] Furthermore, it has been postulated that testosterone levels in the critical period of brain development for sex dimorphism may be lower than normal in those males who become homosexual or transsexual.[3] In addition, homosexual females have been said to have higher testosterone levels than normal heterosexual females.[4] These data, like those of the oestrogen feed-back effect in males, have not been replicated. Furthermore, girls with congenital adrenal hyperplasia (adrenogenital syndrome), who have significantly elevated androgen levels, do not show any increased tendency for homosexual behaviour. Similarly, changes in the H–Y antigen, a cell-surface component that is usually associated with all male tissues, do not explain sexual discrepancies.[5] This is not to deny that syndromes of discrepant hormonal dysfunction can be related to some forms of sexual behaviour. The difficulty is that group studies have not always borne out the correlation suggested by individual studies. To the endocrinologist interested in behaviour, it would seem that transsexualism might develop out of a childhood or idiosyncratic experience in a particular family setting, especially in the case of males.[6] This argument is not as convincing in the case of female transsexuals.

The diagnosis of transsexualism remains a psychological task[7] and the major role of the endocrinologist is often limited to excluding problems of somatic intersexuality. When man demonstrates dominance of mind-brain over body, with development of a distinct cerebral component to human sexuality, discrepant features may be primarily the result of cerebral factors.

It must also be borne in mind that cerebral stress, the taking of alcohol and addictive drugs, and the administration of drugs for treatment of other illnesses may all interfere with blood and tissue hormone levels.

## Male-to-female transsexualism

When first seen as patients, these persons form a diverse group. They include those who have lived for so long and so successfully in the female role that they are unable to present themselves as males. Some of them, trying to be female, become so effeminate that they attract attention or so confused that they fail to relax. Others, including many transvestite impersonators, who may never desire sex reassignment, are expert in changing from one sex role to the other. It is almost as if they have multiple personalities, one for their male appearance and one or more for their female appearance. This changing of roles may reflect indecision. On the other hand there are some, despite their protestations to the contrary, who still appear clumsy and look ill-at-ease or embarrassed, as though they have some difficulty in adopting the role that they claim is rightfully theirs. Their present identity is obviously a new guise. Sometimes, it is a bony frame with obvious muscular development that cannot be hidden which leads to doubt about the person's gender. At other times, it may be sheer height, size of hands and feet, and the physical mould in which they are cast that invites exposure of the true biological identity. For some, without cosmetics, there is no confusion of identity, for the facial contour with beard and laryngeal prominence clearly indicate the effect of androgens (male sex hormones), although with cosmetics and judicious dressing the illusion may be nearly perfect. The most distressing patients of all seeking help are those whose bearing, dress, and attitude reveal them to be men awkwardly dressed in women's clothing.

Often deportment and gait, particularly a hurried walk or run, will suggest male development of muscles even in those who at rest appear presentable as women. The disparity in clinical presentation emphasizes the fact that some are well-versed and established in their role and others are not. Of the former, except for the relatively young, it is seldom that anyone is seen before oestrogen (female sex hormone) medication has been started, mostly self-administered and often without prescription. Oestrogenic substances such as stilboestrol, ethinyloestradiol or contraceptive pills are procured without prescription from friends, the dosage being empirical and often variable. This means that the description of endocrinological status before oestrogen therapy is difficult. Furthermore, even those who have been ambivalent about their transsexualism may have occasionally taken hormones to gauge their effects. While it is true that oestrogenic therapy may be used intermittently with complete recovery from its effects, long-term effects can occur depending upon the dosage and duration of therapy.

Manifestations of oestrogen medication include chloasma (the so-called 'mask of pregnancy', a type of facial pigmentation), nipple pigmentation, and sometimes pigmentation of the central line of the anterior abdominal wall (linea nigra). Gynaecomastia (breast enlargement) of varying degree, or turgescence of the nipples is commonly present. Testicular atrophy, assessed by reduction in size and loss of turgor of the testes, may occur. An alteration in the voice and reduction in body hair may be of a more subtle nature and not always readily discernible. Changes in body contours from the male to female type and a reduction in muscle bulk appear after significant de-masculinization. History-taking may elicit loss of erections, impotence, and ejaculatory failure if sexual play has involved these responses, but as the true transsexual, at this stage of development, does not usually care for genital stimulation, such a history may not be available. Oestrogens can depress libido (sexual desire) and some feel threatened by such a change.

A feature of continuing hormone therapy for transsexuals is that of medical practitioners being invited to provide continuity of therapy prescribed by someone else. Communication may fail to confirm the involvement of the other doctor, who may even deny that the patient has seen him or her. Under these circumstances, the transsexual appears to have lied and, consequently, some medical practitioners become unwilling to prescribe further hormone therapy. In their concern to avoid desultory medication and through fear of criticism, such patients may not reveal how they came to start hormone therapy. In fact the complete history of the patient's therapy may only become fully available when mutual trust between doctor and patient has been established.

Some ambivalent persons start oral oestrogen medication only to become nauseated. The same oestrogens may later be tolerated well, implying that the original nausea was possibly a psychological response to doubts about changing gender roles.

An increased blood plasma level of thyroxine-binding globulin is a good indicator of oestrogen medication when this has been denied. Some reports have suggested significant differences in plasma levels of testosterone and its free, or biologically active, component, associated with corresponding differences in pituitary gonadatrophins (LH and FSH),[8] between heterosexual and transsexual males. Differences in the range of androgen metabolites between heterosexual and homosexual males and transvestite and transsexual males have also been described. However, such results must be viewed with some scepticism. A multiplicity of factors may affect the results, e.g. the effects of medication in transsexual males, the effects of infections with secondary changes in some homosexual males, and the effects of alcohol and drug abuse. A prospective study of hormonal changes in transsexual males has not been carried out because there is no method for assigning developmental potential. Also, some transsexual males have started oestrogen medication before puberty or early in pubertal development, thus showing the greatest oestrogen effects, although most transsexuals have not started medication before established pubertal development, or even later, to offset these effects.

Among male transsexuals examined before seeking oestrogen medication, the hormonal parameters appear to be normal and not significantly different from those of other males whether heterosexual, homosexual, or bisexual. The exceptions to this have been in males with Klinefelter's syndrome (47, XXY genotype), the XYY syndrome, and forms of hypogonadism either of developmental origin with inadequate testicular descent, or secondary to hypothalamic-pituitary disease, or primary testicular disease. In each of these disorders, lowered testosterone levels in plasma are often found. However, in the former group, an unusual percentage of elevated LH and FSH values have been recorded suggesting primary testicular damage.[9] This is also found in untreated subjects and may be related to the inguinal position of the testes when the penis is held in the perineal position, as is so often the case in male transsexuals. Males with persistent pubertal gynaecomastia, and a consequent alteration in body image, show no significant changes in hormonal parameters compared with those in normal males. Thus, it would appear that plasma levels of testosterone, dihydro-testosterone, dehydroepiandrosterone and its sulphate, 17-hydroxy-progesterone and oestradiol are usually within the normal range.[10] In addition, the gonadatrophin and prolactin levels are essentially normal. Occasionally, however, prolactin levels are above the normal range, often resulting from oestrogen medication.[11] The effects of an intravenous oestrogen injection upon gonadatrophin, testosterone or androgen levels have never been examined.[12] As indicated previously, it has been claimed that homosexual and transsexual males do not respond in the same manner as their normal heterosexual counterparts in terms of gonadatrophin levels after oestrogen injection.[13] Luteinizing hormone may be less depressed in homosexual and transsexual males after oestrogen injection and subsequently attain higher levels than in heterosexual males, a so-called positive oestrogen feedback effect.

The effects of androgens are mostly revealed in the physical features and build of male transsexuals. Thus, in many of them, the facial moulding, receding scalp hairline and baldness, laryngeal prominence, and particularly the shape of the nose and appearance of the hands and feet, have a distinctly male appearance. Masculine features are often apparent in the skin, muscle, apocrine gland secretion, and body hair distribution. Some male transsexuals may have elevated FSH values and reduced semen volume with oligospermia. However, testicular biopsy has not been undertaken to determine tubular histology in such cases.[14]

The development of pubertal gynaecomastia, so frequent in males as to be regarded as physiological, has seemingly led some to question their sexuality. The process varies from a plaque-like area beneath the nipple to a distinct female type of breast, and has been a confirmatory feature of transsexualism for some of those people who have queried their sexuality. At the stage of puberty when the pubarche is well advanced, plasma levels of testosterone and dihydrotestosterone have not attained values seen in mature adults. In some otherwise normally-developing males, erectile impotence and a knowledge of such hormonal levels has produced indecision about their sexuality. Furthermore, in males with relatively hairless skin or an effeminate beauty at adolescence, notwithstanding their other features of maleness, similar plasma androgen levels have confirmed an indecisive sexuality and served as a rationalization of their dysphoria. However, it is important that these androgen levels should be interpreted in a physiological setting and not compared with those of adult males. In some males, body fat distribution has not receded as is usual at puberty. Such individuals retain an androgynous quality, in that breasts, thighs, buttocks, and abdomen are more rounded, giving the body a less than male appearance. This condition, which was once likened to dystrophia adiposogenitalis, is not infrequent and, whilst a normal variant of development, can help to rationalize transsexualism in the mind of the affected person. In passing, it must be remembered that alcohol abuse can also lead to depression of plasma levels of testosterone and dihydrotestosterone with elevation of FSH levels.

Transsexual males who started oestrogen therapy close to puberty show more feminine features with less muscle development than do those who start oestrogen therapy much later in life. Facial hair growth may be less than expected and there is less likelihood of baldness. Often the nipples are well oestrogenized, with gynaecomastia, and the testes are small, with diminished sensation or tenderness on palpation. A small penis, probably due to oestrogen medication, occurs in some individuals.

Once transsexualism seems defined and accepted by male transsexuals, oestrogen medication is commenced. Thereafter, most have low plasma testosterone and dihydrotestosterone values, within the female range and without diurnal variation. The corresponding plasma LH and FSH values are low or suppressed while dehydroepiandrosterone and its sulphate are often consistently in the lower part of the normal range. Plasma prolactin values vary from those found in normal males to those commonly found in women taking an oral contraceptive. Much less commonly, significantly elevated prolactin values have been found, sometimes as high as those seen in association with a prolactin-producing tumour of the pituitary gland. Discharge of secretion from the nipple (spurious lactation) is rare but becomes a reinforcing sign that suggests a female breast. Moistness of the nipple, claimed by some transsexuals, is harder to assess. Spider naevi (dilatation of capillary vessels in the skin) as a sign of oestrogen excess seldom occur, but facial, nipple, and linea nigra pigmentation is frequently seen with larger doses of oestrogens. A soft, small, diffuse goitre, which may be delineated by radionuclide scanning techniques, is not unusual in association with oestrogen medication. The plasma thyroxine (T4) and triiodothyronine (T3) levels confirm increased thyroxine-binding globulin (TBG) levels so often seen with oestrogen therapy. The free indices for T4 and T3 are normal, as is pituitary thyroid-stimulating hormone (TSH).[15] Sex-hormone-binding globulin levels are increased and this factor needs consideration when evaluating other hormonal data, including androgen indices.[16] Plasma cortisol levels can be elevated with a normal diurnal variation in the presence of normal levels of adrenocorticotrophic hormone (ACTH). These features all reflect the effects of oestrogen administration. Usually such hormones would not be measured unless there were other reasons, such as obesity. It is also worth remembering that oestrogen therapy may alter the results of oral glucose-tolerance testing.

Those transsexual males who have presented while married, or shortly after separation or divorce, and who have fathered children, have obviously manifested normal male capabilities. Some claim that fantasies were necessary to maintain their sexual activity in marriage. Some, after 20–25 years or so of marriage, have LH and FSH values above normal that could be due to an ageing effect. Some have denied erectile potency and have claimed that, although they could masturbate, heterosexual intercourse was not possible, as it was perceived by them to be homosexual (woman with woman). Some claim that they were only able to have intercourse by fantasizing that they themselves were women. Yet others may have had few or no problems apart from ejaculatory impotence at times. However, many have experienced a disinclination for, or dislike of, the effort and emotion involved in sexual intercourse.

Examination of subjects reveals a variety of appearances as already described. It is difficult to believe that some are other than women, while others obviously appear as males with varying degrees of sophistication in female attire. Some have had an augmentation mammoplasty (surgical enlargement of the breasts), reconstructive surgery of the face, or an orchidectomy (removal of testicles). Usually those awaiting genital surgery maintain their penis in the perineal position between the thighs. Consequently, the atrophic testes retract into the inguinal canals and the pubic skin folds give some semblance of labia majora. Indeed, some clinicians have failed to recognize the true nature of the external genitalia, particularly when the pubic hair has a clean horizontal upper margin as seen in most biological women. The penis is often soft to palpation and its examination is disliked. The scrotal skin is finer than the normal androgenized scrotum. Fat distribution generally reflects oestrogen effects but is variable in relation to basic bodily habitus. Depending upon the duration of oestrogen medication, the scalp hair may have a female outline but there may be commencing baldness which, if extensive, has to be hidden by a wig. Except for those who started oestrogens close to puberty, the laryngeal prominence, or Adam's apple, is distinctly masculine in appearance. Younger subjects generally show less male characteristics in their skin and have a lighter beard and less body hair. Others show the effects of waxing or electrolysis to remove excessive facial and body hair. The voice may be quite feminine in quality if oestrogen therapy has been started close to puberty, but more often it is a modulated, deeper voice. In most male transsexuals, the male cast of the face, the male type of skin and extremities, the male method of sitting and spontaneous mannerisms reveal the undeniable effects of androgens, and thus the true biological sex.

When an orchidectomy has been carried out, plasma LH and FSH levels rise and become significantly elevated if oestrogen administration is suspended. Orchidectomy is normally an important part of gender reassignment surgery. Sometimes, however it is performed unwisely at the patient's request. After orchidectomy, plasma testosterone and dihydrotestosterone values fall within the low female range. Shortly before any type of surgery, oestrogen therapy is suspended as it may contribute to poor wound healing, keloid scars and thrombo-embolic disease. The latter is especially prone to occur in those who also smoke tobacco. After cessation of oestrogen medication, some subjects complain of increased hair growth. For most male transsexuals, hypertrichosis (excessive hair growth) is a worrying problem. Depilation by wax treatment or electrolysis is sought and may be extensive. Additionally, anti-androgen medication may help to reduce the hair growth. For example, cyproterone acetate, in an oral dose of 100 mg or more daily, combined with oral oestrogen can have an ameliorating effect. Also, spironolactone, in a dose of 200–300 mg daily, and medroxyprogesterone can be used. Cyproterone acetate is more effective after orchidectomy than before, even though oestrogens have mostly depressed gonadotrophin production. Cyproterone acetate, spironolactone, and medroxyprogesterone acetate often reduce sexual drive, which is confusing for some subjects. Sometimes the prescribed oestrogen medication in married transsexual males may have been intended to reduce gender dysphoria and libido when, in fact, it has enhanced the gender identity disturbance.

The actual oestrogen doses utilized before orchidectomy are often considerable in the effort to suppress testicular activity, demasculinize, and oestrogenize. With cyproterone acetate alone, LH seems to increase or escape after a period of suppression and testosterone levels may rise after initial suppression. Consequently, there may be a plateau effect for body hair growth. This is mostly overcome by concomitant oestrogen medication. The oestrogen is usually given orally as stilboestrol, ethinyloestradiol, dienoestrol, or Premarin. Alternatively, oestrogen is prescribed as oestradiol valerate by intramuscular injection, the dosage used or demanded varying from 10–30 mg weekly. It is not unusual for the individual patient to claim that the oestrogen dosage is less than that given elsewhere, because of different preparations or a desire for greater oestrogen effect. With high oral oestrogen dosage, nausea and vomiting may occur and liver function tests may show adverse changes. However, to date, nodular hyperplasia or histological changes in the liver akin to those associated with the oral use of anabolic steroids, have not been reported, although the possibility should be considered. Large doses of oestrogens may result in oedema or hypertension in some subjects. Evidently oestrogens can increase plasma renin activity sufficiently in predisposed persons to induce hypertension. The effect of oestrogens on blood pressure cannot be disregarded and a family history of high blood pressure may be significant. Furthermore, oral oestrogen administration may be associated with an increased tendency to blood clotting leading to thrombosis and embolism. Fortunately this complication is unusual and has not been found when ethinyloestradiol dosage is kept below 200 µg daily. Following sex reassignment surgery, medication needs re-evaluation. Theoretically, there is less need for high doses of oestrogen, but many subjects are so accustomed to a certain level of effect that they respond adversely to a reduction in dosage. Whereas a post-menopausal woman, or a young woman who has had her ovaries removed, requires 10 mg of oestradiol valerate by injection at approximately 3-weekly intervals, most transsexuals claim that a similar injection every 3–7 days is essential for their well-being. The dosage of ethinyloestradiol before surgery should probably not exceed 200 µg daily, and after surgery this dose can be reduced, although there is often a need to maintain an oestrogenizing effect for some time. Some patients ask for Premarin as they want natural oestrogens rather than those of the synthetic type. Often the oestrogen is combined with a progestational steroid, such as medroxyprogesterone acetate, given in a dose of 5–10 mg orally daily for ten consecutive days each month. Theoretically, there is a possibility of carcinoma developing in the gynaecomastic breast but this is rare. Medroxyprogesterone acetate can induce secretion of fluid from the breast, a side-effect that may be distressing to some. The high levels of plasma prolactin that may result from oestrogen therapy can be reduced with bromocriptine, which may have a place along with spironolactone in the treatment of unwanted body hair. Some argue against the use of progestogens, believing their effect to be subjective. Nevertheless, psychologically some transsexuals desire a 'hormone rhythm'. When body hair growth is a problem before surgery, it often continues to be so afterwards. Cyproterone acetate in an average daily dosage of 100 mg, combined with an oral oestrogen, is variably effective in reducing hair growth. It may also reduce libido, decrease skin sebum production, and increase plasma prolactin levels. Plasma levels of cortisol may rise and those of dehydroepiandrosterone and its sulphate may fall.[17] The most common side-effects of cyproterone acetate administration are tiredness, weight increase, and occasionally breast soreness. These symptoms may be combined with the tiredness and nausea that some subjects experience with large doses of oestrogens. Programmes of hormone administration given in different centres vary. For ease of administration some simply suggest the taking of an oral contraceptive preparation containing an oestrogen and a progestogen.

Plasma lipid levels should be checked before and after commencing oestrogen therapy. An initial absence of hormone-related oedema and hypertension does not preclude their later appearance. The possibilities of neoplasia developing in oestrogen-stimulated breasts and of enlargement of skin naevi and of keloid scars in association with oestrogen therapy after gender reassignment surgery should always be remembered.

Some reassigned male transsexuals have found that their sexual activity after genital surgery has been less than satisfying, while intercourse has often been painful (dyspareunia). Sometimes the dyspareunia is due to dryness of the neovagina and can be avoided by the use of a lubricant during intercourse. On the other hand, problems with intercourse may result from unreasonable hopes and desires. Although denying that they believed that they would become like women, and realizing that intercourse might not be entirely satisfactory, many have had complaints. Some have adopted a lesbian association with women. Others, who were asexual, have simply used a vaginal dilator and hoped to find a partner in due course. Others, after attempting intercourse and finding it unsatisfactory, have separated from their partners. A number find intercourse lacks erotic value and is therefore unsatisfactory. Some work as call-girls suggesting that intercourse is satisfying for the partner. Others have drifted to massage parlours or prostitution and have offered their services in these situations. It is important to remember that excessive oestrogen medication can inhibit libido.

Finally, what do such persons become? Leaving aside those whose lives may have been damaged by an incomplete or inadequate operation, and those who subsequently found that the operation could not be reversed and committed suicide, the results of treatment seem to vary from adequacy to a complete renewal of life. Some have never felt happier or more at ease with themselves, having died to their old personality to be reborn, as it were, into the new female personality. Clinically, some pass so well as women, with no hint of androgen effect, that it is possible to relegate the past. Others are equally feminine and perhaps more sophisticated or artistic but the past is recalled. Even the tallest may become so feminine, with the end-result of surgery so disguised, that they can be examined for insurance and permanency of employment and the past history not be suspected. Others will never look more than masculinized women because of their skin and physical features, the stigmata of their androgenic development, but these may be forgotten in conversation with them because of their acquired feminine behaviour and mannerisms. These are carried into their daily lives and lead to family acceptance, notwithstanding that they remain transsexuals to themselves but at ease with their condition. Others may be at ease and have a confidence that they never had before surgery but remain masculine, and their very bearing as they sit and talk with people causes biological women or transsexuals of the earlier group to regard them as men or transsexuals remaining in a transitory phase. The two groups seem to have inadequate common ground beyond a diagnosis. Perhaps the former group comprises better-educated persons and the latter group less socially able individuals, but these may only represent the extremes. At the end of the diagnostic spectrum are those who are transsexual in all criteria but who cannot contemplate surgery or cross-dress. They may live a divided life and stress the inadequacy of surgery to correct their basic problem. They can quote examples to show that surgery is not remedial but they may use hormone therapy to reduce symptoms or feel better. Some may have limited homosexual patterns but call themselves women and by so doing are happier in themselves.

## Female-to-male transsexuals

Female transsexuals seem less common than male transsexuals but this may be more virtual than real. None the less, the lesbian-style relationships in which many of them are found may give more comfort or solace than the male homosexual relationship. Furthermore, they have more outlets for their personality and come to terms with their problem earlier than males because of the nature of the female sex drive. It also seems possible that idiosyncratic upbringing of female individuals can lead to disturbances that produce trans-sexualism. A number have had intercourse with a male partner only to find it distressing or nauseating. Others have adopted sexual liaisons with discrepant sexual behaviour that is more expected of perverse male activity. Some have maintained a lesbian-style marriage for many years and wish to consolidate their social position. Although they regard themselves as living as man and woman, they may have purchased a house as man and wife with names altered by deed poll. Others have aggressively claimed that they are lesbian and demanded a hysterectomy to rid themselves of menstruation. They have difficulty expressing their distress and, like some male transsexuals, are regarded as suffering from schizo-phrenia. Some simply regard themselves as transsexuals, having developed through a lesbian-style phase or having been 'tomboys' all their lives. While some are asexual, others seek a full male expression of sexuality.

There is an underlying aggression in the group which may only reflect a fear of misunderstanding. As is the case with male trans-sexuals, they come from all branches of society and the symptoma-tology is a counterpart of that of the male. Female-to-male transsexuals have an intense dislike of their breasts and usually apply binders to hide them. Whereas males may attempt ampu-tation of the penis and castration, female transsexuals rarely mutilate their breasts. Dislike or revulsion of menstruation is common. Some attempt to increase muscle development to appear more masculine and shave the facial hair to increase its growth. On the other hand, androgenized females do not become transsexual and are most distressed about their androgenic features.

With such varying symptomatology, it is unlikely that one or more hormonal factors responsible for female transsexualism could be discerned. Some have periods of amenorrhoea and investigation may suggest an androgenizing polycystic ovary syndrome. Even though this condition may produce symptoms as a result of androgenic substances produced in the abnormal ovaries, true transsexualism does not regress when the ovarian condition has been cured.

When plasma androgen levels are measured, notwithstanding reports that plasma levels of testosterone are increased in female transsexuals, plasma levels of testosterone and dihydrotestosterone are normal or similar to those found in otherwise normal, non-virilized women with steroid-induced hirsutism.[18] Plasma levels of dehydroepiandrosterone and its sulphate are also normal, while those of LH and FSH are appropriate, either for normal women or for those with designated ovarian disorders. Similarly, plasma levels of oestradiol, 17-hydroxyprogesterone, and prolactin are within the normal range.[19] Progesterone values correspond with those seen in women with normal ovulatory cycles or with designated ovarian disorders.[20]

Clinically, there appears to be no separate hormonal abnormality underlying female transsexualism. However, it might closely resemble the clinical picture associated with idiopathic or steroid-induced hirsutism in women. Such women, however, give very different histories from those with transsexualism. Usually, virilizing features develop later in life, secondary to adrenal dyshormonogenesis or ovarian tumours. The virilizing features are anathema to such patients who seek every means to rid themselves of them. On the other hand, the female transsexual does everything possible to achieve virilization which is regarded as essential for peace of mind.

On clinical examination, female transsexuals appear to be essentially female apart from their dressing, deportment, and behaviour, which tend to be that of the stereotyped male. Hairstyles are often decidedly masculine and hirsutism is present in some, with seborrhoea and odorous sweating. The voice is often distinguishable from that of a biological male. Breast development is variable but not out of keeping with that of the normal biological female. The external genitalia are those of the normal female, although occasionally there is some clitoral enlargement secondary to male sex hormone administration. The uterus is palpable in most, except when it has been previously removed by hysterectomy. Female transsexuals often register embarrassment when physical examination of the breasts is performed as part of routine medical assessment.

Generally speaking, in most female transsexuals, oestrogen has been effective in morphogenesis. The behaviour pattern is either a distinctively masculine one that cannot be relaxed, or an assumed one that appears masculine but can be relaxed. When female transsexuals are first seen, evidence of androgen medication is less common than the evidence of oestrogen medication in their male counterparts.

The majority of female transsexuals request reduction mammoplasty and androgen therapy for masculinizing purposes. Testosterone esters such as Sustanon 250 (Organon) 250 mg, or Primoteston Depot (Schering AG) 250–500 mg, given by intramuscular injection at intervals of two weeks, give adequate masculinization. It is important for patients to realize that breast size does not regress under the influence of testosterone therapy, nor do the external genitalia change apart from some enlargement of the clitoris and thinning of the labia minora, both of which are variable.

Unfortunately, hopes of treatment are often unrealistic. By analogy with females affected by adrenal dyshormonogenesis, only those subject to potent androgen influence early in foetal life develop a 'penile' urethra. Those affected later do not develop a satisfactory phallus nor one that allows reconstruction to provide an effective 'penis'. Whilst it may appear superficially normal, it is seldom adequate to establish a complete phallic urethra, let alone being adequate for vaginal intercourse. When the operative results of skin tube phalloplasty, with or without muscle or prosthesis within the skin tube, and without a urethra passing throughout the length of the phallus, are discussed with patients, most are dissuaded from embarking upon this type of surgery. Although some deny that this is of great importance to them, the final result without a functional phallus can create further identity difficulties. For this reason, some patients seek a sculptured prosthetic phallus that can be attached to the pubic area and left in place. The median raphe can be constructed after vaginectomy (removal of the vagina) but, notwithstanding testosterone therapy, appearance of body and external genitalia are not sufficiently masculine for the critical observer. The end result for the female transsexual seems always less than satisfactory, even more so than for females affected by congenital adrenal hyperplasia producing pseudo-hermaphroditism. The inadequacy of surgery in males with gross hypospadias (incompletely developed penile urethra) or with some intersex states, suggests that, even in the presence of erectile prostheses, urethral problems and the insoluble problem for those who want some form of 'ejaculation', do not engender optimism about operative results of phalloplasty in female transsexuals in the future.

The hormonally-treated female transsexual usually appears quite masculine and is sometimes bearded. Often the transformation has been so successful that few people in the community would have any reason to suspect the underlying biologically female sex.

As mentioned earlier, most female transsexuals desire removal of excess breast tissue so that the anterior chest wall is as flat as it is in the biological male. Despite the androgen-induced amenorrhoea, most request abdominal total hysterectomy and bilateral salpingo-oöphorectomy (removal of both ovaries and Fallopian tubes). In addition, many request that the vagina be closed by a surgical procedure such as colpocleisis (occlusion of the vagina) or removal (vaginectomy). However, these procedures are sometimes delayed in case the vaginal tissues might be required for construction of external male genitalia at a future date.

After reassignment surgery, female transsexuals are unable to practise vaginal intercourse without some artificial phallus. Partial non-vaginal intercourse may occur in the absence of surgery, with satisfactory stimulation and response. Knowing this, some female transsexuals have refused surgery in the belief that it has little to offer. They continue to be maintained on injections of testosterone esters at intervals of three to four weeks. Those who have subsequently received tablets of methyltestosterone have usually found that such preparations are not as effective subjectively as the injections and have complained that androgenization was lost. Whilst hormonal therapy in the male can cause unrecognized indecision about identity to become apparent, in the female transsexual this has not occurred. Indeed such persons often demonstrate a braggadocio during the administration of male sex hormone which may be its consequence or the result of a decision to live out their perceived maleness. In some, partial surgery does not bring peace of mind and they feel that it cannot really alter their being.

As with male transsexuals, female transsexuals have arranged 'marriages', even though these are not yet legally recognized.

## Conclusions

It would seem that in only a few male or female transsexuals has it been possible by endocrine therapy to reverse morphogenesis so that adequate gender-role transformation can be established ultimately with the aid of surgery. For some, encoded behaviour, both mental and physical, is so strong that features of the primary biological sex persist as reminders of the past. In a fortunate few this is not so, and it is almost impossible for them to recreate the past and reconcile what they were before reassignment with their present state. The improved self-esteem and acceptance of these persons in society, and even by their children of a prior marriage, might seem pragmatic sanction for such reassignment procedures. However, there are some failures ending in tragedies, and the end result for former spouses and children cannot yet be stated.

# 8   Voice, Speech and Language

## Considerations in the management
## of male-to-female transsexualism

*Jennifer M. Oates and Georgia Dacakis*

In the past ten years, it has become clear that effective management of transsexuals requires a multidisciplinary approach, with the discipline of speech pathology playing an important role in the social adjustment of these individuals. Interpersonal communication, the domain of the speech pathologist, is a primary factor affecting the perception and acceptance of the transsexual in society.[1] Without skill training in this area, it is doubtful whether many transsexuals could be considered successfully rehabilitated.

Male-to-female transsexuals repeatedly complain of situations in which their voice characteristics in particular betray their biological sex. The most common instance occurs in telephone conversations where, despite the distinct introduction, 'Hello, this is *Miss* Jones', the listener responds by addressing Miss Jones as 'Sir' or 'Mr Jones'. Many clients subsequently resort to the inconvenience of personally attending to their affairs rather than risking offence over the telephone. The list of situations in which the transsexual's voice and other communication characteristics betray her biological masculinity is seemingly endless. The warm expression of the shop assistant asking 'Can I help you Miss?' suddenly changing to a look of bewilderment, or indifference; the stares, comments, and abuse directed to a previously anonymous person all contingent on the transsexual speaking, are everyday reminders that, despite constant efforts to buy appropriate clothes and makeup, she has not yet been fully accepted by society. It is no wonder that many clients reject their voice and speech characteristics—a complete rejection which is reflected in statements such as 'I hate my voice, I just don't want it, I hate it . . . I hate it'.

A review of the literature also supports the importance of training in communication skills in the rehabilitation of transsexuals. The most obvious contribution is to society's perception and acceptance of the transsexual's gender identity and the consequent alleviation of discomfort and anxiety in social situations.[2] Kalra has stressed that voice, speech, and language skills are significant in the improvement and reinforcement of the client's self-image.[3] Further, it has been suggested that training in communication skill allows the client to make a more realistic appraisal of the preferred sex role before making the irreversible decision to have surgery.[4] Gender reassignment teams may also consider the transsexual's progress in this area in determining whether or not the client has successfully developed modes of behaviour appropriate to the preferred sex role in the preoperative transition period. Finally, it has been noted that, without professional guidance in this area, the transsexual's own attempts to alter voice, speech, and language characteristics can result in bizarre, unskilful behaviours reminiscent of an unsuccessful female impersonator, and in physical damage to the voice production mechanism.[5]

Before speech pathology management is outlined in the remainder of this chapter, readers should recognize that a small number of transsexuals will not require modification of communication characteristics. Some clients will present with voice, speech, and language features that are already consistent with female behaviour; these features have resulted physiologically and/or through gender role learning in childhood. Others will demonstrate that, within their social network, voice, speech and language characteristics are not significant indicators of gender. This is well illustrated by a transsexual from a rural society who claimed that many of the women in her network had 'lower voices and more facial hair' than she had!

I     Sex-associated voice, speech and language characteristics as a basis for therapeutic intervention

To assist the male-to-female transsexual in altering voice, speech, and language characteristics, the speech pathologist would ideally base therapy on objectively established features which distinguish female and male communication patterns. Such features are referred to as speech markers. The picture of female and male speech markers that has emerged from research efforts is limited by an uneven concentration of research and by large discrepancies in subject selection, design, sampling, and measurement techniques between studies. Nevertheless, the data that have been reported provide an initial basis for the speech pathologist's work.

The most informative clues to a speaker's sex are in the areas of voice production and intonation patterns, with pitch level being most frequently cited.[6] The approximate mean pitch level (as measured in Hertz) is 128 Hz for adult males and 227 Hz for females.[7] Thus, female voices average 1.7 times higher in pitch than do those of males. This difference is due to the vocal cords of females being shorter and less massive than those of males. Pitch ranges for adult males and females overlap considerably however; the approximate range for males is 60 to 260 Hz while that of females is 128 to 520 Hz. It should also be noted here that the sex difference in speaking pitch is significantly reduced in the older age groups above fifty years.[8]

Speech markers in the areas of vocal loudness and voice quality have received some research attention. Studies by Yanagihara *et al.* and Markel *et al.* have determined that males speak with greater loudness levels than females; the mean loudness level (as measured in decibels) was 67 dB for males and 64 dB for females.[9] Differences in voice quality between the sexes have not been clearly delineated. Although it has been established that females have shorter vocal tracts, speak with larger mouth openings and smaller degrees of lip rounding, and show greater irregularities in the frequency of vocal cord vibration, the effects on voice quality perceptions have not been fully evaluated.[10]

A review of several studies of inflectional pitch changes and intonation patterns has revealed further speech markers of sex. McConnell-Ginet, and Pellowe and Jones, demonstrated that white, middle-class women in the United States and England utilized a greater variety of intonation patterns than did men.[11] Pellowe and Jones's work also indicated that men used a much greater proportion of falling pitch tones, while women used more rising tones.[12]

Less significant markers of the sex of the speaker can be found in the features of speech sound articulation, syntax or grammar, usage of vocabulary and conversational style and content. In the area of articulation, numerous examples from English language studies demonstrate that females utilize more correct, standard speech sounds.[13] Examples here include the more frequent use by females than by males of the standard production of the verb ending /ing/ as opposed to the nonstandard /in/, and the more common tendency for males to alter the voiced fricative /th/.

Sex differences in the use of grammatical form have not been found frequently, particularly for English languages.[14] Speech markers in vocabulary usage, however, have been cited more often. Perhaps the most widespread belief about men's speech as compared with women's is that it is characterized by 'coarser' vocabulary; an investigation of the use of profane and obscene expletives in a limited American population by Bailey and Timms provides tentative support for this view.[15] Similarly, women's vocabulary is reputed to be more polite than men's. Only one study supporting this view has been reported; Hartman demonstrated that a sample of American women used more forms of politeness than did their male counterparts when interviewed by college students.[16]

The use of adjectives by males and females has also been the focus of considerable investigation. Swacker, for example, found that in a picture description task, college women more often prefaced definite numerical items by adjectives of approximation (*'about* six books') than did men.[17] Hartman also demonstrated that women used many more evaluative adjectives, such as 'lovely', 'delightful', 'wonderful' and 'cute'.[18]

Examination of the topics, content and style of men's and women's speech suggests several additional speech markers. Three studies conducted in the 1920s using tape-recorded conversations on city streets in the United States and England, and a more recent study by Aries and Johnson, demonstrated that women talked more about intimate topics, people, and clothing, while men primarily discussed finance, politics, work, and sport.[19] Research evidence also indicates that women's speech is characterized by more words implying feeling and psychological state, while men's speech shows an orientation towards objects and actions.[20] Empirical evidence concerning assertiveness in speech is mixed; the sole consistent finding is that men interrupt more often than women, especially in mixed-sex conversations.[21]

In addition to sex markers in verbal communication, it is important to examine non-verbal language differences between males and females, as transsexuals often request guidance from speech pathologists in areas of gestural and postural behaviour. It has been suggested, on a subjective basis, that there are sex differences in behaviours, including eye contact, facial expression, posture, head and body movements, and arm gestures, but very little objective data are available to support this contention.[22] The majority of research has been limited in scope and highly specific for factors such as communication of attitude rather than for more global markers of sex. The non-verbal feature of eye contact has received some relevant investigation, however. Findings from the studies of Exline *et al.* and Mehrabian and Friar suggest that females have more eye contact with their addressees than do males, and that males show greater variability in their eye contact than do females.[23]

In summary, investigations of voice production and intonation have demonstrated that females as compared to males utilize a higher pitch level, lower vocal loudness, a greater variety of intonation patterns and more rising pitch tones. Although speech markers of voice quality are likely, these have not been clearly established. Examinations of articulation and language provide limited evidence that women use more correct speech sound articulation and polite vocabulary than do men, and a greater proportion of evaluative adjectives and adjectives of approximation, more words implying psychological state, and less profane and obscene expletives.

Women's conversational topics may focus more on people, personal matters and clothing, while men may discuss finance, work, politics and sport more frequently. Finally, women may interrupt less than men during conversation, and women may have more frequent and less variable eye contact with their addressees than do men. Further, non-verbal markers have been suggested on a subjective basis, but little data have been reported in this area. For more detailed reviews of sex markers in speech, the reader is referred to Haas *et al.*[24]

The application of these research findings on speech markers to the speech pathologist's work with transsexuals is limited by four factors. Firstly, the above-mentioned differences between male and female speech could be due to a coincidental correlation of sex with another social division, such as occupation or ethnic background, and with other psychological variables, such as intellectual level or anxiety.[25] Much of the research in this area has used *speaker sex* as the only determinant of speech differences and has neglected to examine the effects of other social and psychological factors.

Secondly, a particular sex marker may be relevant only for a specific sub-group of the population: because research has been frequently confined to small circumscribed samples (white American college students, in particular), generalization to the entire population or application to a particular transsexual may not be valid. Thirdly, the research data reported above do not provide information concerning the *relative* contribution of speech markers to the perception of maleness or femaleness. As it is not clear which markers are the most important determinants of perceptions of the sex of the *speaker*, priorities in therapy are difficult to ascertain. Finally, it is important to keep in mind that changes in social processes are likely to result in changes in the relative significance of speech markers of sex. This factor will be more significant for markers which are a function of gender learning rather than biological sex. Findings from studies in the 1920s may not hold for the 1980s and beyond. Thus, although we can be relatively confident that biologically determined markers such as pitch and voice quality will remain unchanged, the importance of learned features, such as usage of vocabulary and topics of conversation, may well alter as the relations between the sexes change.

The research base for the speech pathologist's work in this area is confounded by one further consideration. There has been some investigation of what are often referred to as speech stereotypes: these are widespread *beliefs* about men's and women's speech which may or may not be objectively based. Information about speech stereotypes is valuable in two respects. First, it appears that commonly held expectations people have of the speech characteristics of their own and the other sex exert real pressures to behave in accordance with those expectations, particularly in unfamiliar situations. During the initial transition period, many of the transsexual's social interactions will certainly involve novel situations. Second, a knowledge of speech stereotypes provides insight into what is often assumed by the transsexual client; the client's goals often arise largely from stereotypical beliefs.

Speech stereotypes reported in the literature are derived from informal speculations and from direct evidence of people's beliefs. Informal reports abound in the literature. The writings of Jesperson and Lakoff, for example, assert that women's speech contains more euphemisms, apologies, tag questions and unfinished sentences than does that of men.[26] Women are said to talk more about domestic and family issues and to use more emotional, tentative and non-assertive speech styles than men. Additionally, women are reputed to be more verbose than men.

One of the few researchers to collect direct evidence of the prevalence of speech stereotypes was Kramer.[27] He presented secondary and tertiary students with a list of fifty-one speech characteristics to be rated according to the degree to which they believed the item differentiated the sexes. Features stereotyped as female were the use of clear enunciation, a high pitch, gentle, smooth and fast speech with a wide range in rate and pitch, good grammar, polite speech and gibberish. Females were also considered to be concerned about the listener, to talk about trivial topics, and to use open, enthusiastic and emotional speech. Features stereotyped as male were the use of a deep, loud and forceful voice, swear words, slang, and dominating, demanding, militant and blunt speech patterns. Males were additionally viewed as showing anger, coming straight to the point and demonstrating a sense of humour in speech.

The relationship between speech markers and stereotypes is not well understood, but there are enough data to demonstrate that many of the widely held beliefs about men's and women's speech are subjective and have no basis in reality. A commonly cited stereotype of women's speech, for example, is the use of tag questions. The use of tags as in the statement, 'I am assertive, *aren't I?*' is consistently attributed to women.[28] This belief is not supported in observational studies of men and women, where no consistent differences between the sexes in actual use of tag questions have been found.[29]

To summarize, the investigation of sex-associated voice, speech, and language characteristics is far from complete. Further research is required to generate a more comprehensive data base of speech markers, to discover the social and psychological divisions that determine the distribution of speech markers, and to specify the relative importance of speech features for speaker sex identification. Until research data in these areas are reported, the validity of the speech pathologist's management procedures for transsexuals remains tentative, particularly when dealing with speech markers that are a function of gender learning. Therapy in the area of speech markers which are biologically determined can be undertaken with much more confidence.

# II   Management of the communication problems of male-to-female transsexuals

Alteration and modification of the voice, speech, and language characteristics of the transsexual may be approached through both medical and speech pathology intervention.

## Medical intervention

Medical procedures have been concerned with only one communication feature, vocal pitch level. The primary aim has been to elevate the transsexual's pitch level close to the mean pitch level for females. Although hormone therapy in the adult female-to-male client will alter pitch, it generally does not have a noticeable effect on the voice of the mature male-to-female client.[30] Surgical modification of the vocal folds, on the other hand, can produce a marked increase in pitch. The primary approach here has involved surgical alteration of the length, mass and/or tension of the vocal cords.[31] Donald, for example, has recently described a procedure where the outer layers of the anterior third of both vocal cords are removed to allow a web of tissue to develop across the larynx as healing takes place.[32] This effectively shortens the vocal cords and therefore increases pitch level. The procedure described by Donald, however, remains in experimental stages. There is concern that long-term adverse effects on voice quality and control have not yet been evaluated and may negate the benefits of the increased pitch.[33] Further, as indicated in the previous section of this chapter, there are many important contributions to female communication patterns apart from pitch level. Surgical management alone is likely to be unsatisfactory.

## Speech therapy intervention

There is a paucity of literature pertaining to the management of the communication problems of transsexuals; only three clinical reports have been cited to date. Two were single case studies where the primary therapeutic goal was to increase the client's pitch. In the first study, a thirty-two-year-old male-to-female transsexual was able to increase her habitual pitch from 150 Hz to 200 Hz after four months of weekly therapy, while in the second, a forty-nine-year-old transsexual increased her habitual pitch from 145 Hz to 165 Hz after seven one-hour therapy sessions.[34] Neither author described the procedures utilized to increase pitch, although auditory self-monitoring and imitation of the speech pathologist's models appeared to be the major mechanisms underlying change. The third study was again a single case study, but in this instance a more comprehensive communication skills training approach was reported.[35] The major therapeutic target was non-verbal behaviour. Behaviour modification with video feedback and modelling was effective in modifying a twenty-year-old client's skills in areas such as facial expression, head and body movements, and gestures. However, because the data base concerning sex-differentiated non-verbal behaviour is limited, subjectivity in the choice of therapeutic targets was a primary limitation of this study.

Although the above studies present some limited guidelines for speech therapy intervention, a more comprehensive therapeutic approach is required.[36] Attempts should be made to assess and modify where appropriate, not only pitch level and non-verbal behaviour, but also intonation patterns, voice quality, vocal loudness, vocabulary usage, articulatory precision, and conversational styles. While it is not within the scope of this chapter to describe detailed procedures, the following is a recommended outline for the management programme.

The initial phase of management involves videotaping and audiotaping the client's presenting communication characteristics in conversations and structured tasks such as reading. Such baseline data are gathered from role-paying, and clinical and natural situations to allow valid perceptual analysis of voice, speech, and language features. Where possible, technical instrumentation is utilized to objectively measure pitch level, intonation, voice quality, and vocal loudness. Appropriate devices include fundamental frequency indicators, microprocessor-based pitch analysers, spectral analysers and sound pressure-level meters.

Following assessment, an individual programme and goals of therapy are developed based on established speech markers of sex, the client's needs, and the results of baseline evaluation. Standard speech therapy techniques for disorders of voice, articulation and language form the basis of this programme; the reader is referred to the texts of Moncur and Brackett *et al.*[37] The underlying mechanisms for change in these areas are imitation of the speech pathologist's models and of other female speakers, and training in self-monitoring skills. Visual, auditory and kinaesthetic feedback are utilized in order to develop accurate self-monitoring; this is achieved through the use of fundamental frequency indicators, video playback, audiotape recording and other appropriate biofeedback procedures.

Important features about which the speech pathologist should caution the client during therapy are a deterioration in the client's vocal quality and the development of vocally abusive behaviours, such as excessive throat clearing. Such behaviours might result if the client attempts to produce an unrealistically high-pitched voice with unnecessary tension of the chest, neck, and larynx. In these cases, careful revision of the client's goals and routine counselling to eliminate vocal abuse will be required.

Finally, an essential component of the speech pathology programme is the generalization of skills acquired in the clinic to the client's home and social environment. She must be guided in practising therapy techniques regularly and in transferring skills to everyday situations. Monitoring of the client's performance outside the clinic is achieved through analysis of tape recordings of conversations at home, and feedback from family members or friends. It is also invaluable for the speech pathologist to observe the client's communicative behaviour in her usual environment.

## The outcome of intervention and prognostic factors

The outcome of intervention cannot be cited unequivocally because of the limited amount of published data concerning the results of attempts to modify the communication characteristics of transsexuals. Available clinical reports, however, indicate that therapy outcomes are positive for the majority of clients. The case studies and clinical findings of Yardley *et al.*, and Oates and Dacakis, all demonstrated that therapeutic procedures resulted in significant and desirable changes in the areas of pitch level, intonation pattern, vocal intensity, articulation, and non-verbal behaviour.[38] In addition to analyses conducted by the authors, the transsexuals involved in these studies reported increased confidence in their ability to present as females and stated that they were now far less often mistaken for males in face-to-face or telephone situations.

Although the outcome of therapy is likely to be favourable for the majority of transsexuals, there are a number of factors which might adversely affect the prognosis for change in communication skills. Such negative factors include the presence of a large larynx with long and massive vocal cords, a wide discrepancy between the presenting and target communication characteristics, particularly if the client has used vocally abusive or bizarre behaviour, and has a limited ability to discriminate between appropriate and inappropriate voice, speech, and language features. The transsexual's knowledge and understanding of the range of sex differences in communication also affects prognosis; clients who consider that pitch level alone is important do not often achieve optimum communication patterns. Further negative prognostic indicators include interruption of the therapeutic programme due to a client's psychosocial problems, uncertainty concerning the diagnostic status of the client in cases where psychiatric disorder, homosexuality, or transvestism have not been excluded, and discrepancies between the transsexual's goals and those which can be safely and realistically addressed in therapy.

Although the preceding discussion has highlighted the limited nature of research in the area of sex-associated voice, speech, and language characteristics, a lack of reports concerning comprehensive speech pathology management, and a number of negative prognostic factors, there are many overriding considerations which encourage speech pathology intervention programming for transsexuals. These include positive treatment outcomes, the very high motivation levels of the majority of clients, the speech pathologist's sound therapeutic base in all areas delineated as speech markers of sex, and the fact that the transsexual's communication problems cannot practically be held in abeyance until the relevant research is complete.

# 9    Primary Medical Care for Transsexuals

## How can the general practitioner help?

*Murray Barson*

This chapter deals only with aspects of the medical care of individuals, genetically male, who wish to be women. The author has no experience with the primary care needs of transsexual women who wish to be men. In common with most medical practitioners, he had no relevant undergraduate training in the primary care of either male or female transsexuals and admits that at his first professional encounter with a transsexual woman he was somewhat nonplussed and quite ignorant of the special needs of this group. To whatever extent he can claim knowledge of this subject, he owes a great deal to the transsexual clients who have consulted him.

At the first contact with the patient one must attempt to determine that one is in fact dealing with a transsexual. Requests for oestrogens or a preference for female dress are not infallible indicators of transsexuality. Although distinguishing between transvestism and transsexuality should be fairly simple as a medical history is taken, a few transvestites themselves may be confused about their own needs when first coming to terms with feelings of ambivalence regarding masculinity/femininity, cross-dressing, and sexual preferences; delusional desire for sex change is not uncommonly a symptom of psychosis; genital dysphoria, in the patient's own mind, may be confused with gender dysphoria. Mis-diagnosis can lead to inappropriate management. Occasionally one encounters a man, either homosexual or heterosexual who, for his own particular needs, desires a degree of feminine appearance, including breast development, but who has no desire to adopt the female role, and different criteria apply to the decision regarding hormone therapy. The request for oestrogens does not establish the diagnosis, nor justify automatic prescription.

Not all transsexuals, no matter how classical the history, are appropriate for gender reassignment surgery. While the details of assessment are the concern of specialists, the general practitioner can look for ambivalence regarding sex role, psychological problems, and impulsive or inappropriate decisions prompted by external factors. Supportive counselling over a lengthy period may be necessary and repeated contacts will generally enable one to gain the patient's trust and to better understand her needs.

Many transsexual 'women' are well-informed regarding medical aspects of their adopted sex role, but others may need information about such things as hormones, cosmetic surgery (including breast augmentation), control of unwanted hair, genital surgery, and sexual function before and after genital change. Not all of the medical information which circulates among transsexuals is accurate. There is, for instance, a whole folk-lore of unfounded beliefs about the efficacy of certain forms of oestrogen, their dosages, and side-effects.

The male-to-female transsexual's first approach to a general practitioner is often with a request for oestrogen and she will most likely have ascertained from others that the doctor is amenable to prescribing these. She may have had an unfortunate previous experience with doctors and be initially defensive, aggressive or anxious. The doctor's sympathetic acceptance of her transsexuality and awareness of her special needs may encourage her to raise other matters of concern. She needs access to primary care for problems unrelated to gender change, and in fact may often be neglecting such problems due to uncertainty about doctors' reactions to transsexuals. Most transsexuals are determined to achieve optimum female appearance, will be definite in requesting a prescription, and will not be seeking advice as to whether or not they should take oestrogens. Many will already be using hormones, often in excessive doses, which are readily obtainable from non-professional sources. A doctor may limit his interaction with such clients to a prescription of the tablets requested and this may be the only response desired by the client. However, the responsible practitioner must ensure, as a minimum, that there are no contra-indications to administration of oestrogens and that the risks of chronic oestrogen use are appreciated. Questions intended to determine contra-indications or delineate other needs may be perceived as hesitancy or refusal to prescribe. An early statement of willingness to help, including providing tablets, together with a brief description of some of the hazards of oestrogens and the need to carefully select the appropriate form and dosage, may set the patient at ease.

Information relevant to the use of oestrogen may be gained precisely by direct questioning. A history of thrombosis, hypertension, cerebral or coronary vascular disease, diabetes, epilepsy, migraine, hepatic disease, or malignancy should be excluded. A family history of some of these conditions may be a relative contra-indication and should also be sought. The increased risks to cardiovascular health of tobacco when combined with high-dose oestrogens should be stressed. Breast self-examination can be taught, and some mention made of the possibility of prostatic problems.

Information should also be sought regarding past and present sexual activities. This may indicate the need for investigations to rule out sexually-transmitted diseases. It also serves to demonstrate the doctor's willingness to discuss sex, a problem area about which some patients might otherwise be reluctant to ask for help.

Physical examination should include measurement of weight and blood pressure, breast examination, assessment of liver size, genital examination and a urine test for glucose. Rectal examination of the prostate is indicated for older patients, or any with symptoms of urinary obstruction. After genital surgery there is an increased risk of urinary tract infection and occasional cultures of urine may be justified even in the asymptomatic patient.

Most transsexual 'women' at some time need endocrinological, dermatological, and often psychological advice or treatment. A general practitioner may feel able to deal with most of these areas, but one should also be aware of whatever special services for transsexuals exist in local public hospitals, and which specialists will deal sympathetically and competently with transsexuals' problems. When referral is made to a public hospital for treatment, a brief telephone call to the resident staff may prevent embarrassing confusion or delay, particularly in deciding on a male or female ward if admission to hospital is likely. One would hope that admitting officers, clerical staff and nurses could deal sensibly and efficiently with such matters. It is ironic and lamentable that a person may be accepted as a woman in all aspects of life except when dealing with 'the system' of a big hospital.

As well as breast augmentation and major genital procedures, surgery may be indicated for removal of scars or tattoos, or may be indicated to alter a formerly acceptable masculine nose that sits less comfortably on a 'woman's' face.

Decisions regarding gender reassignment surgery will generally be made after the co-ordinated assessment of the patient by staff of a hospital gender dysphoria clinic. The general practitioner often knows the patient well and may have invaluable information relevant to assessment.

The doctor should know where help may be sought regarding voice re-training, vocational counselling, non-verbal communication skills, dress, and deportment appropriate to the adopted sex role. Transsexual support groups exist in most cities and some state and federal departments may have some special arrangements for transsexuals. Many factors influence the success with which a transsexual may adopt the female sex role. Body shape, hair growth, voice production and facial characteristics that are less masculine than usual all confer an advantage. Support of family and friends is also important. One encounters transsexuals who will clearly always have difficulty in passing as women, and one must admire the courage with which some face this predicament. Some never achieve social acceptance. Many have continuing emotional problems due to pre-existing psychological factors. Many too are lonely, frustrated, and incur loss of income and status in adopting the female role. Considerable insight into the dilemma of the transsexual in our the realization that invariably these women knowingly accept the problems of changing sex, and prefer this new role to the state of constant conflict they experience in living as men.

While it is important to be able to empathize with the difficulties transsexuals may labour under, it is important also to look beyond their gender dysphoria to their total health care. Many gender reassignment clinics prefer their patients to be in the care of a general practitioner who can co-ordinate medication and pick up problems of dosage or of conflicting medications, whether prescribed or not. In return, the general practitioner is often regarded as a valuable liaison between the patient and the gender clinic team. It may often be the general practitioner who is told by the patient of problems before or after surgery which she is unwilling or embarrassed to discuss with the surgeons, psychologist, or psychiatrist. In such cases, accurate feedback to and liaison with the clinical team is maintained by the general practitioner. Finally, in addition to the necessity of providing liaison with other health professionals, advice and warning about medication, and management of transsexual patients with regard to their gender dysphoria and reassignment (if carried out), the general practitioner is often the best placed to advise relatives of the patient. Information provided by him or her is usually highly relevant and of great assistance to the psychologists and psychiatrists assessing the transsexual or putative transsexual, and of considerable use in assessing the patient's adjustment when not directly seeking reassignment.

In the final analysis, the general practitioner is ultimately responsible for the general health of the transsexual in areas not immediately related to feminization or reassignment. As such, the responsibility for primary care of the individual patient makes the general practitioner an important member of any gender assessment team.

# 10    Gender Reassignment Surgery

## I    Pre- and post-operative nursing care

*Lorraine Clarke and Margaret Stubbings*

This chapter is based upon the experience of nursing staff who have cared for transsexuals in a large teaching hospital in Melbourne. Few nurses have knowingly come into contact with transsexuals and most have little idea of the problems these people have to contend with during their daily lives.

After discussion amongst the nursing and medical staff about hospital admission of patients with gender dysphoria, it was decided to admit male-to-female transsexuals to a gynaecological ward, and female-to-male transsexuals to a male surgical ward. This has been successful, and in most cases the transsexual patients have related well to other patients within these wards.

## Pre- and post-operative care of male-to-female transsexuals at the time of genital reassignment surgery

Genital reassignment is a complicated operation and is described in detail elsewhere in this chapter. The patient is admitted to hospital three days before surgery and is started on a 'bowel preparation' regime, to cleanse the bowel pre-operatively. This is necessary because the surgeon is operating in an area close to the rectum which may be inadvertently injured. As part of the bowel preparation the patient is given a low-residue (low-fibre) diet, thereby obviating the need to open the bowels post-operatively, with inevitable straining that might displace the newly-grafted skin tube lining the vagina. The low-residue diet is maintained for the first ten days post-operatively. As for all patients undergoing major surgery, nothing should be given to eat or drink for at least four hours before the operation.

A blood sample is taken from the patient for grouping and cross-matching two or three units of blood, which is then available in case excessive bleeding occurs during the operation.

The night before the patient is due to have her operation the pubic area has to be shaved. It is usual for her to do this herself and have it checked by one of the senior members of the nursing staff. If the patient is unable to shave herself, this should be done by a nurse.

On returning from the operating theatre, the patient has both an intravenous infusion running and an in-dwelling urinary catheter draining the bladder.

The intravenous infusion is maintained until the haemoglobin and red blood cell count is checked post-operatively. If these parameters are low, the patient will require a blood transfusion. On the other hand, if they are within normal limits, the intravenous line is removed. As the area in which the surgeon is operating is very vascular, it is not uncommon for quite heavy bleeding to occur. Under these circumstances the patient will be returned to the ward with a blood transfusion running.

The urinary catheter usually remains in place for ten days to prevent the new urethral opening from closing up as it heals. As urinary tract infections are a common problem with long-term bladder catheterization, all precautions are taken to prevent infection. In this regard, it is important to ensure that the patient drinks copious amounts of fluids, that temperature charts are closely monitored and that regular specimens of urine are collected for microbiological examination. Any evidence of urinary infection is an indication for appropriate antibiotic treatment.

There are two common methods of looking after the genital wounds: either the wounds are completely covered with a pressure-dressing that remains untouched for seven days, after which the patient returns to the operating theatre to have tension sutures and drainage tubes removed and the vaginal pack changed, or the dressings are kept in place with an abdomino-perineal binder and changed in the ward at approximately four-hourly intervals.

As is to be expected, most patients are anxious to see their new genitalia. Before they do so, it is advisable to explain to them that the area will be swollen and unsightly for several days, and that the appearance will improve greatly as time passes.

Sometimes there is a tendency for the patient to bleed from the vascular tissue surrounding the new opening of the urethra. Close observation of this area by the patient and nursing staff is therefore recommended. If any bleeding occurs it should be reported to the surgeon immediately.

During the first week after the initial operation, the patient should remain in bed, thus allowing the skin graft in the new vagina to heal. Strain on this area could cause the graft to prolapse.

As mentioned above, a week after the initial operation, the patient returns to the operating theatre for inspection of the genital area and changing of dressings. Following this procedure, it is most important that a soft vaginal dilator remain in the vagina so that patency is maintained, otherwise shrinkage could occur. At this stage the patient should be instructed how to make soft vaginal dilators and how to insert them. The dilators are normally made by packing a condom with a piece of foam rubber or soft plastic, cut to the appropriate length and width. Insertion is facilitated by liberal application of a lubricant to the dilator.

Ten days after the initial operation, the urinary catheter is removed and the patient encouraged to pass urine naturally. As the external urethral opening is still somewhat swollen at this stage, it is not uncommon for the urinary stream to spray to a variable extent. Until it gradually returns to normal, a perineal pad can be used to help direct the stream.

Usually the patient is discharged from hospital two weeks after the surgery has been performed. She is supplied with material for making vaginal dilators and instructed again about their correct use and maintenance of vaginal hygiene.

## Pre- and post-operative care of female-to-male transsexuals

Female-to-male transsexuals are admitted to hospital on two separate occasions, the first time for bilateral mastectomy, and the second time for hysterectomy and removal of the ovaries and Fallopian tubes.

By and large the pre- and post-operative care of these patients consists of routine observations and nursing care, the only difference being that they are nursed in a male surgical ward.

No operations to construct a penis have been attempted at our hospital because of the lack of success with the operation elsewhere.

## Psychological aspects

It is most important that nursing staff treating these patients have frequent and ready access to senior personnel (both nursing and medical) attached to the gender reassignment clinic. They should be encouraged to discuss freely the problems associated with nursing such patients.

Transsexuals have spent their life-time distressed about their sexuality. While most of the nursing staff feel comfortable with their own sexuality, they often find this challenged after association with transsexuals. This may cause some members of staff to avoid such patients if possible or to display less than usual interest in their welfare.

As the patient who has undergone surgical reassignment is in hospital for about two weeks, she may become quite familiar with the nursing staff. This may lead to open discussion about all aspects of life with junior nurses, some of whom are quite young and naïve. When transsexuals relate intimate details of their sex lives to such nurses it can be disturbing or even shocking to some, while others become quite distressed and need psychological counselling and support. Transsexuals should be made aware of this before they are admitted to hospital, if such problems are to be prevented.

Our experience with nursing transsexuals at the time of gender reassignment surgery has convinced us that nurses can do a great deal to help such people at a time of stress in their lives.

# II   Cosmetic surgery

*Murray Stapleton*

This chapter outlines various non-genital surgical procedures that are occasionally called for in people who have had their gender reassigned.

## *Breast surgery*

### Augmentation mammoplasty

Prosthetic augmentation of the female breast has been carried out now for many decades. It is a procedure that is usually sought by the woman who suffers from post-lactation breast atrophy, but it is also used for those with small or asymmetrical breasts, and after radical mastectomy in the course of breast reconstruction surgery. Male-to-female transsexuals request augmentation mammo-plasty when breast enlargement following hormonal therapy is inadequate. Surprisingly perhaps, breast enlargement achieved by hormonal stimulation alone in male-to-female transsexuals is such that augmentation mammoplasty is requested less frequently than might be expected.

The operation involves the subcutaneous insertion of a prosthesis consisting of an envelope of silastic material which may be filled with a silicone gel or normal saline. The prosthesis is placed in a surgically-created cavity, usually behind the existing breast tissue, or less commonly, beneath the pectoralis major muscle on each side.

In Australia the operation is usually performed under a general anaesthetic, but in the United States of America and elsewhere it is often done in a plastic surgeon's office under local anaesthesia. While the procedure contributes greatly to the sense of well-being in all patients in whom it is indicated, it suffers from the complication of scar contracture around the walls of the surgically-created cavity. This leads to the breast becoming firm in consistency and distorted in contour, consequent upon the natural and expected contraction of scar tissue that is seen elsewhere in the body as a normal component of the healing process. Why should this happen? Research suggests that it may be related to the absence of an epithelial lining in the created surgical cavity or to leakage of silicone granules from the prosthetic envelope with stimulation of increased scar tissue formation. Furthermore, it is not yet understood why this phenomenon can occur in one breast rather than the other or why it may develop some twelve months after the original operation. Interestingly, not all patients who have had an augmentation mammoplasty of this type develop a contracted scar tissue capsule around the prosthesis.

The placement of the prosthesis beneath what breast tissue a patient possesses makes possible self-examination of the breasts for the palpation of lumps. Although patients often ask whether this type of mammoplasty is likely to stimulate breast cancer, they can be reassured that there is no evidence to support such an idea.

## Reduction mammoplasty

The female-to-male transsexual on the other hand, usually seeks an operation to reduce the size of the breasts. Such patients can be divided into two major groups: those with large breasts and those with small breasts.

The operation to reduce large breasts is performed frequently for women who are troubled by large, pendulous, heavy breasts. In the female-to-male transsexual, particular problems may be encountered when offering this procedure. The principles of the operation are that the nipple must be kept viable and be moved from a position on the apex of the breast to a position on the chest wall, while at the same time reducing the size of the breast.

For small breasts, the operation commonly performed is analogous to that used for males with gynaecomastia (enlarged breasts) where, by lifting a flap of areolar skin, one is able to dissect the breast tissue away from the skin and from the fascia covering the pectoralis major muscle underlying the breast.

Both types of operation should be carried out in hospital under general anaesthesia. Furthermore, both procedures, because of the large cavity created, are frequently complicated by some degree of post-operative haemorrhage which should be watched for carefully during the recovery period.

## Cosmetic surgery of the face

The field of facial cosmetic surgery is growing with alarming speed, stimulated by the progress made in cranio-facial surgery. This new field of surgery has involved detailed study of the facial skeleton using computerized tomography and three-dimensional radiology. Information from this work highlights the fact that there are only very minor differences between the male and female facial skeletons.

Conversion of the facial features from those of one gender to those of another presents the plastic surgeon with one of the greatest surgical challenges. However, it must be realized that the appearance of an attractive female face does not come from the facial skeletal features alone, but rather from the facial skin features.

### Augmentation of the facial skeleton

It is now possible to augment the facial skeleton, comprising the cheek bones and the jaw, to highlight features which in some patients would be regarded as attractive. Using split rib-bone grafts or artificial preparations, suitably moulded augmentation of the jaw and cheek bones can be carried out from within the mouth. Other procedures may be offered to remove bone from the facial skeleton, although these would rarely be required for transsexuals.

### Facelift

This procedure has merits for the ageing patient who presents with redundant skin in the region of the eyelids and neck. It is an operation which strips up the skin of the face through incisions which are hidden in the scalp hairline and around the ear. It should be regarded as a major operation as branches of the facial nerve are liable to be injured during their separation from the overlying skin. Such surgery is not commonly sought by transsexuals.

## Dermabrasion

This procedure is offered to correct the scarring resulting from facial acne. It is of limited value, but occasionally patients with deep pitting of the face may derive cosmetic improvement from it. Dermabrasion is carried out with an air-driven, rotating abrasive disc, preferably under general anaesthesia.

## Rhinoplasty (modification of the nasal anatomy)

There is no such thing as a typically male or female nose. When rhinoplasty is sought by a transsexual patient, therefore, the surgeon should enquire closely about the deformity which is giving the patient problems. The upper part of the nose is supported by bone and, since the overlying skin is usually quite fine, it is possible to move and correct almost any deformity in this region. The lower part of the nose, however, presents problems that can be far more difficult to correct. This part of the nose has much thicker skin with far more sebaceous activity and, even with complete removal of the under-lying cartilages, the nasal shape may not be altered significantly, thereby limiting the possibility of a perfect result. Furthermore, the patency of the nasal airways should always take precedence over a patient's desire to have a finely contoured nose. There is little point in altering the appearance of the nose if this results in loss of respiratory function.

Rhinoplasty may be performed under local or general anaesthesia. Post-operatively, the patient wears an immobilizing splint of plaster of Paris or a pre-formed aluminium former, which fits over the nose. Immobilization is maintained for approximately seven days.

## Removal of abdominal wall fatty tissue (lipectomy)

Another operation that may be performed is lipectomy (re-moval of abdominal wall fatty tissue). While this procedure is not often sought by transsexual patients, it is sometimes of value for those who have a redundant roll of skin and subcutaneous tissue over the lower abdominal wall. The removal of this is achieved by an extended transverse abdominal incision. The abdominal skin and fat is mobilized from the underlying abdominal wall musculature. The procedure may or may not involve a transposition of the umbilicus depending on the amount of tissue removed.

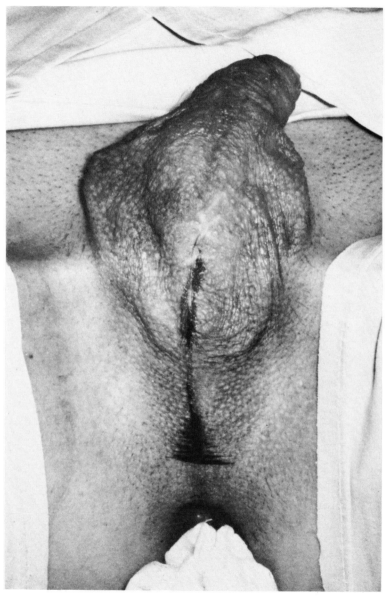

Fig. 1   The line of the initial incision in scrotum and perineum

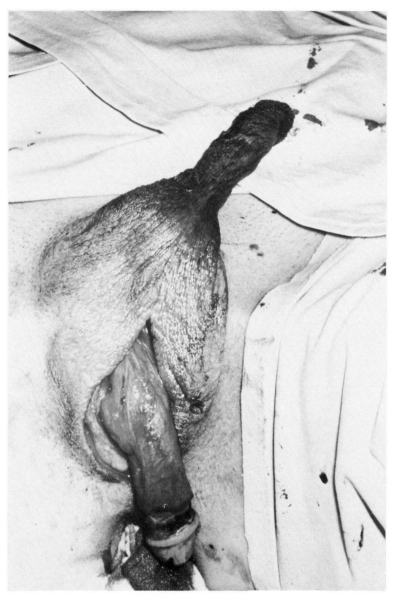

Fig. 2    Removal of penile skin as a tube after circumcision of skin at the coronal sulcus
of the penis

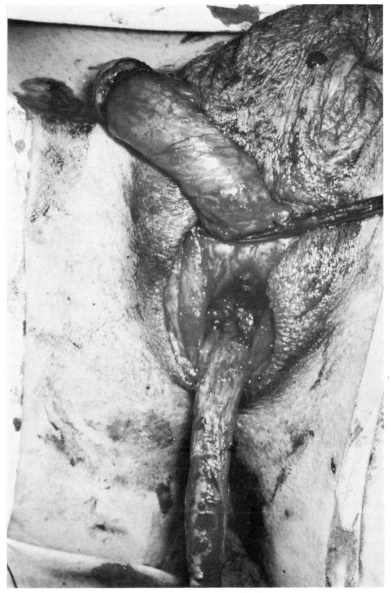

Fig. 3 Separation of the corpora cavernosa of the penis from the penile urethra and surrounding corpus spongiosum. The urethra has been divided and the urethral bulb dissected from the pubic symphysis

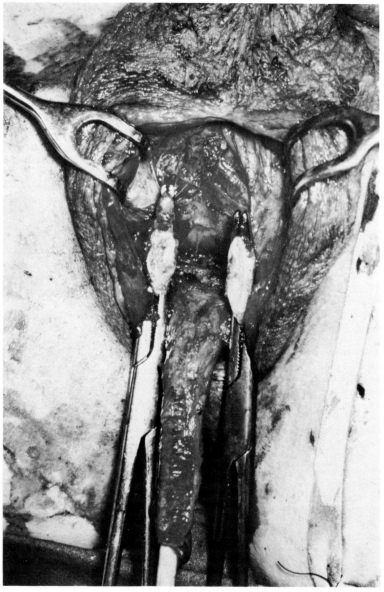

Fig. 4　The ligated stumps of the corpora cavernosa after removal of their major portions

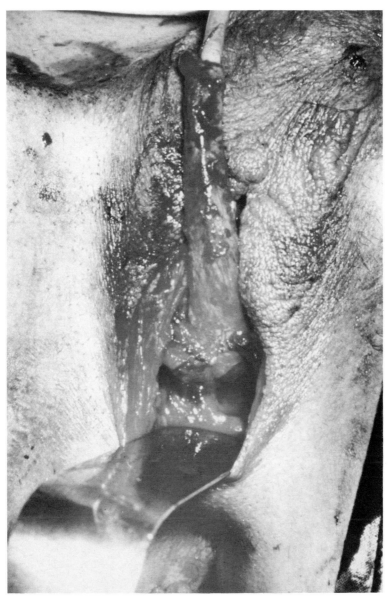

Fig. 5  The vaginal cavity has been created by dissection between the bulb of the penis anteriorly and the anal canal posteriorly

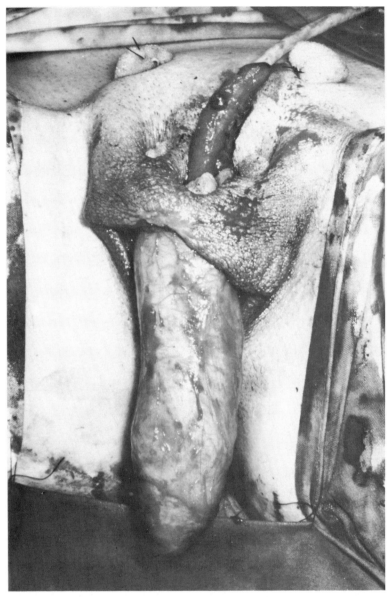

Fig. 6   The penile skin tube has been turned inside out and packed with gauze and the penile urethra has been brought through an incision in the anterior flap of skin

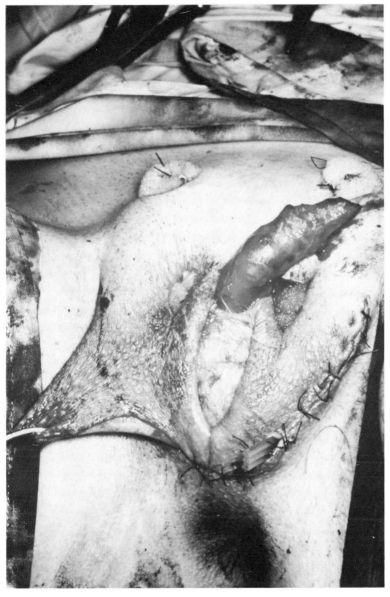

Fig. 7 The penile skin tube packed with gauze has been inserted into the newly-created vagina and scrotal skin is being fashioned into labia

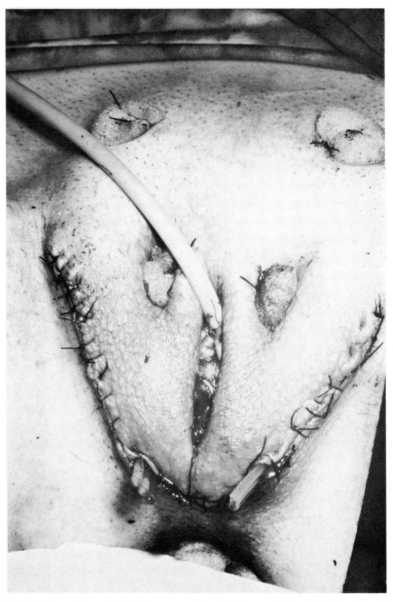

Fig. 8   The penile urethra has been removed so that its opening is at the skin surface of the newly-created vulva; a urinary catheter is protruding from the urethra. This is the usual appearance of the site immediately after completion of reassignment

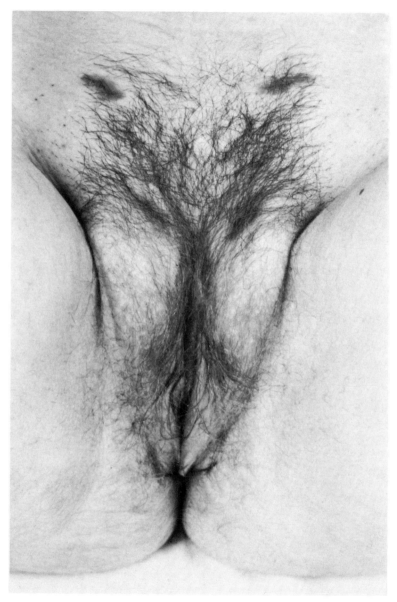

Fig. 9 The external genitalia viewed from the perineal aspect six weeks after male-to-female surgical genital reassignment

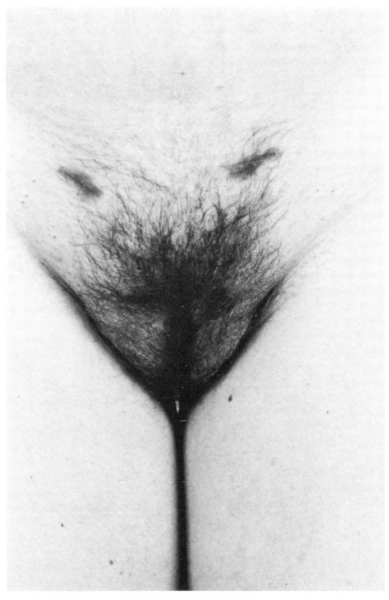

Fig. 10   The external genitalia viewed from above six weeks after male-to-female surgical genital reassignment

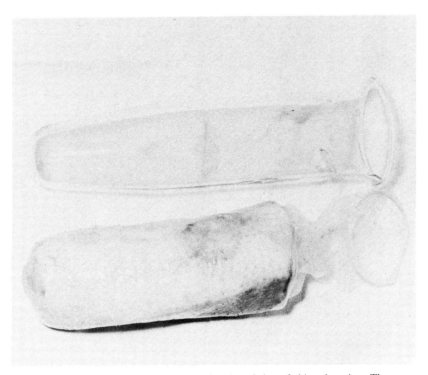

Fig. 11 A glass dilator used to estimate the size of the refashioned vagina. The amount of gauze packing used to fill the dilator is measured and then inserted to distend the condom, which is shown with the skin graft behind it and ready for use

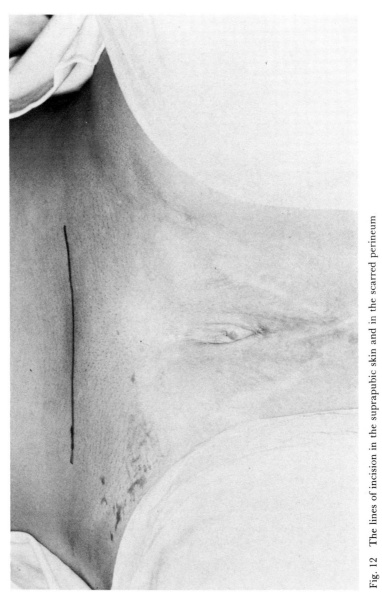

Fig. 12   The lines of incision in the suprapubic skin and in the scarred perineum.

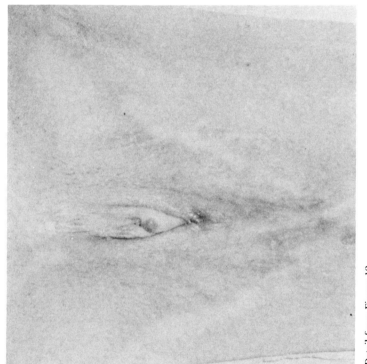

Detail from Figure 12.

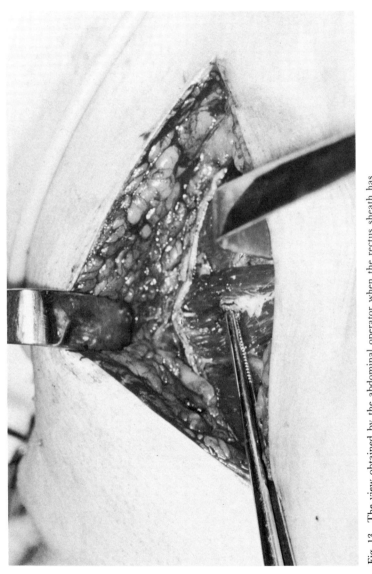

Fig. 13 The view obtained by the abdominal operator when the rectus sheath has been opened

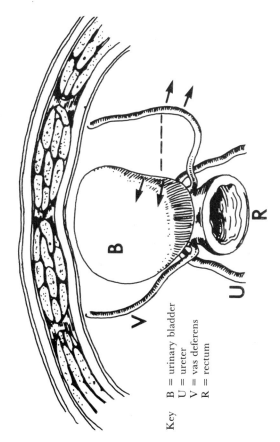

Key  B = urinary bladder
     U = ureter
     V = vas deferens
     R = rectum

Fig. 14  A diagram to show the line of incision between the urinary bladder and vas deferens

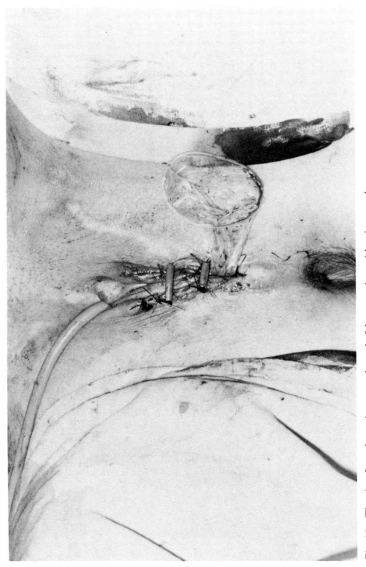

Fig. 15 The view from the perineum at the end of the operation, with urinary catheter and condom in position

The latter process is termed abdominal lipectomy, but there is a new operation, suction lipectomy, which should still be regarded as somewhat experimental. It involves the insertion of a cannula beneath the skin and into the fatty subcutaneous layers. When suction of approximately 720 mm mercury is applied to the cannula, fat can be removed. The advantage of this procedure over a standard abdominal lipectomy is evident in areas of body contours. This applies particularly to the upper thighs and buttocks where a standard lipectomy procedure involves the use of a lengthy incision. Suction lipectomy may be used in the male-to-female transsexual to sculpture a body shape that appears more feminine.

## Removal of tattoos

Occasionally male-to-female transsexuals present with tattoos on various parts of the body, dating from an earlier phase of life when every attempt was made to portray a very masculine image, all to no avail. Such pigmented designs in the skin mar the transition to the female role and male transsexuals invariably request their removal.

This is usually performed by surgical excision of the affected skin with its replacement by a skin graft from another part of the body. More recently, the laser has been introduced as a possible alternative method for dealing with tattoos. However, the extent of subsequent scarring has been disappointing and may limit extensive use of the laser for this purpose.

# III   Male-to-female surgical genital reassignment

*Lena McEwan, Simon Ceber and Joyce Daws*

## History

The surgical treatment of gender dysphoria is a relatively recent development, with Abraham's report in 1931 being the first to describe surgical procedures used in the management of transsexualism.[1]

Although this was followed by sporadic attempts to treat the condition, mainly in Europe, very little attention was paid to it until 1953 when Hamburger *et al.* reported a comprehensive study on the role of surgery in treatment of the transsexual.[2] By and large, this consisted of psychotherapy, hormonally-induced castration with occasional gonadal castration (removal of testicles), and penectomy (removal of the penis). Construction of a vagina was rarely attempted. Among Hamburger's patients was the famous Christine Jorgensen. In 1964 Benjamin reported on ninety-one transsexuals, thirty-one of whom had undergone surgery and, of these, twenty-five had had a vagina constructed.[3] Of the 100 transsexuals reported on by Pauly in 1965, eleven of the forty who had undergone surgery had had a vagina constructed.[4]

In women, construction of the vagina was pioneered by Dupuytren in 1817.[5] Split skin grafts for lining the vagina were introduced by Heppner in 1872,[6] Abbe in 1892,[7] and McIndoe and Counsellor, both in 1937.[8] Baldwin used a free graft of intestine in 1907.[9] Local pedicle flaps of labial and thigh skin were described by Graves in 1921 and Frank in 1927,[10] while in 1935 Kanter and Wells allowed the dissected vaginal cavity to heal by secondary epithelialization.[11]

For vaginal construction in males, Gillies and Millard in 1957 suggested the use of penile skin as a pedicle flap to line the neo-vagina.[12] Several modifications of this technique have since emerged. These include the use of an open (filleted) or tubed penile skin flap, and a choice of anteriorly- or posteriorly-based pedicles.

In some cases, to provide for sufficient vaginal depth, a split-thickness skin graft and/or scrotal tissue have been utilized together with a pedicle graft of penile skin for lining the vagina. When the group at Johns Hopkins Hospital, Baltimore, began to treat male-to-female transsexuals, Jones *et al.* developed an operative technique whereby the newly-formed vaginal cavity was lined with a flap of penile skin anteriorly, and a perineal skin flap posteriorly.[13] In 1970 Edgerton and Bull reported the use of a posteriorly-based penile tube pedicle flap for lining the vagina.[14] At a second-stage operation three to four weeks later, the posterior pedicle was partially divided and scrotal tissue was used to form labia (lips) surrounding the vaginal opening.

Although Laub and Fiske, at Stanford University in 1974, advocated a free split skin graft,[15] Fogh-Anderson, in Denmark in 1969, used full-thickness penile skin as a free graft for lining of the vagina.[16]

In 1971 Stuteville *et al.* described a vaginal reconstruction technique using an anteriorly-based inverted penile tube,[17] and it is this which has formed the basis of the operation used at the Queen Victoria Medical Centre in Melbourne.

## Operative technique

The patient is admitted to hospital three days before the operation. The bowel is prepared with twice daily enemas and a Neomycin washout is given on the evening before operation. A low-residue diet is commenced and the perineum is thoroughly shaved. Neomycin IG orally twice daily and Metronidazole 200 mg thrice daily are also given to reduce the potential risk of infection spreading from the rectum to the surrounding tissues.

At the time of anaesthetic pre-medication, the patient is given 5000 international units of Sodium Heparin subcutaneously, and electrical stimulators are applied to the calf muscles, when the patient is placed in the lithotomy position at the beginning of the operation, to prevent deep venous thrombosis. A 14- or 16-gauge catheter is inserted into the bladder.

Using the diathermy knife, a vertical incision is made, splitting the lower half of the scrotum and extending posteriorly to within 2 cm of the anus (Fig. 1). This incision is deepened until the corpus spongiosum of the penis is displayed. A plane between Buck's fascia and the dartos fascia is developed by blunt dissection up to the penile coronal sulcus. A circumcoronal incision then allows the penis to be pulled out of its skin tube (Fig. 2). The penile suspensory ligaments are divided, freeing the corpora from the pubic symphysis. Each testis is exposed and the corresponding spermatic cord is followed to the external inguinal ring where it is ligated with No. 1 chromic catgut, divided, and allowed to retract into the inguinal canal. Several No. 1 chromic catgut sutures are used to close the external inguinal ring.

The plane between the penile corpus spongiosum and corpora cavernosa is identified near the urethral bulb and is developed distally on to the penile shaft. The urethra is divided and the corpora are clamped temporarily while the urethral bulb is freed from the underside of the pubic symphysis (Fig. 3). Each corpus is then clamped at its base parallel to the inferior pubic ramus, divided, and the stump oversewn with No. 1 chromic catgut (Fig. 4).

The central tendon of the perineum, extending from the bulbospongiosus to the sphincter ani externus muscles, is divided (Fig. 5), and, with one finger in the rectum, a plane is developed by blunt dissection between the prostate and Denonvilliers' prerectal fascia anteriorly and the rectum posteriorly. Dissection is continued to the level of the pelvic peritoneum. The cavity is checked carefully for communication with the rectum and any major bleeding is controlled. A 5 cm vaginal ribbon-gauze pack is inserted into the cavity.

The open distal end of the penile skin tube is oversewn with two layers of 4/0 Dexon: one layer is in the skin and the other in the dartos fascia. The tube is then inverted and packed with 5 cm vaseline ribbon-gauze. The site where the urethra will come through the skin flap is chosen as posteriorly as possible and incised vertically in diamond shape (Fig. 6).

The lower anterior abdominal wall skin and subcutaneous tissue are undermined for a short distance and tension sutures of No. 1 nylon are placed to hold the distally advanced abdominal wall skin to the periosteum over the pubic tubercle and to the origin of the adductor muscle tendons. The urethra is fed through the prepared aperture in the skin flap and the tension sutures are tied firmly over plastic foam bolsters.

The pack is removed from the new vaginal cavity which is inspected again to ensure that all bleeding has ceased. The packed penile skin tube is then inserted into this cavity. If a shortage of penile skin limits the advancement of the tube, several centimetres can be gained by vertically sectioning the dartos muscle and fascia in the mid-line at the base of the skin tube.

The excessive scrotal remains are split vertically until the apex of the split can be sutured comfortably under slight tension to the lower end of the original skin incision. The redundant skin and scrotal contents left on each side are trimmed to form labia (Fig. 7), and sutured with 3/0 Dexon after corrugated drains have been placed along each side of the vaginal skin tube.

The urethra is shortened and sutured to the skin with 4/0 interrupted Dexon sutures (Fig. 8). The wound is dressed with tulle-gras gauze and combine padding held in place by tight 7.5 cm elastoplast strapping applied from the buttock around to the opposite anterior abdominal wall on each side.

On the seventh post-operative day, the patient is returned to the theatre. The vaginal pack is removed and the cavity inspected. If the posterior skin fold is too far anterior, which is often the case, it is divided vertically and re-sutured transversely. A condom filled with foam rubber is then placed in the neovaginal cavity.

After returning to her bed, the patient is taught how to remove, make, and replace the condom pack. She is instructed to keep it in place except when removal is necessary for micturition or defaecation. The catheter is removed from the bladder on the tenth day and the patient allowed home on the fourteenth day after initial surgery.

At approximately four weeks post-operatively the patient is given a rigid vaginal dilator to use for fifteen minutes twice daily. Sexual intercourse may commence six weeks after the patient has left hospital.

# Results

From November 1976 to October 1982 sixty-eight patients underwent male-to-female genital reassignment surgery at the Queen Victoria Medical Centre, Melbourne. Follow-up data were available for fifty-seven of these patients. Thirty-eight (55 per cent) had been followed up for over twelve months and twenty-three of these had completed a detailed questionnaire and undergone a physical examination. These twenty-three patients will be referred to as the 'core group'.

## Length of hospitalization

This varied from two to six weeks. When patients had an uncomplicated post-operative course, the average length of stay in hospital was fourteen days.

## Complications

The significant operative complications that occurred are shown in Table 10.1. There were no deaths and no major medical complications such as pulmonary emboli or myocardial infarction.

**Table 10.1  Complications of male-to-female genital gender reassignment surgery in sixty-eight male transsexuals**

| 68 patients | |
| --- | --- |
| Rectal perforation | 4 |
| Rectovaginal fistulae | 1 |
| Haemorrhage (requiring return to operating theatre) | 6 |
| Neovaginal prolapse | 2 |
| Necrosis of vaginal skin tube | 4 |

Early in the series, two patients had rectal injuries requiring temporary colostomies. One injury was noted at operation and immediate colostomy was performed, while the other was noted at the examination under anaesthesia one week after the initial operation. Once again, a colostomy was performed immediately. Following these problems, it was decided to prepare the bowel of all patients pre-operatively so that any rectal injury noted at the time of operation could be immediately repaired. This occurred on two further occasions and there were no untoward consequences. One patient presented with a high rectovaginal fistula six weeks after operation. This was repaired three months later and has remained closed. However, because of scarring the vagina is short.

Post-operative bleeding within the newly formed vaginal cavity and from the urethral mucosa-to-skin suture line was troublesome early in the series. Two patients developed a prolapse of some of the neovaginal skin due to haemorrhage and four patients had to be taken to theatre for control of haemorrhage from the urethral mucosa-to-skin suture line. Since the introduction of the pressure dressing technique there have been no major post-operative haemorrhages.

Four patients had necrosis (death) of a significant portion of the vaginal skin tube. This was noted at the examination under anaesthesia. Subsequently all of them were found to have short vaginas.

## External genitalia

The overall appearance of the external genitalia was regarded as satisfactory in every patient within the core group and a typical result is illustrated (Figs 9, 10). One patient required reduction in the size of the labia. More detailed results of surgery on the external genitalia have been as follows.

### Urethra

Although the urethral opening is placed well posterior at operation it tends to migrate forward during the post-operative period due to tissue tension and contraction of scar tissue. The opening was in a satisfactory position in thirteen patients of the core group and too anterior in nine. One patient required revisional surgery of the urethral orifice for a stricture. Seven patients have had the urethra shortened to place the opening more posteriorly.

In some patients the urethral bulb is large and surrounded by dense musculature. These patients tend to develop a lump which appears in the vaginal introitus during sexual arousal and may obstruct the vaginal cavity. Two patients have undergone further surgery to reduce the size of the urethral bulb with a satisfactory result.

### Posterior vaginal fold

A fold of skin is present at the posterior margin of the vaginal opening, at the point of inversion of the skin, which was previously at the ventral aspect of the base of the penis. This fold is initially useful in helping to retain the intravaginal packing. It is often divided at the time of the first dressing to allow better access to the vagina. In some patients the fold has persisted, leading to painful intercourse, or collection of urine in the vagina. Six patients required revisional surgery of the skin fold.

## Vagina

Table 10.2 shows the length and breadth of the vaginal cavity obtained in fifty-six patients. Thirty-six patients (65 per cent) had vaginas which were adequate for sexual intercourse, that is, greater than 10 cm deep and at least 35 mm or two finger-breadths wide. In the core group 78 per cent of patients with adequate vaginas were having vaginal intercourse and surprisingly, eight of nine patients with inadequate vaginas were also having vaginal intercourse.

**Table 10.2  Vaginal dimensions in male transsexuals reassigned as females**

| Vaginal length | Core group | Others | Vaginal width | Core group | Others |
|---|---|---|---|---|---|
| > 15 cm | 7 | 3 | > 35 mm | 18 | 30 |
| > 10 cm | 6 | 20 | > 25 mm | 2 | 2 |
| < 10 cm | 9 | 10 | < 25 mm | 1 | |
| Unrecorded | – | 1 | Unrecorded | 1 | 2 |
| | 22 | 34 | | 22 | 34 |

## Orgasmic function

Within the core group, sixteen of the eighteen patients having vaginal intercourse reported having orgasm. Three of the five patients not having intercourse could obtain orgasm by masturbation. Overall, 83 per cent of the group had the capacity to reach orgasm.

## Patient satisfaction

Patients in the core group were requested to grade various aspects of the genital and sociological results of their operation on a scale of 1 to 4. The results are set out in Table 10.3. These figures confirm that most patients were satisfied with the results of operation in most areas. The greatest area of dissatisfaction was related to inadequate vaginal depth which interfered with sexual activity.

**Table 10.3   The degree of satisfaction experienced by male transsexuals after reassignment as females**

| | Patient grading | | | |
| --- | --- | --- | --- | --- |
| | IV | III | II | I |
| Genital appearance | 19 | 3 | | |
| Vaginal depth | 6 | 10 | 3 | 3 |
| Genital sensation | 18 | 3 | 1 | |
| Orgasmic ability | 14 | 7 | | 1 |
| Self image | 21 | – | 1 | |
| Work situation | 19 | 3 | – | |
| Social life | 18 | 2 | 2 | |
| Sexual life | 11 | 7 | 3 | 1 |
| Overall result | 18 | 3 | | |

I   Poor or worse
II   Fair or unchanged
III   Satisfactory or some
     improvement
IV   Good to excellent

One patient (not in the core group) committed suicide six months after a technically successful operation. This appeared to be related to loss of her job, boyfriend, and self-esteem. Shortly before her suicide she stated she had no regrets whatsoever about having had the operation.

*Secondary surgery*
Table 10.4 summarizes the secondary operations that were carried out up to October 1982 in the core group of patients.

**Table 10.4   The frequency and nature of secondary surgical procedures in 23 male transsexuals reassigned as females**

| Secondary surgery | No. of procedures | |
| --- | --- | --- |
| Vaginal lengthening | 4 | |
| Urethral repositioning | 3 | 17 procedures |
| Urethral bulb reduction | 4 | in 9 patients |
| Labial reduction | 1 | |
| Posterior skin fold revision | 5 | |

The most challenging technical problem has been that of the short vagina, one of the commonest complications of gender reassignment procedures. However, abdomino-perineal vaginoplasty, a technique utilizing a combined abdominal and perineal approach, has allowed a safe lengthening of the organ. The two-way approach has been used to lessen the risk of trauma to the bladder or rectum which may result in troublesome fistula formation resulting in passage of urine or faeces from the vagina.

The patient is admitted two days before the operation for mechanical cleansing of the bowel by the use of enemata and bowel washouts. A low-residue diet is given. The night before operation 1 gm Neomycin antibiotic is given orally, and this dose is repeated with the premedication for anaesthesia.

Under general anaesthesia a split skin graft is taken from the thigh. This skin is subsequently prepared for use by stretching it over a mould which is fashioned by the packing of a condom (Fig. 11).

The patient is placed in a modified lithotomy position using Lloyd-Davies stirrups with a pad under the pelvis. A Foley urinary catheter is inserted into the bladder, which is emptied. A transverse skin incision is made within the pubic hair line (Fig. 12). This is deepened through the rectus muscle sheath and beyond its lateral margin: the rectus abdominus muscles are separated vertically and the peritoneal cavity is opened transversely (Fig. 13).

At this point in the operation, a moderate degree of head-down Trendelenburg tilt of the operating table is helpful to assist in displacing the small intestine, which is then packed out of the surgical field. A self-retaining retractor is inserted to facilitate exposure of the pelvic cavity. The position of the bladder is identified by palpation of the balloon of the Foley catheter and an incision is made in the peritoneum, lateral to the bladder and medial to the vas deferens (Fig. 14). A space is developed beside the bladder and deepened towards its base by blunt dissection. Meanwhile the perineal operator has incised the scarred vagina and dissects upwards towards the fingers of the abdominal operator. If concern is felt about the proximity of the rectum, an assistant can insert a finger into it via the anal canal to provide guidance.

Once a meeting has occurred between the operators within the curve of the stretched levatores ani muscles laterally, the space is developed, haemostasis is secured, and the mould with overlying skin graft inserted. The visceral peritoneum is closed over the mould and the parietal peritoneum is closed with continuous No. 1 Dexon sutures after any abdominal packs have been removed. The muscles are approximated with interrupted Dexon, and subcutaneous and subcuticular sutures of Dexon are used to complete wound closure.

The perineal operator inserts the condom and closes the perineal incisions (Fig. 15). The urinary catheter is left in the bladder until the first dressing is done eight to ten days later.

Soon after this time the catheter is removed and the patient can take showers or baths and can be instructed to insert the condom herself. Most patients can leave hospital after ten days. Six weeks later, sexual intercourse may be commenced.

A neovaginal condom mould is worn continuously (except for purposes of toilet and intercourse) for six months until the tendency for the skin-grafted vagina to shrink is overcome. A glass dilator is then used intermittently if regular intercourse is not occurring.

## Conclusion

The results confirm that the decision by the transsexual to undergo sex-change surgery must be based on the patient's acceptance that the results may not be perfect or even ideal. The complication rate is significant and the final results are unsatisfactory with regard to vaginal adequacy in 35 per cent of cases. However, a significant proportion of these patients' vaginal inadequacy can be corrected by further surgery of the abdomino-perineal type.

# IV   Female-to-male surgical genital reassignment

*William A. W. Walters*

Female-to-male sex reassignment surgery involves several separate operations as follows: removal of the enlarged female breasts and their reconstruction as male breasts, removal of the uterus, Fallopian tubes and ovaries by abdominal total hysterectomy and bilateral salpingo-oöphorectomy, closure of the vagina, and construction of a penis (phalloplasty) with fashioning of a scrotum to house artificial testes.

The first two procedures are standard ones without any special technical problems. However, the second two procedures, which are sometimes combined, can provide technical difficulties that render ultimate success in terms of a functional phallus unlikely. It is one thing to have a tube skin graft that looks somewhat like a penis suspended from the pubic region, but quite another to have this graft functional in urinary and sexual terms.

Basically, phalloplasty consists of raising a tube of skin, subcutaneous tissue, and sometimes muscle, usually from the anterior abdominal wall, detaching it from its upper attachment and swinging it downwards towards the lower limbs. This results in the tube of skin hanging in a dependent position from its remaining lower attachment in the suprapubic region. Further skin flaps are mobilized in the pubic region to construct a scrotum into which two prosthetic testes are placed.

The skin lining the vagina is sometimes used to construct a penile urethral tube along the ventral surface of the phallus so formed. Alternatively, a segment of a vein removed from the patient's leg, for example, can be used for this purpose. Closure of the vagina is usually carried out at this time and is a straightforward procedure. However, if the vaginal skin is not required for urethral construction, the vagina can be closed at the time of the hysterectomy.

The newly created phallus can be made intermittently rigid or erect by implantation within it of a simple system of plastic tubes that can be distended with fluid from a reservoir, usually placed beneath the skin in one or other groin. An additional bulb attached to the system and containing valves is implanted beneath the skin of the scrotum. The groin fluid reservoir can be activated by gentle digital pressure on one side of the bulb thereby allowing fluid to distend the tube system to produce phallic erection. Digital pressure on the other side of the bulb results in fluid returning to the reservoir with return of the phallus to its resting state.

While phalloplasty can be quite successful in some patients it involves a series of operations, all of which may be attended by complications requiring prolonged hospitalization. This may lead to frustration and depression in the patient with adverse effects on any current emotional relationship.

In our opinion, until surgical techniques improve, phalloplasty should be avoided in female-to-male transsexuals. An acceptable alternative to most patients is the wearing of a phalloscrotal prosthesis, or model of the penis and scrotum, constructed out of suitable pliable plastic material. Such prostheses can look quite realistic, and each patient can be provided with two, one with a non-erect phallus for wearing inside the clothing and one with an erect phallus for coital purposes. Both prostheses are held against the pubic region by straps that pass around the body.

In our experience, female-to-male transsexuals are most concerned about ridding themselves of the two obvious physical manifestations of femininity—large breasts and a uterus that menstruates. While they also desire a phallus, most can accept not having a phalloplasty until this surgical procedure is attended by a more successful outcome.

# 11   Welfare Services for Transsexuals
## Non-medical assistance
### Sue Harding

Most transsexuals have special psycho-social problems which can hinder their integration into society in their chosen gender role. Unfortunately, there is still much ignorance and prejudice about the phenomenon of transsexualism within Australian society, and consequently welfare services, by and large, are ill-equipped to assist transsexuals to make the difficult transition from one gender role to the other.

The purpose of this chapter is to briefly indicate the major areas of difficulty confronting the transitional transsexual and to make some suggestions about possible areas of social work involvement. The writer is drawing on some eight years' experience of working with transsexuals within the confines of an income maintenance (Social Security) department where the workload is not exclusively comprised of transsexuals.

This chapter is biased in two ways. Firstly, it relates to the Australian way of life; its organization, its legislature, and its social norms and values. Secondly, the information relates mainly to pre-operative transsexuals. It should not be presumed, however, that post-operative transsexuals do not require welfare services nor that the difficulties encountered by female-to-male transsexuals are identical with those of male-to-female transsexuals.

## Social work with transsexuals

Every 'true' transsexual wishes to become socially and sexually integrated into society in their chosen gender role. A major step towards achieving this goal is sex-reassignment surgery which is subject to a protracted pre-operative assessment period. During this time a person's ability to merge into society without being recognized as an anomaly is closely evaluated.

Transsexuals undergoing assessment invariably experience crises and depression. The waiting period prior to surgery is a turbulent and stressful time because it is often one of inadequate emotional support, being a time of estrangement from family and previous friends, and a time when there is difficulty forming new, substantial relationships. Often, too, pre-operative transsexuals are unemployed, and while they are trying to live on an inadequate income (Social Security) they are also attempting to convincingly establish themselves in the opposite sexual identity. In the space of two to five years they are trying to achieve what it has taken a 'normal' man or woman many more years of conditioning to achieve.

In terms of ability to cope with every-day life situations, transsexuals could be said to be psychologically and socially disabled by virtue of their past gender history. It is argued that in just the same way as Western society, in particular, has seen fit to develop special services and programmes to assist other specific disability groups, so there is a need for organizations to provide services to assist transsexuals to fit into society in their chosen gender identity. There is therefore a dual role for social workers whose day-to-day work brings them in contact with transsexuals: first, in the area of casework with individuals, their families, friends, and others, and, second, in the area of community development. The latter is concerned with community education, the development of appropriate services, and with acting as agents of change in respect of administrative practices within government departments and in the area of law reform.

Social work with pre-operative transsexuals is time-consuming because of the long lead-up time to surgery and because they consider their every-day difficulties urgent and intractable. The social worker must be able to endure intense transference of feelings when counselling a transsexual in crisis. Feeling comfortable with the phenomenon of transsexuality is a prerequisite to working in this field. The worker needs to be able to relate to the transsexual as if he or she were a 'normal' man or woman, despite a sometimes unconvincing appearance. Usually, transsexuals are not amenable to counselling perceived as not helping them achieve their goals; their 'blocking' mechanisms are well developed.

Male-to-female transsexuals often have an exaggerated view of womanliness, and few are in tune with the Women's Liberation movement. The female social worker should be willing to act as a model for clients who may have no close 'normal', female friends from whom feedback on appearance and behaviour can be gained. Lack of self-confidence is a major component in their depression.

It is important to allow the upset transsexual the opportunity to 'let off steam' in a safe environment, as this can prevent acting out in socially unacceptable ways. 'Manipulative' is a common label affixed to transsexuals. While we are all capable of being manipulative at times, transsexuals do have these tendencies well-developed through a lifetime of being non-assertive. This is exacerbated by the assessment process which requires the client to play a passive role in isolation from the decisions which will affect his or her future life.

One frequent consequence is hostility towards members of the treating team, and the social worker needs to help transsexuals to express this anger and then to channel their energies into constructive activities. Sometimes training in assertion can be helpful.

Work with these clients is challenging and rewarding. They have enormous motivation to change and their progress is rapid. A social worker in this field is professionally well equipped to create a network of relevant services to support the efforts of the pre- and post-operative transsexual.

## Major areas for social work involvement

### Appearance

#### 'Going public'·

The timing of this important event is dictated by many considerations such as family, finances, employment, accommodation, and of course self-confidence and appearance. All these issues need to be addressed prior to deciding 'when' and 'how' the person is going to communicate his or her serious intent to live life in the opposite gender role.

Once the decision has been taken, some male-to-female transsexuals opt to adopt an incremental approach over some time to changing their appearance, preferring to move from a wholly masculine appearance to that which is 'unisex' by letting their hair and nails grow longer but not wearing cosmetics or nail polish, and by wearing jeans and flat shoes rather than dresses and high-heeled shoes. Others prefer to make a complete and immediate change.

Throughout their waking hours, transsexuals strive to achieve their concept of the ideal. Often they have a distorted body-image which exaggerates their least attractive features out of all proportion. They constantly make comparisons with others and can become inordinately self-conscious about a feature. The two most troublesome features to the male-to-female transsexual are the voice and beard.

#### Voice—pitch and speech

Intonation as well as pitch is required for a convincing presentation. In addition, the style of speech may require modification, particularly in the case of transsexuals who in earlier life have attempted to convince themselves and others of their masculinity by adopting a 'macho' style of address.

Some, by conscious effort, are able to raise their pitch to a satis-factory level. Others find it impossible to modify their masculine voices. Sometimes transsexuals avoid speaking or tend to whisper. In these cases referral to a speech therapist may be helpful. Although, for several reasons, speech therapy may not produce significant changes, the therapist can ensure that, by whatever means are employed to raise the pitch, damage to the vocal cords is avoided. Singing and/or drama classes may also improve vocal presentation.

When all else fails, shortening of the vocal cords by an ear, nose and throat surgeon can raise the pitch of the voice. Simultaneously, surgery can reduce the prominence of the thyroid cartilage (Adam's apple) to improve the cosmetic appearance of the throat. The risk of vocal trauma, however, must be emphasized.

### Complexion

The face receives more scrutiny than any other part of the body; thus the quality of skin and character of facial hair are crucial to self-confidence. While hormones cause some feminization of the male-to-female transsexual's complexion, facial and body hair, once established, will continue to grow, though the rate of regrowth may be reduced.

Facial hair is removed through shaving, waxing, electrolysis and anti-androgens. Shaving is least satisfactory, particularly if the hair is dark, for it is visible through the skin as a shadow. Also, shaving is such a stereotypical male act that even hirsute biological females avoid it. Removal of hair by waxing creates a more feminine com-plexion, but is time-consuming and needs to be perfected by constant practice. Electrolysis is the only depilation method that is reasonably permanent. However, it is painful, expensive and slow, and scarring can result. Drugs (e.g. cyproterone acetate) for hirsutism have pro-duced good results in some transsexuals, but, as these are still ex-perimental, they are not widely available.

Topically applied preparations for excess hair growth from phar-macists do not seem to be widely accepted, probably because of their lack of effectiveness.

Androgen therapy in the case of female-to-male transsexuals is most effective in bringing about beard growth and deepening of the pitch of the voice. Unfortunately it tends to cause acne, which can be psychologically upsetting.

### Cosmetic surgery

Nose refinement (rhinoplasty) and breast augmentation (mammo-plasty) can assist to align the body more closely with the feminine stereotype. Results are not always satisfactory and the risks should be discussed before a decision is made.

It is worth mentioning here that visible tattoos are a handicap because of widespread employer prejudice, since tattoos are associated with delinquency and criminality. Their removal by plastic surgery or other methods should be seriously considered.

### Cosmetics, clothing and deportment

Early in the transition, cosmetics tend to be used to camouflage beard, shadow and poor skin. When coupled with unsuitable colours, the results can be garish. Cosmetic attendants in large city departmental stores can be a valuable source of advice.

Clothing is dependent upon choices which enhance the best aspects of the figure and which minimize the least attractive. Some city stores advertise clothing for the 'large woman', although this usually means 'wider' rather than 'taller'. For the unemployed transsexual, good clothing can be obtained cheaply from a variety of 'thrift' shops belonging to religious organizations. Female underwear for the male-to-female transsexual whose appearance is still unconvincing can generally be purchased without undue embarrassment from each city's main shopping area.

Obtaining fashionable footwear for the woman who takes a shoe-size larger than 9½B is difficult and the male-to-female transsexual with a wider foot finds it even more difficult. A few specialty shops can, however, meet most needs up to a size 12 for women, and can supply narrow men's footwear for female-to-male transsexuals. Shoes can also be made to order.

Walking, sitting, and eating are accomplished by studying and then copying the way in which other men and women make these actions. The social worker should allow his or her client the opportunity to practice these new behaviours and should point out behaviours which do not conform to their client's chosen gender identity. Classes in deportment through mannequin schools are expensive. Transsexuals should be wary of signing up for numerous classes before determining their effectiveness. They would also be well advised to telephone beforehand to ascertain if there is willingness to assist transsexuals.

## Establishing identity

### Change of name by deed poll

Provided there is no intention to deceive, anyone can change his or her name by deed poll. The new name should be registered with the

Registrar-General's Office. It is then a relatively simple matter to obtain a change of name on driver's licence, general insurance policies, taxation and medical insurance files, and other such documents.

## Birth certificates

In Australia birth certificates are unalterable. This fact places transsexuals in a difficult and embarrassing position when they are required to produce their birth certificate to prove their identity, for instance when applying for a passport.

It is incongruous that while the medical profession has recognized the need to treat such people through eventual surgery, the law of the land has not yet addressed itself to the legal status of pre- and post-operative transsexuals.

## Passports

The purpose of a passport is to prove one's identity and place of birth when travelling overseas. It is not used to prove one's gender. It is therefore unfortunate that the Australian application form for a passport requires a person to state whether he or she is male or female. It also asks if a person has been known by any other name.

When a transsexual lodges the completed application form, it should be accompanied by the original birth certificate or extract of birth registration, together with a certified copy of the deed poll which explains why the person's claimed name differs from the name on the birth certificate. There may be other documents which are also required, for example a marriage certificate. This procedure does not prevent the Department of Immigration and Ethnic Affairs issuing that person with a passport in the new female (or male) name with the biological gender shown as the opposite to that indicated by the name, appearance, and behaviour.

To date, efforts to bring about a change in the department's administrative practices and policy has not succeeded, and will not succeed while the law fails to recognize the surgically-changed gender identity of transsexuals.

## Life assurance policies

Since the risk factor differs between men and women, it is important that the life assurance company be advised that a policy holder is a transsexual. Otherwise claims may be rejected and policies cancelled.

## School and tertiary examination results and certificates

In the experience of the writer, provided the transsexual has proof that he or she has changed name legally, state education departments have shown themselves willing to re-issue certificates and the like in the person's new name.

## Employment references

Many past employers have proved willing to re-issue references with the changed name. The importance of references in obtaining employment cannot be stressed enough.

In all cases mentioned in this section, the transsexual should be prepared to produce a letter from the medical team stating that he or she is a transsexual undergoing assessment for sex reassignment surgery and is required to dress and live completely in his or her chosen sexual identity.

## Family counselling

Some transsexuals marry and have children in an effort to resolve their identity confusion. Frequently, by the time a person presents for treatment the marriage has broken up, but sometimes treatment is sought while the person concerned is still living with spouse and children. In either case, contact with the other family members can achieve a better understanding of the condition. Through counselling, fears that the children will become transsexual can be allayed and anger and grief can be worked through so that plans for the future can be formulated.

Divorce is a prerequisite for sex reassignment surgery, giving rise to ethical and moral conflict, particularly in the case of Roman Catholics. Discussing the issue with a knowledgeable and sympathetic priest can be beneficial to both partners.

This is a time when the family is also in need of practical advice on such matters as housing, schooling, income maintenance for wife and children, referral for legal advice, and so on.

Parental counselling is not always possible or indicated, particularly where the transsexual has previously broken all ties with his or her immediate family. The transsexual may not even live in the same part of the country as his or her parents. Where close ties with parents, brothers, and sisters do exist, family members will sometimes accept contact with a social worker, but it should not be the responsibility of the social worker to appraise them that their son or daughter is a transsexual: this is the responsibility of the transsexual. Role-playing with the social worker can be helpful in practising how to go about breaking the news as tactfully as possible.

Many family members think, like the community at large, that transsexualism is some sort of perverted sexual practice. It can therefore be helpful for the family members to have access to simply written articles on what transsexualism is all about. Such articles, together with counselling, can assuage feelings of revulsion and guilt, particularly on the part of the parents.

The needs of children in a marriage which has broken up or is about to go through divorce should not be overlooked by the parents or the counsellor. Children often accept the transsexual parent once they are enabled to understand the nature of the condition and if they receive reassurance that divorce does not mean the loss of the love of the transsexual parent. Obviously the wife of a male-to-female transsexual will need to have some measure of acceptance and understanding of her husband in order to allow the continuation of the relationship between him and the children.

## Employment

### *Unemployment*

The unemployed transsexual who is trying to survive on Social Security payment is also attempting to convincingly establish a new sexual identity. During this crisis period many prefer not to confront the problem of finding a job while they are worrying about their appearance and their voices and beards. However, long periods of unemployment are a severe handicap in today's labour market. It is a well-known fact that two or more years of continuous unemployment nearly always results in a person becoming permanently unemployable.

In addition, transsexuals often lack a relevant previous employment history. A person who has worked all his adult life in male-type occupations is probably not going to have any experience of female-type work and will not possess suitable references. Such a person should be referred for vocational advice, assistance with presentation, and training in job-seeking skills. Sometimes on-the-job training or further education for a suitable career is required to provide them with saleable skills in their new gender identity.

Failure to be punctual for early morning appointments is a characteristic common to many male-to-female transsexuals, probably due to their time-consuming cosmetic routine discussed earlier. This habit needs to be eliminated if employment is to succeed, unless shift work is contemplated.

### *The transsexual who is currently employed*

When a transsexual makes the decision to change sex he or she often resigns from his or her employment. However, quitting a job immediately upon embarking on treatment is to be discouraged until alternatives have been explored. When the person's appearance and presentation are satisfactory, employers should be approached with a view to keeping the transsexual employed in the new gender identity. Some countries have anti-discriminatory laws which, in effect, would be supportive of someone who wished to remain in the same job or who could be transferred to another job.

While the responsibility to approach an employer lies primarily with the transsexual, the social worker can act as an advocate through educating the employer and reassuring him that a transsexual employee has not changed his or her personality or lost all work skills through changing sexual identity.

A strategy that the writer has employed with some success is that of helping the transsexual put the request 'to change sex on-the-job' to the employer *prior* to adopting male or female attire. This is then followed up by the social worker inviting the employer to meet him or her and the transsexual for a joint discussion on the implications. The employer should have an initial private discussion with the social worker so that fears and prejudices can be frankly aired; then, at a pre-arranged time, the transsexual, wearing the attire of his or her chosen identity, should join in the discussion. This enables the employer to confront reality rather than be left to imagine what the employee will look like cross-dressed.

The use of male or female staff toilets is a common objection put forward by employers. Again, valuable ground work can be put in by the transsexual talking to his or her fellow employees and gaining their understanding and support. Usually, if the new appearance and behaviour closely conform to society's expectations of 'maleness' and 'femaleness' then fewer objections tend to be raised. Where prejudice and discrimination are being experienced by the transsexual at work, advice and support from unions should be sought if the person is a union member.

Not all employed transsexuals can confront the issue of remaining in the same job. They may experience intolerable real or imagined pressure from work-mates which forces them to resign. In these instances, they should immediately register for work and Social Security benefits and, in so doing, should explain fully the circumstances leading them to abandon their jobs.

*Employment in the chosen gender identity*

Many pre-operative transsexuals are able, because of their good appearance and work skills, to find suitable employment. The difficulty arises though, when employment is dependent upon a medical examination, which is usual in the case of government positions. The transsexual would be advised to first enquire about the organization's policy regarding employment of transsexuals, either pre- or post-operatively.

## Accommodation

Usually changing sex necessitates moving house. Finding suitable alternative accommodation can be an onerous task, particularly if one is unemployed and cannot share accommodation with anyone else. Landlords can be particularly unsympathetic where unemployment exists and where a person's presentation is at odds with the landlord's expectations. Sometimes a letter from the medical team or social worker can help sway the landlord's decision to lease in favour of the transsexual. Government housing authorities too can be enabled to exercise compassion if the social worker acts as an educator and advocate.

The staff of men's or women's hostels, while offering cheaper accommodation, is not usually keen on accommodating transsexuals. Moreover, even if a transsexual's appearance and behaviour are good, hostel accommodation does not usually afford sufficient privacy. The close proximity to others puts the transsexual in danger of being discovered as such.

## Quality of life issues

### Sexual counselling

This is a neglected area, but a troublesome one to many. In the main, transsexuals hope to attract as sexual partners 'normal' men or women. Prior to surgery they often feel inhibited in seeking these sorts of relationship, some having homosexual relationships prior to, and sometimes after, surgery. Sexual preferences are as varied among transsexuals as they are in the general community, but the important factor is that they desire sexual relationships in which their male or female identity is essential to those relationships. Many, however, feel obliged to give the appearance of wanting or having a so-called normal heterosexual relationship. Thus a candid exploration of their current sexual needs, expectations, and fears can go a long way towards helping them accept their own particular developing sexuality. People with intractable sexual difficulties should be referred to an experienced counsellor.

### Spiritual support

The importance of religion to the transsexual should not be

overlooked. Unfortunately, transsexuals are not welcomed by some religious groups and churches. Furthermore, the necessity of obtaining a divorce in order to undergo sex reassignment surgery is at odds with Anglican and Roman Catholic teaching. However, some priests of both denominations can be constructive and supportive in helping the transsexual to consider the various ethical issues involved in reassignment.

### Self-help groups

There is an absence of viable self-help groups for transsexuals in Australian. In the main transsexuals prefer to identify with 'normal' people and, while they may indicate a desire to get involved in community activities, in practice many tend to become spectators rather than participants. Most will describe themselves as 'loners' by necessity and circumstance, and since many lack self-confidence it is a difficult task to motivate them to join activities in the mainstream of society.

Sometimes male-to-female transsexuals will readily accept the idea of learning traditional female crafts such as cooking and dressmaking, and many organizations offer a wide choice of community classes at little cost.

## Miscellaneous issues

### Police harrassment

Australian society adheres rigidly to stereotypic male and female sex roles. As a consequence, it does not recognize homosexuality, transvestism or transsexualism. In most states it is illegal to practice homosexuality or to cross-dress in public.

Nowadays however, most police forces in Australia are familiar with transsexualism. Nevertheless, anyone undergoing assessment for sex reassignment should carry a letter from the medical team explaining the necessity to cross-dress and, as a precaution, this letter should be carried at all times.

### Medical and hospital insurance

Changing one's sex is a costly business. Unless transsexuals are eligible for free medical and hospital treatment, they should take out insurance cover at the highest level if they are contemplating undergoing assessment for eventual sex reassignment. Some insurance companies do not cover the cost of elective surgery such as rhinoplasty or mammoplasty. All companies have a qualifying period before a person is entitled to claim on their insurance.

## Marriage and adoption of children

Until laws are changed, no pre- or post-operative transsexual is able to obtain a legal marriage in Australia, or to adopt children.

## Future directions

Insufficient resources are available for research. The psycho-social needs of transsexuals and their families are largely neglected, as are adequate follow-up services for post-operative transsexuals.

Transsexualism has existed in societies for centuries, and is likely to continue for a long time to come. It cannot be ignored. The community needs to be educated and laws changed to enable the transsexual to take his or her place in society without stigma or discrimination.

# 12    Ethical Aspects
## Is gender reassignment morally acceptable?
*William A. W. Walters*

From a survey of the philosophical literature, it is apparent that there is no simple definition of ethics. We can probably best describe it as the science of morals, which is that branch of philosophy concerned with human character and conduct.[1] The province of ethics is to seek the reasons for conduct being called right or wrong, good or bad, and why it can actually be said to be so; to discover the principles and aims of morals; to define the nature of the good and its relationship to the right.[2] It is important to appreciate that ethics does not attempt to lay down any definite rule for conduct since that would imply a universally accepted ideal which cannot be found. Rather, it seeks to help us ask the right questions concerning our motives, decisions and actions so that we are being rationally self-conscious and acting responsibility. We could sum up these ideas by describing ethics as a systematic attempt to avoid taking anyone or anything for granted.[3] In the Western world the moral teachings of the Judaeo–Christian religious traditions have provided the basis for ethical behaviour, but their influence in this regard, especially in education, appears to be declining, and any teaching of morality and ethics in future may have a largely secular basis.

Because of the relatively recent recognition of transsexualism as a specific entity and the introduction of sex reassignment as the preferred form of treatment of the condition, personnel concerned with the care and management of transsexuals are 'breaking relatively new ground' in an ethical sense.

## The definition of sex and gender

According to nature, the transsexual has been born of one or other biological sex. Why try to convert him or her to the opposite sex? The answer to this question must take account of the definition of sex and, in particular, of sexual identity. Is the sex of an individual determined by the chromosome constitution, the genital anatomy, the presence of ovaries or testes, the hormonal secretions determining secondary sexual characteristics, by how the individual is viewed by society, or by how the individual regards his or her own sexuality (the psychological gender)? While all of these factors are important, ultimately it is the psyche that has the overriding influence in the determination of gender identity. Hence, the entirely organic approach is inadequate for a complete understanding of gender identity.

In those people in whom the body image conflicts with the psychological conviction of gender identity, there are only three possible approaches to management: either the psychological gender identity can be changed so that it is in keeping with the biological sex, the latter can be changed so that it is in keeping with the psychological gender, or the individual can be advised to live in the biological or desired sex roles without surgery.

While there is some difference of opinion about the most appropriate clinical management of secondary transsexuals (in whom the gender disturbance first appears in adolescence or later life) there seems little doubt that the most appropriate management of primary transsexuals (in whom the gender disturbance was evident in early childhood) is complete gender reassignment, including genital surgery.[4]

If the primary transsexual is obliged to live in the role of his or her biological sex without reassignment, varying degrees of suffering and depression may result, culminating in self-mutilation or suicide. This raises the obvious ethical question of whether it is morally right to withhold gender reassignment when the consequences might be so disastrous.

Medical practitioners concerned with gender reassignment would be well advised to conduct such work in teaching hospitals rather than in private hospitals. In the former institutions, it is easier to form an interdisciplinary medical and paramedical group of specialists to look after the diverse needs of transsexuals. Such groups provide ethical safeguards for the patient and individual members of the medical team. In addition, the teaching hospital environment ensures that only work of a high standard will be conducted with proper assessment of therapeutic results.

## The natural law

One of the main ethical objections to gender reassignment is that it operates against the natural law. The concept of natural law is one of the classical Christian approaches to general ethical questions. It dominated medieval moral theology and still forms the basis of Roman Catholic thinking. A wide definition of natural law would be that there are certain precepts or norms of good and right conduct discoverable by all mankind.[5] In other words, the natural law is revealed by man's conscience. Natural laws are claimed to be universal and to apply to all men, though in practice they need clarification through revelation and reinforcement by the teaching authority of the Church. Any deliberate interference with normal bodily functioning is, according to this law, a violation but may be justified on one of two grounds: firstly, the principle of totality, whereby any diseased part of the body may be removed or otherwise modified if its malfunctioning constitutes a serious threat to the whole; or, secondly, the principle of double effect, whereby a good action is not forbidden even if one of its unintended consequences is evil. If one adhered to this philosophy, much of medical practice would be unacceptable in that to some extent it interferes with normal bodily function.

On the other hand, Protestant Christian ethical thinking has tended to concentrate on general questions about the nature of man and the quality of a truly human life as made possible in those who have responded to God's grace. Love, freedom and forgiveness have been favorite themes. For example, situation ethics is determined basically by love and is a person-centred rather than a principle-centred ethic. Contemporary discussions on the nature of health and the social dimensions of medicine open up interesting possibilities for the recovery of something like the Biblical perspective, in which health was seen as one part of a much larger quest for wholeness of personal and social life.

Consequently, if one was to formulate a view based on the theology of natural law, one would conclude that transsexualism should not be treated by sex reassignment, whereas if one was to take the Protestant viewpoint one could argue that, by contributing to the wholeness of personal and social life, gender reassignment in transsexuals is morally acceptable.

## Surgery for treatment of a psychological condition

From within the medical profession a not uncommon view has been expressed that gender reassignment is ethically unacceptable in that it is a form of psychosurgery. The latter was a term applied to the surgical treatment of various psychiatric states (e.g. schizophrenia and depression) by operations on the brain, such as prefrontal leucotomy. This procedure was introduced in the 1930s and was carried out in the succeeding fifteen to twenty years. It has now fallen into disrepute and has been severely criticized on ethical grounds as it often changed the personality so drastically that people were no longer 'themselves'. Furthermore, the changes they experienced were irreversible. While gender reassignment surgery does not involve brain surgery, it could be construed as a form of psycho-surgery in that it is a surgical treatment for what appears to be primarily a psychological problem. Certainly, in terms of the identity of the person, gender reassignment, including the genital surgery, is a vitally important procedure with just as far-reaching implications for the transsexual, in terms of personal identity, as psychosurgery had for the psychiatric patient. On the other hand, transsexual surgery is quite different from psychosurgery in that there is no operative procedure on the brain. The analogy is there-fore unsatisfactory and can be dismissed.

## The removal of sex organs

It is often claimed by those who object to gender reassignment that healthy organs are being removed, and that this is contrary to the very basis of medical treatment which aims to preserve or restore normal bodily function. However, this is not the case. Although removal of the penis and testes in male transsexuals ablates male reproductive function, the transsexual does not possess this function anyway because he cannot behave sexually as a male, having the irreversible conviction that he is female. Furthermore, not only does he avoid using the genitals for sexual purposes, but he may mutilate them beyond repair in an attempt to rid himself of what he sees as a gross abnormality or deformity. In addition, after several years of oestrogen therapy the testes become atrophic and can no longer be regarded as normal organs.

The intent of the surgery is also important ethically in that its aim is to have a therapeutic effect. It is not simply a question of removing organs because they are not appealing to the patient but of removing organs to make way for the construction of other organs to resemble those of the biological female. As a result, the individual will be able to function sexually, whereas before operation sexual function was not possible.

Human sexuality has a much wider function than that of repro-duction alone. It is an expression of love and affection and brings pleasure, satisfaction and stability to human relationships. In the surgically reassigned transsexual these sexual functions are now possible in a way that they were not before surgery.

## Hormonal therapy

This can be accompanied by complications of life-threatening magnitude, such as thromboembolism, hypertension, cardiovascular disorders and, less seriously, interference with metabolic functions. Therefore, it is mandatory that transsexuals taking hormones in high dosage be under the care of an appropriate medical adviser. The aim in therapy should be to administer the lowest dose of hormone necessary for adequate feminization or masculinization (within limits) and for adequate suppression of gonadal function. Blood levels of hormones should be monitored as a guide to therapy. After surgical gender reassignment, the dosage of hormones can be reduced. The doctor has an ethical obligation to explain the risks of hormonal therapy to the patient and, as far as possible, to ensure that it is administered in the correct manner.

While taking hormones, every patient should be seen regularly for assessment of cardiovascular status, liver function, examination of breasts and pelvic examination.

## Informed consent

Gender reassignment, especially its surgical component, has such wide implications for the patient's future that full and detailed consent must be obtained. The patient must understand all implications of the procedure, and sign a special consent form which is witnessed by a lawyer who has attested to the patient's understanding of the document. The patient must also realize the limitations of surgery and understand its possible risks and complications. Obviously, it is not wise for gender reassignment to be carried out in married persons or in minors where consent involves other parties. Where transsexuals have married and have children, the effects of gender reassignment on the family need serious consideration by the medical team. Under such circumstances, the medical management will affect not only the patient but other persons intimately related to the patient, and whilst the doctor's prime duty is to his patient, he also has a wider duty to the family and to society.

## Confidentiality

Confidentiality is extremely important in this field of medicine as there are serious implications for the patient should it be breached. Therefore it would be wise if medical practitioners obtained written consent from the patient before divulging any information about that patient, even to other medical practitioners.

# Research

Whilst a number of studies have indicated that 80 per cent of reassigned transsexuals achieve a satisfactory result in terms of personal well-being, other studies have found a lower success rate.[6] From this, some would argue that the reliability of the treatment in improving the patient's condition is questionable and that therefore the surgery should not be done at all, especially as it is irreversible. Attention is drawn to the occasional patient in a number of studies who has reverted to the original sex role or who has committed suicide subsequent to reassignment.

There is no doubt that there is still a need for a proper long-term follow-up study of patients who have been surgically reassigned and that most of the studies published so far reveal deficiencies in this respect. Nevertheless, the general consensus of opinion around the world that gender reassignment is, on balance, more effective than any other treatment for this condition would seem to indicate that a case for abolition of such treatment cannot be upheld in the present state of knowledge. Obviously there is an urgent need for research in this area. Providing all the usual ethical procedures in relation to the conduct of clinical research are observed, one can make a strong case for conduct of such research on ethical grounds, because until our knowledge of the condition increases we are not in a position to be dogmatic about the efficacy of gender reassignment as currently practised. One might conclude, therefore, that there is indeed an ethical obligation to conduct research into the causes and management of transsexualism.

# Socio-economic aspects

Gender reassignment usually involves a two-year period of fairly intensive medical and surgical treatment and it might well be asked whether the community can afford this. It is alleged by some that the reassignment procedure is principally a cosmetic one and that there are many people with more urgent conditions requiring medical treatment who should occupy hospital beds. This is a difficult ethical question because it eventually centres on individual versus community needs and the allocation of scarce medical resources. Is it morally justifiable to provide sophisticated medical services for a minority in the community when there are urgent community needs of a more general nature, such as housing, education, geriatric care, and environmental protection, affecting a much greater proportion of the population? If it is agreed that facilities can only be provided to treat some of the transsexuals in the population, then how should selection procedures operate? Should they be determined by selective criteria? If so, how are the criteria to be decided upon? Or should the selection be on a random basis? Three positions can be discerned. Firstly, the all-or-none principle; if all patients cannot receive equal treatment, then no patients should be treated, as to treat some at the expense of others is morally wrong. Secondly, selection of some patients could be made by application of medical and utilitarian standards. Thirdly, random selection could be used to eliminate criteria based upon general social worth. Arising out of a consideration of these three positions, one could draw attention to three issues that are particularly relevant to making decisions about allocation of health care resources, namely, prospects of treatment effectiveness, the role of social worth, and the moral acceptability of random selection.[7] Generally, socio-economic aspects of health care in all fields continue to provide ever-increasing problems requiring solution.

## Future possibilities

Ethical problems are likely to arise when transsexuals request that they be allowed to marry; to adopt children; or to have embryos transferred to their peritoneal cavities in the hope that they will develop as abdominal pregnancies and result in normal living children.

## Marriage

Obviously most transsexuals see marriage as one of the important corollaries to gender reassignment. However, many of them are unaware of their ethical obligations in this regard. It might be argued that it would be important for a reassigned transsexual to indicate to the spouse-to-be that he or she was not born as a biological member of the sex to which he or she appeared to belong, and that consequently he or she was unable to bear children. If they were to marry and it was subsequently discovered by the spouse that the person he or she had married was not of the biological sex he or she purported to be, then it could be alleged that a gross deception had been perpetrated.

## Adoption of children

A number of transsexuals who have been reassigned wish to adopt children. The ethical problems that arise in this regard relate to how the community regards the rearing of children. If it believes that two people, one of each biological sex, are required for the rearing of children, then it is unlikely that it would favour the adoption of children by transsexuals who have been reassigned. On the other hand, there are a number of single parents who successfully rear their children and I do not know of any evidence to suggest that reassigned transsexuals would not be capable of the task.

## Abdominal pregnancy

The development of *in vitro* fertilization procedures has raised the possibility that an embryo could be transferred to the peritoneal cavity of a male-to-female transsexual and might, in the presence of adequate hormonal stimulation, grow adequately as an abdominal pregnancy, resulting eventually in the birth of a normal living child by abdominal delivery. Important ethical considerations arise in this situation as abdominal pregnancy is recognized as a life-threatening condition. For example, it may cause internal haemorrhage with a threat to the life of the bearer of the conceptus, and in most surveys of abdominal pregnancies a high foetal mortality has occurred.[8] Therefore, it could be argued that the intentional development of abdominal pregnancies would be unethical. Certainly most members of the medical profession would be highly critical of their colleagues becoming involved in such procedures. On the other hand, it might be argued that so long as the patient understands the risks, it is her decision as to whether the possible outcome of a living child warrants the risks involved. It could be argued also that the community condones people taking life-threatening risks in other situations, so why not in this one? This argument, however, seems to lose sight of the foetus. When there is an appreciable risk of foetal morbidity, abnormality, and mortality, the mother does have to think not only of her own desires and welfare but also of those of the foetus.

## Personal viewpoint

Personally, I hold the view that gender reassignment is morally justifiable in that its aim is therapeutic. In particular, it seeks to improve the quality of life of the transsexual by allowing him or her to become better integrated in society, with peace of mind. In this regard, several studies have indicated that it is attended by a significant measure of success.[9]

On the other hand, I would urge extreme caution when considering requests by transsexuals to adopt or bear children, as another party, namely the foetus or child, is involved under such circumstances. To depart from our traditional and well-tried methods of parenting and rearing children would be a very serious matter. In my view, decisions of such import cannot be left with the individual patient and doctor but require the sanction of society before being implemented.

# 13  Legal Aspects
## Should the law be changed?

*Douglas Graham*

The purpose of this chapter is to analyse some legal aspects of transsexualism, including the legality and legal consequences of sex reassignment surgery.

Transsexualism has been defined as 'an obsession to belong to the opposite sex which is not practically reversible by psychological or other medical treatment'.[1] It must be distinguished from hermaphroditism, which is a 'congenital condition of ambiguity of the reproductive structures so that the sex of the individual is not clearly defined as exclusively male or exclusively female'[2] and from other sexual anomalies. It must also be distinguished from transvestism, although the distinction may only appear to be one of degree; transvestism being 'the act of dressing in the clothing of the opposite sex'[3] and being usually attributed to a psychological compulsion.

## *The legality of sex reassignment surgery*

Having regard to the fact that the transsexual is physiologically a member of one sex, that the purpose of surgery is to render him anatomically a member of the other sex (at least to outward appearances), and that the procedure is irreversible, it is understandable that extreme caution must be observed, especially considering the fact that both the diagnosis of the condition and the decision to undertake the procedure depends, in the end, upon an evaluation of the subject's own assertions.

The first question in relation to transsexualism for consideration by lawyers is the legality of the surgical procedure itself. Under the common law, it is possible that the procedure would have constituted the offence of mayhem.[4] In Australia and the United Kingdom this has been replaced by various statutory offences which cover wounding and the infliction of grievous bodily harm. In the United States legal opinion on the legality of the procedure has been divided, partly because of the continued existence of mayhem as a crime in some states.[5] However, there is no decision on the point. In 1969 an English legal writer suggested that orchidectomy and mastectomy could be performed safely in England for therapeutic purposes but doubted whether the procedure could be justified in the then state of medical knowledge. He said:

> The law would countenance such an operation if full consent of the patient is obtained and if the operation is for a proven therapeutic purpose. Otherwise the operation is a criminal assault even if consent is given. What is therapeutic depends upon the state of medical knowledge and public opinion at any given time.[6]

A slightly more liberal view was expressed in 1970 by the High Court in England in the celebrated case of *Corbett* v. *Corbett (orse. Ashley)* to which further reference will be made hereafter, as follows:

> There is obvious room for differences of opinion on the ethical aspects of such operations but, if they are undertaken for genuine therapeutic purposes, it is a matter for the decision of the patient and the doctor concerned in his case.[7]

The diligence of an American legal researcher has revealed a number of decisions and statutory provisions in non-common law countries including Switzerland, Argentina and Belgium.[8] In the Belgian case charges were laid against doctors following the death of a transsexual as a result of blood clotting after reassignment surgery. The prosecution claimed that the surgery was not justified because it had been performed simply to pacify the patient not to cure him, but the doctors claimed that the procedure had been carried out to restore the patient's psychiatric balance and to facilitate his social adjustment. The Court noted the existence of a conflict of medical opinion upon the procedure and concluded that it should not decide which was the more proper view where there was no question about the expertise and integrity of the conflicting opinions. The prosecution also contended that there could not have been a valid consent to the procedure but the Court held that the patient had been intelligent and well-balanced and his consent could not be negated merely by his sexual abnormality.

The question of consent to the procedure raises issues of peculiar difficulty. The reasoning of the Court in the Belgian case illustrates the contradiction: if the justification for the procedure is the restoration of the patient's psychiatric balance it seems difficult to conclude at the same time that the patient is well-balanced. Bearing in mind that major elective surgery bringing about irreversible consequences including sterility is involved, the need to ensure that a genuine and informed consent has been given cannot be overstressed. Although the transsexual may well be psychologically healthy, the fact that the specific disorder, which is the occasion for the procedure, causes an obsessive desire that the procedure be undertaken must create very real difficulties in arriving at a conclusion that the giving of consent to the procedure was the result of a genuine and informed decision on the part of the patient.

## Legal position of the transsexual

In the case of a transsexual who has not undergone surgical reassignment but who lives in the role of the opposite sex, either independently or as part of the early phase of treatment, certain conclusions can be reached with confidence. There is no prohibition against assuming the role and attire of the opposite sex unless it were done as part of a scheme to obtain a pecuniary advantage by deception. It is no offence to appear in a public place in the attire of the opposite sex.[9] A purported marriage between a male and a male-to-female transsexual before reassignment surgery would be held to be no marriage at all on the same basis as purported marriages between homosexuals have been held to be incompetent in the United States[10] and in Canada.[11]

Sexual activities between a male and a male-to-female transsexual before the reassignment surgery would constitute the offence of gross indecency between male persons.[12] In some jurisdictions that offence is only committed where one of the parties to the act is under a specified age.[13]

The position of the transsexual after surgical reassignment is not at all clear. The very few decisions which have dealt with what were admittedly cases of transsexualism have arisen in two contexts. One class of case has arisen where a surgically reassigned transsexual seeks an amendment to the official birth records in order that a birth certificate can be obtained which specifies the new sex. The other class of case has arisen where the transsexual has gone through a ceremony of marriage after reassignment surgery.

It seems to be generally accepted that a reassigned transsexual will seek to have birth records altered so as to conform to the new gender identity, as a confirmation, or even as a vindication, of the new identity and to avoid problems and embarrassment which arise in relation to such matters as the sex shown on passports.

In a Scottish case decided in 1957, the Court refused to direct the alteration of the transsexual's entry in the birth records pursuant to a statutory power to correct erroneous entries, the grounds being that the power was only available to correct entries which were erroneous when made, and that the physiological changes in the person concerned (who had not been surgically reassigned) were insufficiently advanced to justify a correct entry in any event.[14] The Court, whilst expressing sympathy to the applicant, observed that

sympathetic considerations 'would not all point in one direction' because 'sympathy would also be required to be extended to the feelings of the wife and children.'

The experience of the United States in this area has been relatively limited, the reported decisions being few in number and
conflicting in their results.[15]

Under the Victorian law, the Government Statist is required to
register particulars of all births that happen in Victoria in a
particular statutory form which provides for the recording, *inter alia*,
of the sex of the child.[16] The Victorian Act contains the following
relevant provisions:

40. If the Government Statist is satisfied whether by declaration or
otherwise that any particular in any entry in a register is incorrect, he
may endorse a correction of such entry in the margin without any alteration to the original incorrect particular, and such correction shall be
signed by him and marked with the date upon which the correction is
made . . .

Provided that where the Government Statist is satisfied subsequent to
the registration of the birth of a child at the time of such registration the
sex of the child was mistaken and application is made to change the
particulars of the sex and of the christian name or other name of the child
to accord with the actual sex of the child the Government Statist may
alter the original particulars in the Register of Births with respect to the
sex and to such christian or other name, shall sign the correction, and
shall mark it with the date upon which the correction was made.

40A. Every certified copy of an entry corrected in accordance with the
proviso to section 40 shall omit the incorrect particulars and include the
correct particulars unless the Government Statist directs the certified copy
to be a copy of the original entry showing all marginal notations made
therein.

The general power of amendment of entries which are incorrect
would probably be held to be available only in the case where the
error occurred at the date when the birth was notified to the
Government Statist or at the time when the entry was originally
made. The manner of amendment is significant in that the original
incorrect particular stands and the correction is endorsed in the
margin of the register. A birth certificate which mirrored a corrected
entry in that form would not supply the particular demands of the
transsexual even if the correction could be made. But it is the
proviso which enables the Government Statist to alter the original
particulars in cases where 'at the time of such registration the sex
of the child was mistaken' which is of more interest, especially since
the next section enables the issue of a birth certificate which does
not disclose the fact of amendment on its face. The proviso to section

40 and the new section 40A were enacted in 1971 in order to deal with a case where the sex of a child had been mistaken at birth and, as a consequence, an incorrect birth entry had been made. Under the previous law, the entry could be corrected but the fact that a correction had been made would have had to appear in the entry and in any birth certificate which was issued. The provisions would not assist the transsexual to obtain a new birth certificate because they are only applicable in cases where the sex of a child was mistaken at the time of the registration. Whatever may be encompassed by the word 'mistaken' it is unlikely that a court in this country would hold that any mistake on anyone's part occurred at the time of the registration of the transsexual's birth.

In all other states and in the A.C.T., legislative provision is made for the correction of incorrect entries in registers of births. In N.S.W.,[17] Queensland,[18] Western Australia,[19] and Tasmania[20] power is given to correct an 'error of fact or of substance'. In South Australia[21] power is given to correct 'incorrect particulars', while in the A.C.T.[22] there is power to correct any 'error, mis-statement or omission'. It is very doubtful whether any of these provisions would authorize the alteration of the relevant entry in the register of births following surgical reassignment. A birth certificate issued in Queensland following the correction of an entry will normally not include the original particulars, but elsewhere it would appear that the certificate will show both the original and the altered particulars.

Throughout Australia a change of name effected by deed poll may be recorded by registration of a copy of the deed in the appropriate government office. In some parts of Australia power exists to record particulars of the change of name in the relevant entry in the register of births, but both the entry and any birth certificate would record the original and the altered name.[23]

The courts did not confront the legal problems which arise when a transsexual goes through a ceremony of marriage until very recently, at least not consciously. The courts administering the matrimonial law of course had met with cases of curable and incurable structural defects rendering a spouse incapable of sexual intercourse.

The Court's concern arose from the central significance of capacity to consummate as an essential ingredient to the validity of marriage:

> Without that power neither of the two principal ends of matrimony can be attained, namely a lawful indulgence of the passions to prevent licentiousness, and the procreation of children, according to the evident design of Divine Providence.[24]

The fundamental problem which arises in relation to such a marriage derives from the essential nature of marriage itself. This is clearly spelt out by statute in Australia: ' "Marriage" according to law in Australia is the union of a man and a woman to the exclusion of all others, voluntarily entered into for life.'[25] The question, therefore, is whether the courts will recognize a reassigned male-to-female transsexual as a 'woman' and a reassigned female-to-male transsexual as a 'man' for the purposes of this definition. There are two decisions in point, one English and one American.

The English case was *Corbett* v. *Corbett*.[26] The Petitioner sought a declaration of nullity in respect of the marriage he had entered into with the Respondent on the ground that the Respondent was a man. The Respondent was registered and brought up as a boy. He had been diagnosed as a transsexual and, after some psychiatric treatment and hormone treatment, had eventually undergone sex reassignment surgery. The trial Judge was Sir Roger Ormrod, a distinguished judge with qualifications in medicine as well as law. Evidence was received from nine members of the medical profession, the areas of specialty including obstetrics and gynaecology, psychiatry, pathology and the study of human metabolism. All medical witnesses agreed that there are at least four criteria for assessing the sexual condition of an individual, namely chromosomal factors, gonadal factors, genital factors and psychological factors. The Judge summarized his conclusions on the medical evidence as follows:

> The respondent has been shown to have XY chromosomes and, therefore, to be of male chromosomal sex; to have had testicles prior to the operation and, therefore, to be of male gonadal sex; to have had male external genitalia without any evidence of internal or external female sex organs and, therefore, to be of male genital sex; and psychologically to be a transsexual. The evidence does not establish that she is a case of Klinefelter's syndrome or some similar condition of partial testicular failure, although the possibility of some abnormality in androgenisation at puberty cannot be excluded. Socially, by which I mean the manner in which the respondent is living in the community, she is living as, and passing as, a woman, more or less successfully . . . It is common ground between all the medical witnesses that the biological sexual constitution of an individual is fixed at birth (at the latest), and cannot be changed, either by the natural development of organs of the opposite sex, or by medical or surgical means. The respondent's operation, therefore, cannot affect her true sex. The only cases where the term "change of sex" is appropriate are those in which a mistake as to sex is made at birth and subsequently revealed by further medical investigation.[27]

The Judge went on to point out that over a great many areas the law is indifferent to the sex of an individual, it being irrelevant to most of the relationships which give rise to contractual and tortious rights and obligations and to the greater part of the criminal law. But the sex of the parties is of essential importance in the relationship of marriage, being the union of one man and one woman. He then said:

> The question then becomes, what is meant by the word 'woman' in the context of a marriage, for I am not concerned to determine the 'legal sex' of the respondent at large. Having regard to the essentially heterosexual character of the relationship which is called marriage, the criteria must, in my judgement, be biological, for even the most extreme degree of transsexualism in a male or the most severe hormonal imbalance which can exist in a person with male chromosomes, male gonads and male genitalia cannot reproduce a person who is naturally capable of performing the essential role of a woman in marriage. In other words, the law should adopt in the first place, the first three of the doctors' criteria, i.e., the chromosomal, gonadal and genital tests, and if all three are congruent, determine the sex for the purpose of marriage accordingly, and ignore any operative intervention. The real difficulties, of course, will occur if these three criteria are not congruent. This question does not arise in the present case and I must not anticipate, but it would seem to me to follow from what I have said that the greater weight would probably be given to the genital criterion than to the other two. This problem and, in particular, the question of the effect of surgical operations in such cases of physical inter-sex, must be left until it comes for decision. My conclusion, therefore, is that the respondent is not a woman for the purposes of marriage but is a biological male and has been so since birth. It follows that the so-called marriage of September 10, 1963, is void.[28]

The American case is that of *M.T.* v. *J.T.* decided in 1976 by the Appellate Division of the Superior Court of New Jersey.[29] The Plaintiff (wife) and the Defendant (husband) were married but had separated and the Plaintiff sought an order for maintenance. The Defendant's answer to the claim was that the marriage was void because the Plaintiff was a male. The Plaintiff was a male-to-female transsexual who had undergone reassignment surgery before the marriage with the knowledge of the Defendant and at his expense. Evidence was given on the Plaintiff's behalf by her own physician who had a speciality in 'gender identity' and by two psychologists, both with special knowledge in sexual dysfunction. The Defendant called his adoptive father, who was a physician, as an expert witness. It appeared that, so far as the Plaintiff's own physician was aware, no one had tested her to find out what chromosomes she had. Each of the psychologists considered that a person of female psychic gender who underwent sex reassignment surgery should be characterized as a female. The Court declined to follow the decision in *Corbett* v. *Corbett* saying:

Against the backdrop of the evidence in the present record we must disagree with the conclusion reached in *Corbett* that for purposes of marriage sex is somehow irrevocably cast at the moment of birth, and that for adjudging the capacity to enter marriage, sex in its biological sense should be the exclusive standard.

Our departure from the *Corbett* thesis is not a matter of semantics. It stems from a fundamentally different understanding of what is meant by 'sex' for marital purposes. The English court apparently felt that sex and gender were disparate phenomena. In a given case there may, of course, be such a difference. A pre-operative transsexual is an example of that kind of disharmony, and most experts would be satisfied that the individual should be classified according to biological criteria. The evidence and authority which we have examined, however, show that a person's sex or sexuality embraces an individual's gender, that is, one's self-image, the deep psychological or emotional sense of sexual identity and character.

The English court believed, we feel incorrectly, that an anatomical change of genitalia in the case of a transsexual cannot 'affect her true sex.' Its conclusion was rooted in the premise that 'true sex' was required to be ascertained even for marital purposes by biological criteria. In the case of a transsexual following surgery, however, according to the expert testimony presented here, the dual tests of anatomy and gender are more significant. On this evidential demonstration, therefore, we are impelled to the conclusion that for marital purposes if the anatomical or genital features of a genuine transsexual are made to conform to the person's gender, psyche or psychological sex then identity by sex must be governed by the congruence of these standards.[30]

After reviewing some of the American cases already referred to the Court went on:

In this case the transsexual's gender and genitalia are no longer discordant; they have been harmonized through medical treatment. The Plaintiff has become physically and psychologically unified and fully capable of sexual activity consistent with her reconciled sexual attributes of gender and anatomy. Consequently, the Plaintiff should be considered a member of the female sex for marital purposes. It follows that such an individual would have the capacity to enter into a valid marriage relationship with a person of the opposite sex and did do so here. In so ruling we do no more than give legal effect to a *fait accompli*, based upon medical judgement and action which are irreversible. Such recognition will promote the individual's quest for inner peace and personal happiness, while in no way disserving any societal interest, principle of public order or precept of morality.[31]

The decision of the trial judge in favour of the validity of the marriage was accordingly upheld.

As far as the writer is aware, no Australian court has yet had to consider the issue which arose in those two cases. The nearest approach to the problem came in the Family Court decision of *Re Marriage of C and D* (*falsely called C*), which concerned a surgically corrected hermaphrodite, not a transsexual.[32] The Judge in that case was clearly impressed with the approach and reasoning in *Corbett* v. *Corbett* but the applicability of that decision in Australia did not fall for decision.

The chromosome test has certainly loomed large in almost all the cases referred to in this chapter. Except in the case of certain rare anomalies such as Klinefelter's syndrome and Turner's syndrome, the chromosome test seems to yield unambiguous results. It is perhaps from this lack of ambiguity that its decisiveness has tended to flow. That may or may not be justified.

It is appropriate briefly to formulate some conclusions. The legal status in Australia of post-reassignment transsexuals is not altogether clear, either for the purposes of contracting marriage or for other purposes including the criminal law. [The situation may soon alter pending a review of the legal status of transsexuals in Australia currently being undertaken by the Committee of Attorneys-General: Editors]

In the absence of legislation it seems likely that an Australian court faced with the question of the validity of a marriage contracted by a reassigned transsexual in the new role would conclude that the decision in *Corbett* v. *Corbett* should be followed. Further, if the question which Sir Roger Ormrod left open, namely the legal sex of such a transsexual for purposes other than marriage, arose for decision in Australia it seems likely, by extension of the reasoning in that case, that the court would conclude that the transsexual belonged to the pre-operative sex. There are several reasons why those conclusions seem likely and they are substantial, but they lie outside the scope of this chapter.

# 14    Results of Gender Reassignment

## Is it all worthwhile?

*William A. W. Walters, Trudy Kennedy and*
*Michael W. Ross*

The issue of follow-up of post-operative transsexuals is central to the whole issue of the appropriateness of gender reassignment surgery as a form of treatment for gender dysphoria. If, on follow-up, there has been found to be no improvement in the patient, then obviously surgery as a treatment has had little value. If, on the other hand, post-operative transsexuals appear to be improved on some index compared with transsexuals who have not been operated upon, then surgery would appear justified. A second point central to the argument about efficacy of treatment concerns the indices used to assess improvement, and here there is considerable disagreement. Some researchers are prepared to accept an improvement in mental health and happiness as reported by the patient after surgery, while others look for more independent measures, such as increased stability in relationships, work history, number of changes of address, and occupational status. However, this last set of measures makes an inferential leap from improved mental health to improved social and occupational functioning which is by no means certain.

There are certain other difficulties in follow-up studies. First, the results on follow-up depend on the patients initially selected: those teams carefully selecting patients will probably have better results than than those teams taking patients straight off the street. Second, particularly in the case of longer-term follow-up, many patients will be unable to be contacted and probably those who are most readily able to be contacted will be those who have had problems subsequent to surgery and who have remained in touch. Despite these difficulties, however, there have been a number of follow-up studies carried out.

The results of gender reassignment can be assessed in various ways ranging from the purely technical achievements of plastic surgery to the total adaptation of the transsexual to the desired sex-role in the community. The latter would include some measure of the degree of social integration, psychological stability and adequacy of sexual function.

Results can also be assessed after the elapse of varying periods of time following reassignment. Usually the closer to genital gender reassignment surgery the assessment is made the better the results, as patients have not had time for the novelty to wear off and frequently display an enthusiasm and optimism which subsides with the passage of time. Indeed, as the years pass, some reassigned transsexuals realize that they have imperfections compared with biological members of the sex to which they have been assigned and that reassignment has not necessarily brought them the improvement in life they had expected. This is especially likely to occur in people who had personality disorders before surgery was performed. Consequently, results of long-term follow-up (over five years) of reassigned transsexuals are not likely to be as good as results assessed within the first few years after genital surgery.

The selection of patients for reassignment is also a potent factor in influencing the results. In general, the stricter the selection the better the results. Factors that are usually taken into account before surgery is recommended for transsexuals include:

1. the psychological and emotional stability;
2. the effectiveness of adaptation to the desired sex-role;
3. the degree of social acceptance of the person in that role;
4. the equilibrium of the personality;
5. the nature of the physical characteristics.

If, during the two-year assessment, the transsexual has been psychologically stable, well adapted to the desired sex role and accepted readily in that role in society, with a well-integrated personality and secondary sexual characteristics that are not too difficult to alter, prospects for successful reassignment are good. On the other hand, when one or more of these factors are adverse, the chances of success are significantly reduced.

In what has come to be regarded as a study of major importance, Wålinder and Thuwe reported on the results of gender reassignment in thirteen male and eleven female transsexuals followed up for a median of 5.5 and 7.5 years respectively.[1] This was a most detailed study and involved interviews, analysis of questionnaires, collection of data from social registers, and physical examination of patients with gender dysphoria treated in a Swedish clinic. During the interview, questions were asked about work, housing, sexuality, marriage, attitude of relatives and mental health. Extra information of sociological and psychological import, independent of the transsexual, was obtained from social registers. This included places of residence, changes in civil state, social security benefits, alcohol excess, convictions for crime, certification of sickness, and disability pensions. In addition, careful assessment of physical results and their harmonization with the reassigned sex role was made. The transsexual's own opinion of the results as well as the opinion of the investigators were taken into account before a final conclusion was reached about the success of reassignment. Taking the male and female transsexuals together, the outcome was favourable in 80 per cent of the cases, with female transsexuals showing better results than male transsexuals. Although mental health improved generally, social adjustment only improved marginally. Occupation and housing situations improved for one-third of the males reassigned as females, but for only half of the females reassigned as males. In the group as a whole, no striking change in libido was demonstrated, but the rate of marriage after reassignment was higher than one might have expected.

Another important finding of this study was that when candidates for reassignment were immature or disordered in personality with poor interpersonal relationships before surgery, these aspects were unlikely to improve after reassignment.

Certain contraindications to gender reassignment have been recognized in several studies and should be taken into account when deciding upon management.

Among the most important of these are:

1.  the presence of psychosis;
2.  states of mental retardation or dementia;
3.  abuse of drugs, including alcohol;
4.  repeated criminal acts;
5.  lack of support from relatives and friends;
6.  inability to pass successfully as a member of the opposite sex.

Not all of these contraindications need be regarded as absolute, and they may be revised from time to time during the assessment of a candidate when social, psychological or physical conditions change.

Lothstein has drawn attention to the variable results of gender reassignment and attributes this situation to difficulties in diagnosis of true or primary transsexualism.[2] He points out that primary transsexuals (with a history of gender disturbance from childhood) generally have a better outcome from gender reassignment than secondary transsexuals (in whom the gender disturbance first appeared in late adolescence or early adulthood). Lothstein also draws attention to the need for stricter diagnostic criteria so that different sub-groups of transsexuals can be identified who might be more successfully treated by psychological or psychiatric means than by reassignment. A survey of the medical literature suggests that some patients who would otherwise have undergone gender reassignment surgery may adjust to a non-surgical solution through psychotherapy. Moreover, many misdiagnosed gender dysphoric patients need psychotherapy in the first instance, not surgery.

Indeed, gender reassignment surgery should only be considered for a highly selected group of diagnosed gender dysphoric patients. In our clinic in Melbourne, from 1976–82, we performed gender reassignment surgery in sixty-eight male-to-female transsexuals. Follow-up data were available for fifty-six of these interviewed over one to six years after surgery. Twenty-two of these fifty-six patients completed a detailed questionnaire concerning all aspects of life after surgery and reported for physical examination by a surgeon in the clinic. Detailed reference is made to these results in chapter 5. As with other studies reported from other clinics around the world, approximately 80 per cent of our patients reported a good or satisfactory outcome after surgery, despite the fact that the vagina was deemed of inadequate dimensions in 35 per cent of them. While this follow-up of patients has not been long enough in our opinion, it reflects the experience of clinics elsewhere in the world where intensive and prolonged assessment of patients is conducted before final genital surgery is performed. Nevertheless, we entirely agree with Lothstein that more attention should be paid to the assessment of the social and psychological status of reassigned transsexuals than has been the practice so far.

While some medical authorities express complete opposition to surgery for treatment of transsexualism, other workers in the field are of the opinion that surgery is still the best means of coping with a select group of transsexuals. Moreover, the latter group hold the view that one can increase the likelihood of a favourable outcome for the surgically reassigned transsexual by selecting candidates on the basis of their ego strengths and adjustment during the pre-surgery period while living in their new gender role.

Hunt and Hampson followed up results of reassignment in seventeen male transsexuals an average of 8.2 years after surgery.[3] No changes in the levels of psychopathology and only modest gains overall in economic functioning and interpersonal relationships were found. Larger gains were made in sexual satisfaction and degree of acceptance by family members. None of the seventeen transsexuals regretted having had surgery.

Recently Blanchard et al. studied fifty-five male-to-female transsexuals to examine the relationship between psychological and social adjustment on the one hand and progressive stages in gender orientation on the other.[4] The results clearly indicated that gender reorientation is associated with better psychological and social adjustment.

While Meyer and Reter at the Johns Hopkins Hospital, Baltimore, found that sex reassignment surgery conferred no objective advantage in terms of social rehabilitation, and that when the patients who had received gender reassignment surgery were compared with those who had not, there was little to chose between the two groups in terms of social adjustment,[5] a Swedish study conducted by Lundström revealed a different outcome.[6] In this latter study thirty-one gender dysphoric patients were followed up who were not accepted for gender reassignment. All were followed for at least three years from the first time that they were told that gender reassignment surgery was not indicated. Unlike Meyer and Reter's patients, the majority of the Swedish patients persisted in their wish to have gender reassignment surgery and showed a less harmonious life situation than those who had undergone such surgery. Lundström drew attention to those male transsexuals in whom the differential diagnosis borders on effeminate homosexuality (characterized by absence of aversion for their personal sexual characteristics plus great interest in homosexual contacts) and who appear to have good prospects of accepting their biological sex role and reaching a state of contentment without gender reassignment. He also found that patients with cross-dressing behaviour of compulsive type had great difficulty in reconciling themselves to their biological sex role.

As an alternative to gender reassignment surgery, various forms of psychotherapy have been tried;[7] it is difficult, however, to see how much success can be achieved by such therapy alone unless the patient is motivated to accept it.

Intensive psychoanalytic psychotherapy is aimed at stabilizing the transsexual in a non-operated state thereby, hopefully, allowing for adaptation to life without surgery, or at reversal of the cross-gender identity. This form of psychotherapy assumes that trans-sexual ideation is a rigid defence against anxiety-producing gender-role incompetence rather than a developmental disturbance in core gender identity. An attempt is made to reconcile psychological gender with anatomical sex or to make it possible to tolerate the anatomical sex.

A second type of psychotherapy, supportive psychotherapy, is designed to help the transsexual cope with alienation, social rejec-tion and other feelings concomitant with cross-gender identity. In these circumstances, the assumption is made that psychotherapy cannot usually reverse the condition.

The third method, group psychotherapy, aims to help the patient adjust to his or her gender identity without gender reassignment surgery. The emphasis is on informal group discussion which encourages patients to discover their patterns of adjustment to psychological stress.

Fourthly, behaviourally-oriented psychotherapy has as its goal modification of that gender role behaviour which leads to patient and observers labelling the patient as gender deviant, and change of those beliefs which the patient attributes to gender at birth. Here, the assumption is that transsexual ideation and behaviour represent a set of inappropriate responses learned in early childhood, coupled with failure to learn gender-appropriate behaviour from peers due to ensuing social isolation. The most successful programme of this sort to date, utilized in three cases, involved:

1. modification of effeminate gender-role behaviour in male transsexuals;
2. institution of modelling and behaviour rehearsal of gender-appropriate behaviour;
3. fantasy training using shaping, stimulus fading and reinforcement for heterosexual fantasies;
4. electrical aversions for homosexual fantasies.

None of the above psychological techniques has been shown to have any significant measure of success in even a moderate-sized group of transsexuals, and the disadvantages of such methods have not been determined. However, complications following treatment using intensive psychoanalytic psychotherapy have been reported. As anxiety often increases either at termination of psychotherapy or with a decision for surgery, psychological decompensation or suicide may occur. Indeed, Pauly states that transsexual patients have been pushed into psychosis by attempts to challenge and reverse the cross-gender identity.[8]

## *Technical results of genital surgery*

### Male-to-female transsexuals

In the Queen Victoria Medical Centre study, 35 per cent of patients expressed some dissatisfaction with the results of genital surgery.[9] By far the most common complaint was difficulty or pain with sexual intercourse. Physical examination revealed the main reason to be inadequate length of the vagina, thereby limiting penile penetration. Much less commonly, the width of the vagina was inadequate. Rarely were both vaginal length and width too small within the same patient. In some cases, complaints were made that the axis of the vagina was such that when the individual was lying supine the penile entry had to be vertical initially and then required a directional change towards the horizontal, making intercourse difficult. In such cases a minor surgical procedure will correct the situation.

When the amount of skin in the genital region is limited, particularly the amount of penile skin, the results of vaginal construction can be expected to be less than optimal after a first operation. Inevitably, a second operation is required to graft more skin (usually taken from the inner aspect of the thigh) into the vagina to enlarge its dimensions. If this should also fail to increase the capacity of the vagina, a third operation may be necessary. In our experience, a combined abdominal and vaginal operation to assist the placement of skin grafts may achieve the desired result. When such procedures fail, or when the amount of genital skin is deemed to be inadequate in the first place, an isolated segment of colon may be used to form the vagina.

Occasionally patients have been concerned about a pouting of the external urethral meatus and surrounding erectile tissue, which distends during sexual excitation causing a reduction in vaginal circumference at the vaginal opening. During intercourse, the protruding urethral opening may be traumatized, leading to pain, bleeding and subsequent discomfort when urine is passed. In this situation, a minor operation is required to reduce the amount of periurethral erectile tissue.

After initial genital surgery, some patients complain of disturbances of the urinary stream, such as a spraying or spurting of urine too far anteriorly. Sometimes stenosis (narrowing) of the urethral meatus results in a poor urinary stream, difficulty in emptying the bladder and, eventually, complete urinary obstruction. Urethral dilatation under general anaesthesia will usually effect a cure. Alternatively, a simple operation to reposition the external urinary meatus a little more posteriorly may be required in those cases where the urinary stream is diverted too far forwards.

After the first operation, the skin flaps created from scrotal skin to form the equivalent of labia minora and majora in the biological female may be too pendulous or asymmetrical. Should this cause concern to the patient, it is an easy matter to remove some of the excess skin under general anaesthesia.

An important and well recognized hazard of genital gender reassignment surgery is an artificial opening or fistula between the urinary tract (urethra or bladder) or rectum and the newly created vagina. Fistulae can occur as the result of trauma and reduced blood supply to tissues with or without infection. Usually a fistula is recognized at the time of or soon after surgery, but it may not be apparent until several weeks after the patient has left hospital. Such a complication may be induced by rough or faulty dilatation of the vagina so that the dilator perforates the vaginal wall to enter rectum or bladder. Fistulae can be repaired by various operative techniques, both abdominal and vaginal, the nature of which will be determined by circumstances in the individual case.

Narrowing and eventual closure of the vagina will inevitably occur if the vagina is not regularly dilated by use of a vaginal dilator or by sexual intercourse. Once shrinkage of the vagina has occurred, patency can only be restored by further plastic surgery.

Surprisingly, few patients in the Queen Victoria Medical Centre series failed to achieve orgasm after surgery. Such a complaint can usually be corrected by sexual counselling of the patient and her partner.

## Female-to-male transsexuals

The operations of bilateral mastectomy, total hysterectomy and bilateral salpingo-oophorectomy are standard procedures without the number of potential difficulties that may arise after genital surgery in the male transsexual.

On the other hand, phalloplasty (construction of a penis) is a complex multi-stage operative procedure with universally unsatisfactory results so far. Until surgical techniques improve, the female transsexual can be better served by peno-scrotal prostheses obtained from a manufacturer of plastic surgical appliances. In this way some relief of anxiety and embarrassment about physique and inability to function sexually as a male can be achieved.

## Conclusion

It is clear from the literature that successful results of gender reassignment surgery are a function of careful selection of patients initially to exclude any who are not likely to benefit from surgery. It would also appear that continuation of supportive psychotherapy after surgery, perhaps for the first year, is mandatory to ensure the best adjustment of patients to their new role in society.

# Appendix I
## Health Care Services for
## Transsexuals in Australia

The following information is provided by kind permission of the Victorian Transsexual Coalition, comprising members of the Transsexual Community with the assistance of the Queen Victoria Medical Centre, Commonwealth Rehabilitation Service, Department of Employment and Youth Affairs, Committee of Self-Help Groups, Social Biology Resources Centre, Lifeline, and supporting Churches.

Although the information mainly applies to the State of Victoria, Australia, it is included in this book as an example of what can be achieved by a transsexual self-help organization.

The Victorian Transsexual Coalition was established in 1979 as a result of the problems being faced by transsexuals and the helping services, in rehabilitation within the framework of inadequate laws and public misconceptions.

The aims of the organization are as follows:

1.  To research the range of needs of transsexuals and to encourage the development of appropriate services.
2.  To act as a clearing house for information and services pertaining to transsexuality.
3.  To draw attention to political, social and economic processes which discriminate against transsexuals.
4.  To foster and support the self-help group known as the Victorian Transsexual Association.

## The transsexual person: what to do, where to go

These few points are intended as a guide for transsexuals who have come to face their situation and seek professional assistance.

1.  You should obtain from a general practitioner doctor a referral to the co-ordinator of the Gender Identity Clinic and write or make an appointment accordingly.
2.  You should then put your request to join the Gender Reassignment Programme in writing and attach this to your referral.
3.  You should understand that the complexity of the problems facing you are such that miracles will not be performed overnight and certain conditions will be expected of you. The average time of assessment before surgery is two years, and while this seems a long time

it can be used profitably in helping you adapt to the desired sex role. So have patience, be as honest and open as you can and persevere—a wrong decision could be disastrous for you.

4. You should remember that the team is only willing to help those who help themselves—so be reliable, keep appointments and notify cancellations.

## Change of name by deed poll

This information is meant as a guide for residents of Victoria.

It is preferable that you arrange your change of name by deed poll through a solicitor so that all the legal ramifications are explained to you. A solicitor's fee should be in the order of $30 to $50, plus registration fees.

Alternatively you could obtain assistance from one of the Legal Aid offices.

If you choose to register your change of name by yourself, the completed deed poll should then be deposited at the office of:

The Registrar General,
233 William Street,
Melbourne, 3000.

Together with:
Registration Fee $9
Stamp Duty $10

NOTE: This does not alter your birth certificate records.

## Typical letter required for passports and similar formal identification

To whom it may concern

This is to certify that Ms. ——————————————————————— of
——————————————————————— has undergone the procedure of sex reassignment from male to female. The sex change operation was performed on ——————————————————————— at the
——————————————————————— Hospital in ———————————————.
For all intents and purposes Ms. ———————————————————————
should now be regarded as female.

Signed by Co-ordinator,
Gender Identity Clinic

# Guidelines for passports and travel documents

1. Australian passports issued to transsexuals may now show the sex of reassignment, subject to the production by the applicant of medical evidence of reassignment and on provision to the applicant of written advice that the sex indicated in the passport is for that purpose only.
2. You should arrange an interview with the Supervisor of the Passports Section of the Department of Immigration and Ethnic Affairs to discuss the application forms, birth certificates, doctors' certificates and so on, as required. Most departmental officers are briefed on the transsexual situation and are helpful in their duties.
3. Pre-operative transsexuals may obtain an alternative document called a 'Document of Identity' which does not specify sex. However, this document could raise the question of 'Why does this person not have a proper passport?', and in turn promote further investigation. This can depend largely on the immigration officer at the time.
4. There may be specific problems relating to transsexuals travelling overseas regardless of documentation. Certain countries regard the transsexuals in the category of 'undesirable alien' and may not permit entry, regardless of the passport being non-sex or new-sex identified.
5. It is *imperative* that any transsexual contemplating overseas travel makes sure that visas are secured in Australia, and also check where possible the climate of opinion in the country to be visited. The majority of major Western countries should pose no problem on entry other than the embarrassment caused by the sex contradiction.

NOTE: The issue of a passport in the new sex *does not* alter the legal sex status of the person, which remains in accordance with the birth certificate.

# Road traffic authority—driver licence policy

The sex of a licensee is currently indicated by the person's title, that is Mr/Mrs/Miss/Ms. This approach will probably be varied with the introduction of plastic licences and their endorsement with the character 'M' or 'F'.

At this stage there is no proposal to vary the current policy on the procedure for changing a licensee's gender identification on the driver licence. That policy requires a person desiring to change the gender identification to present a medical report stating that a course of treatment is being undertaken preparatory to surgical gender reassignment. On receipt of that report the person's gender identification is changed and the records annotated accordingly.

The Road Traffic Authority's policy in this matter is based on the fact that a driver licence is an authority to drive and that for police enforcement purposes the details of the licensee should reflect the actual physical appearance of the person.

The licence is not an identity document and, consequently, the details therein do not constitute a statement of the legal sex status of the holder.

# Useful addresses

## Spiritual supports

Metropolitan Community Church
(Ecumenical)
P.O. Box 441
SOUTH YARRA VIC. 3141

Christs Community Church
(Ecumenical)
*see above*

'Acceptance'
(Roman Catholic)
P.O. Box 276
CARLTON VIC. 3053.

Ecumenical
32 Lindsay Street
McKINNON VIC. 3204

St Peter's and St Paul's Church
(Roman Catholic)
Dorcas Street
SOUTH MELBOURNE VIC. 3205

## Speech therapy

Prince Henry's Hospital
St Kilda Road
MELBOURNE VIC. 3004

Royal Melbourne Hospital
Grattan Street
PARKVILLE VIC. 3052

Lincoln Institute for Health Services
625 Swanston Street
CARLTON VIC. 3053

## Personal growth courses

Augustine Church Centre for Drama & Growth
Minona Street
HAWTHORN VIC. 3122

## Passports

Australian

Department of Foreign Affairs
Passports Section
6th Floor
Commonwealth Centre
Cnr Spring and Latrobe Streets
MELBOURNE VIC. 3000

British

British Consulate-General
Passports Section
330 Collins Street
MELBOURNE VIC. 3000

## Clubs and self-help groups

Victorian Transsexual Coalition
G.P.O. Box 1991S
MELBOURNE VIC. 3001

Seahorse Club (Vic)
G.P.O. Box 2337V
MELBOURNE VIC. 3001

'The Hub'
Christ's Community Church
144 Adderley Street
WEST MELBOURNE VIC. 3003

Forum Social Club
P.O. Box 175
HAWTHORN VIC. 3122

# Useful directories

Women's Liberation Switchboard can provide additional information on cheap accommodation on request.

Youth Emergency Accommodation
Melbourne City Mission Youth Services
20 Princess Street
CARLTON VIC. 3053

Apartment and Boarding Houses of Melbourne and Inner Suburbs
Hanover Welfare Services
17 Brougham Street
NORTH MELBOURNE VIC. 3051

Travellers' Aid Society of Victoria
(Lists cheap hotels in city)
281 Bourke Street
MELBOURNE VIC. 3000

Commonwealth Rehabilitation Service
Northern Regional Rehabilitation Unit
Department of Social Security
Commonwealth Centre
Corner Spring and LaTrobe Streets
MELBOURNE VIC. 3000

# Appendix II
## Hormone Preparations Available in Australia

The following list of commonly used hormone preparations includes only those available in Australia. For any given preparation the dose in each tablet or injection is listed, along with a notation (NHS) if it is available under the National Health Scheme; otherwise the full cost of the preparation will be borne by the patient. The number of tablets or injections commonly prescribed per prescription is also included. The name of the pharmaceutical company manufacturing each hormone is listed in parenthesis adjacent to the trade name of the hormone.

## Female sex hormones

I Oestrogens:
1. Tablets
    (a) ethinyloestradiol
    
    | | | |
    |---|---|---|
    | Estigyn (Glaxo) | 0.01 mg | 100 NHS |
    | | 0.02 mg | 100 NHS |
    | | 0.05 mg | 100 NHS |
    | Primogyn C (Schering) | 0.02 mg | 100 NHS |

    (b) diethylstilboestrol
    
    | | | |
    |---|---|---|
    | Stilboestrol (Hamilton) | 0.5 mg | 100 NHS |
    | | 1 mg | 100 NHS |
    | | 5 mg | 100 NHS |
    | | 10 mg | 100 NHS |

    (c) oestradiol valerate
    
    | | | |
    |---|---|---|
    | Progynova (Schering) | 1 mg | 21 |
    | | 2 mg | 21 |

    (d) oestriol
    
    | | | |
    |---|---|---|
    | Ovestin (Organon) | 1 mg | 30, 90 |

    (e) oestrone
    
    | | | |
    |---|---|---|
    | Ogen (Abbott) | 0.625 mg | 100 |
    | | 1.25 mg | 100 |
    | | 2.5 mg | 100 |

(f) conjugated equine oestrogens
    Premarin (Ayerst)        0.3 mg  100
                           0.625 mg  60
                           1.25 mg  60

(g) dienoestrol
    Dienoestrol (Hamilton)     0.1 mg  100
                           0.3 mg  100
                           1 mg  100
                           5 mg  100
                           10 mg  100

2. Injections or Implants
  (a) Oestradiol valerate
      Primogyn Depot (Schering)    10 mg/ml vials   3 NHS
      Oestradiol Implants (Organon)  20 mg pellets
                                 50 mg pellets
                             100 mg pellets

II Progestins:
  1. Tablets
    (a) medroxyprogesterone acetate
        Provera (Upjohn)        2.5 mg   25
                          10 mg   100

    (b) dydrogesterone
        Duphaston (Ethnor)      10 mg  50

III Combined Oestrogen-Progestin Preparations (Oral Contraceptives):
A wide variety is available from pharmacists.

## Drugs for suppression of body hair growth

1. Tablets
  (a) Spironolactone
      Aldactone (Searle)     25 mg  100

  (b) Cyproterone acetate
      Only available in Australia on special application to the
      Commonwealth Department of Health.

## Male sex hormones

I Androgens:
  1. Tablets or capsules
    (a) Testosterone undecanoate
        Andriol (Organon)         40 mg capsules  60

(b) Methyltestosterone
Testomet (Protea)

| | | |
|---|---|---|
| | 5 mg | 25,100 |
| | 25 mg | 25,100 |
| | 50 mg | 100 |

2. Injections or implants
   (a) Sustanon 100 (Organon)

| | | |
|---|---|---|
| testosterone propionate | 20 mg | |
| testosterone phenylpropionate | 40 mg per ml amp. | 3 |
| testosterone isocaproate | 40 mg | |

   (b) Sustanon 250 (Organon)

| | | |
|---|---|---|
| testosterone propionate | 30 mg | |
| testosterone phenylpropionate | 60 mg per ml amp. | 3 |
| testosterone isocaproate | 60 mg | |
| testosterone decanoate | 100 mg | |

   (c) Testoviron (Schering)

| | | |
|---|---|---|
| testosterone propionate | 25 mg/1 ml | 3 |
| testosterone propionate | 50 mg/1 ml | 3 |

   (d) Primoteston Depot (Schering)

| | | |
|---|---|---|
| testosterone enanthate | 100 mg/1 ml | 3 |
| testosterone enanthate | 250 mg/1 ml | 3 |

# References

## Chapter 1

1 Sörensen, T. and Hertoft, P., 'Sex modifying operations on transsexuals in Denmark in the period 1950–1977', *Acta Psychiatrica Scandinavica*, *61*, 1980, pp. 56–66.

2 Benjamin, H., *The Transsexual Phenomenon*, Julian Press, New York, 1966.

3 Bem, S. L., 'The measurement of psychological androgyny', *Journal of Consulting and Clinical Psychology*, *42*, 1974, pp. 155–62.

4 Ross, M. W., Rogers, L. J. and McCulloch, H. 'Stigma, sex and society: A new look at gender differentiation and sexual variation', *Journal of Homosexuality*, *3*, 1978, pp. 315–30.

5 Ross, M. W., Wålinder, J., Lundström, B. and Thuwe, I., 'Cross-cultural approaches to transsexualism: A comparison between Sweden and Australia', *Acta Psychiatrica Scandinavica*, *63*, 1981, pp. 75–82.

6 Bentler, P. M., 'A typology of transsexualism: Gender identity theory and data', *Archives of Sexual Behaviour*, *5*, 1976, pp. 567–84.

7 Lothstein, L. M., 'Psychodynamics and sociodynamics of gender-dysphoric states', *American Journal of Psychotherapy*, *23*, 1979, pp. 214–38.

8 Lothstein, L. M. and Levine, S. B., 'Expressive psychotherapy with gender-dysphoric patients', *Archives of General Psychiatry*, *38*, 1981, pp. 924–9.

9 Morgan, A. J., 'Psychotherapy for transsexual candidates screened out of surgery', *Archives of Sexual Behavior*, *7*, 1978, pp. 273–83.

## Chapter 3

1 Meyer-Bahlburg, H. F. L., 'Sex hormones and male homosexuality in comparative perspective', *Archives of Sexual Behavior*, *6*, 1977, pp. 297–325; Meyer-Bahlburg, H. F. L., 'Sex hormones and female homosexuality: A critical examination', *Archives of Sexual Behavior*, *8*, 1979, pp. 101–19; Meyer-Bahlburg, H. F. L., 'Hormones and psychosexual differentiation: Implications for the management of intersexuality, homosexuality, and transsexuality', *Clinics in Endocrinology and Metabolism*, *11*, 1982, pp. 681–701.

2 Dörner, G., *Hormones and Brain Differentiation*, Elsevier, Amsterdam, 1976.

3 Meyer-Bahlburg, 'Hormones and psychosexual differentiation'.

4    Erhardt, A. A., Evers, K. and Money, J., 'Influence of androgen on
      some aspects of sexually dimorphic behavior in women with the late-
      treated adrenogenital syndrome', *Johns Hopkins Medical Journal, 123,*
      1968, pp. 115–22.
5    Money, J. and Matthews, D., 'Prenatal exposure to virilizing
      progestins: An adult follow-up study of twelve women', *Archives of
      Sexual Behavior, 11,* 1982, pp. 73–83.
6    Van Look, P. F. A., Hunter, W. M., Corker, C. S. and Baird, D. T.,
      'Failure of positive feedback in normal men and subjects with
      testicular feminization', *Clinical Endocrinology, 7,* 1977, pp. 353–66;
      Aono, T., Miyake, A., Kinugasa, T., Kurachi, K. and Matsumoto,
      K., 'Absence of positive feedback of oestrogen on LH release in
      patients with testicular feminization syndrome', *Acta Endocrinologica,
      87,* 1978, pp. 259–69.
7    Imperato-McGinley, J., Peterson, R. E., Gautier, T. and Sturla, E.,
      'Androgens and the evolution of male gender identity among male
      pseudohermaphrodites with 5-α reductase deficiency', *New England
      Journal of Medicine, 300,* 1979, pp. 1233–7.
8    Meyer-Bahlburg, 'Hormones and psychosexual differentiation'.
9    Wålinder, J., 'Transvestism, definition and evidence in favor of
      occasional derivation from cerebral dysfunction', *International Journal of
      Neuropsychiatry, 1,* 1965, pp. 567–73.
10   Hoenig, J. and Kenna, J. C., 'EEG abnormalities and transsexual-
      ism', *British Journal of Psychiatry, 134,* 1979, pp. 293–300.
11   Alanko, A. and Achté, K. A., 'Transsexualism', *Psychiatria Fennica,*
      1971, pp. 343–58.
12   Ross, M. W., Wålinder, J., Lundström, B. and Thuwe, I., 'Cross-
      cultural approaches to transsexualism: A comparison between
      Sweden and Australia', *Acta Psychiatrica Scandinavica, 63,* 1981,
      pp. 75–82.
13   Biller, H. B., 'A note on father absence and masculine development
      in lower-class negro and white boys', *Child Development, 39,* 1968,
      pp. 1003–6.
14   Freund, K., Langevin, R., Zajac, Y., Steiner, B. and Zajac, A.,
      'Parent-child relations in transsexual and non-transsexual homosexual
      males', *British Journal of Psychiatry, 124,* 1974, pp. 22–3.
15   Halle, E., Schmidt, C. W. and Meyer, J. K., 'The role of
      grandmothers in transsexualism', *American Journal of Psychiatry, 137,*
      1980, pp. 497–8.
16   Buhrich, N. and McConaghy, N., 'Parental relationships during
      childhood in homosexuality, transvestism and transsexualism',
      *Australian and New Zealand Journal of Psychiatry, 12,* 1978, pp. 103–8.
17   Uddenberg, N., Wålinder, J. and Höjerback, T., 'Parental contact
      in male and female transsexuals', *Acta Psychiatrica Scandinavica, 60,*
      1979, pp. 113–20.
18   Green, R., 'Childhood cross-gender behavior and subsequent sexual
      preference', *American Journal of Psychiatry, 136,* 1979, pp. 106–8.
19   Hellman, R. E., Green, R., Gray, J. L. and Williams, K., 'Childhood
      sexual identity, childhood religiosity, and 'homophobia' as influences

in the development of transsexualism, homosexuality, and heterosexuality', *Archives of General Psychiatry*, *38*, 1981, pp. 910–15.

20 Lothstein, L. M. and Levine, S. B., 'Expressive psychotherapy with gender dysphoric patients', *Archives of General Psychiatry*, *38*, 1981, pp. 924–9.

21 Lebovitz, P. S., 'Feminine behavior in boys: Aspects of its outcome', *American Journal of Psychiatry*, *128*, 1972, pp. 103–9.

22 Green, R., *Gender Identity Conflict in Children and Adults*, Basic Books, New York, 1974.

23 Stoller R., *Sex and Gender: On the Development of Masculinity and Femininity*, Science House, New York, 1968.

24 Lothstein, L. M., 'Psychodynamics and sociodynamics of gender dysphoric states', *American Journal of Psychotherapy*, *33*, 1979, pp. 214–38.

25 Levine, S. B., 'Letter to the editor', *Archives of Sexual Behavior*, *13*, 1984, pp. 287–9.

26 Morgan, A. J., 'Psychotherapy for transsexual candidates screened out of surgery', *Archives of Sexual Behavior*, *7*, 1978, pp. 273–83.

27 Prince, V., *Understanding Cross-Dressing*, Chevelier Publications, Los Angeles, 1976.

28 Steiner, B. W., Satterberg, J. A. and Muir, C. F., 'Flight into feminity: The male menopause?', *Canadian Psychiatric Association Journal*, *23*, 1978, pp. 405–10.

29 Lothstein, L. M., 'The ageing gender dysphoria (transsexual) patient', *Archives of Sexual Behavior*, *8*, 1979, pp. 431–44.

30 Wålinder, J., Lundström, B. and Thuwe, I., 'Prognostic factors in the assessment of male transsexuals for sex reassignment', *British Journal of Psychiatry*, *132*, pp. 16–20.

31 Ross, M. W., Rogers, L. J. and McCulloch, H., 'Stigma, sex and society: A new look at gender differentiation and sexual variation', *Journal of Homosexuality*, *3*, 1978, pp. 315–30.

32 Lothstein, 'Psychodynamics and sociodynamics of gender dysphoric states', *American Journal of Psychotherapy*, *33*, 1979, pp. 214–38.

33 Bentler, P. M., 'A typology of transsexualism: Gender identity theory and data', *Archives of Sexual Behavior*, *5*, 1976, pp. 567–84.

34 McCauley, E. A. and Erhardt, A. A., 'Role expectations and definitions: A comparison of female transsexuals and lesbians', *Journal of Homosexuality*, *3*, 1977, pp. 137–47.

35 Ross *et al.*, 'Cross-cultural approaches to transsexualism'.

36 Hoenig, J. and Kenna, J. C., 'Epidemiological aspects of transsexualism', *Psychiatrica Clinica*, *6*, 1973, pp. 65–80.

## Chapter 4

1 Hore, B. D., Nicolle, F. V. and Calnan, J. S., 'Male transsexualism in England: Sixteen cases with surgical intervention', *Archives of Sexual Behavior*, *4*, *1*, 1975, pp. 81–9.

2 Green, R., 'The significance of feminine behavior in boys', *Journal of*

*Child Psychology and Psychiatry, 16,* 1975, pp. 341–4; Rekers, G. A., 'Atypical gender development and psychosocial adjustment', *Journal of Applied Behavior Analysis, 10,* 1977, pp. 559–71.

3   Ross, M. W., Wålinder, J., Lundström, B. and Thuwe, I., 'Cross-cultural approaches to transsexualism: A comparison between Sweden and Australia', *Acta Psychiatrica Scandinavica, 63,* 1981, pp. 75–82.

4   Zuger, B., 'Effeminate behavior present in boys from early childhood', *The Journal of Pediatrics, 69, 6,* 1966, pp. 1098–1107.

5   Pauly, I. B., 'Female transsexualism: Part 1', *Archives of Sexual Behavior, 3, 6,* 1974, pp. 487–507.

6   Green, R., 'One hundred and ten feminine and masculine boys: Behavioral contrasts and demographic similarities', *Archives of Sexual Behavior, 5, 5,* 1976, pp. 425–46.

7   Green, R., Williams, K. and Goodman, M., 'Ninety-nine "tomboys" and "non-tomboys": Behavioral contrasts and demographic similarities', *Archives of Sexual Behavior, 11, 3,* 1982, pp. 247–66.

8   Rekers, G. A., Crandell, B. F., Rosen, A. C., and Bentler, P. M., 'Genetic and physical studies of male children with psychological gender disturbances', *Psychological Medicine, 9,* 1979, pp. 373–5.

9   Green, R., *Sexual Identity Conflict in Children and Adults,* Penguin, Baltimore, 1974.

10   Stoller, R. J., 'The transsexual experiment', *Sex and Gender,* Vol. II, Hogarth Press, London, 1975.

11   *American Psychiatric Association Diagnostic and Statistical Manual of Mental Disorders* (3rd edition), 1980.

12   Stoller, 'The transsexual experiment'.

13   Hore *et al.,* op. cit.

14   Stoller, 'The transsexual experiment'.

15   Stoller, R. J., 'Etiological factors in female transsexualism: A first approximation', *Archives of Sexual Behavior, 2,* 1979, pp. 47–64.

16   Zucker, K. J., 'Childhood gender disturbance: Diagnostic issues', *Journal of the American Academy of Child Psychiatry, 21,* 1982, pp. 274–80.

17   Freund, K., Langevin, R., Zajac, Y., Steiner, B. and Zajac, A., 'Parent-child relations in transsexual and non-transsexual homosexual males', *British Journal of Psychiatry, 124,* 1974, pp. 22–3.

18   Buhrich, N. and McConaghy, N., 'Parental relationships during childhood in homosexuality, transvestism, and transsexualism', *Australian and New Zealand Journal of Psychiatry, 12,* 1978, pp. 103–8.

19   Pauly, op. cit.

20   Green, *Sexual Identity Conflict in Children and Adults.*

21   Rekers, G. A., Mead, S. L., Rosen, A. C. and Brigham, S. L., 'Family correlates of male childhood gender disturbance', *Journal of Genetic Psychology, 142,* 1983, pp. 31–42.

22   Stoller, 'The transsexual experiment', p. 219.

23   Zucker, op. cit.

24   Goldman, R. and Goldman, J., *Children's Sexual Thinking,* Routledge & Kegan Paul, London, 1982.

25   Ross, M. W., 'Societal relationships and gender roles in

homosexuals', *Journal of Sex Research*, *19*, 1983, pp. 273–88.
26  Newman, L. E., 'Treatment for the parents of feminine boys', *American Journal of Psychiatry*, *133*, 6, 1976, pp. 683–7.
27  Schapira, K., Davison, K. and Brierley, H., 'The assessment and management of transsexual problems', *British Journal of Hospital Medicine*, *22*, 1979, pp. 63–9.
28  Stoller, R. J., 'The transsexual boy: mothers' feminized phallus', *British Journal of Medical Psychology*, *43*, 1970, pp. 117–28.
29  Westfall, M. P., Schatzberg, A. F., Blumetti, A. B. and Birk, C. L., 'Effeminacy II: Variations with social context', *Archives of Sexual Behavior*, *4*, *1*, 1975, pp. 43–51.
30  Schatzberg, A. F., Westfall, M. P., Blumetti, A. B. and Birk, C. L., 'Effeminacy I: A quantitative rating scale', *Archives of Sexual Behavior*, *4*, *1*, 1975, pp. 31–41.
31  Bates, J. E., Skilbeck, N. W., Smith, K. V. R. and Bentler, P. M., 'Intervention with families of gender-disturbed boys', *American Journal of Orthopsychiatry*, *45*, *1*, 1975, pp. 150–7.
32  Rekers, 'Atypical gender development and psychosocial adjustment'.
33  Bates, J. E., Bentler, P. M. and Thompson, S. K., 'Measurement of deviant gender development in boys', *Child Development*, *44*, 1973, pp. 591–8.
34  Rosen, A. C., Rekers, G. A. and Rogers Friar, L., 'Theoretical and diagnostic issues in child gender disturbances', *Journal of Sex Research*, *13*, 2, 1977, pp. 89–103.
35  Zucker, op. cit.
36  Zuger, 'Effeminate behavior present in boys from early childhood'.
37  Goldman and Goldman, op. cit.
38  Thompson, S. K. and Bentler, P. M. 'A developmental study of gender constancy and parent preference', *Archives of Sexual Behavior*, *2*, *4*, pp. 379–85.
39  Green, *Sexual Identity Conflict in Children and Adults*; Stoller, 'The transsexual experiment'; Zucker, 'Childhood gender disturbance'.
40  Winkler, R. C., 'What types of sex-role behavior should behavior modifiers promote?', *Journal of Applied Behavior Analysis*, *10*, *3*, 1977, pp. 549–52.
41  Rekers, G. A. and Lovaas, O. I., 'Behavioral treatment of deviant sex-role behaviors in a male child', *Journal of Applied Behavior Analysis*, *7*, *2*, 1974, pp. 173–90.
42  Person, E. and Ovesey, L., 'The transsexual syndrome in males; I. Primary transsexualism', *American Journal of Psychotherapy*, *28*, *1*, 1974, pp. 4–20.
43  Ross *et al.*, 'Cross-cultural approaches to transsexualism'.
44  Zuger, B., 'Effeminate behavior present in boys from childhood: Ten additional years of follow-up', *Comprehensive Psychiatry*, *19*, 1978, pp. 363–9.
45  Lebovitz, P. S., 'Feminine behavior in boys: Aspects of its outcome', *American Journal of Psychiatry*, *128*, *10*, 1972, pp. 1283–9.
46  Green, *et al.* 'Ninety-nine "tomboys" and "non-tomboys"'; Green, 'One hundred and ten feminine and masculine boys'.

47    Barlow, D. H., Reynolds, E. J. and Agras, W. S., 'Gender identity change in a transsexual', *Archives of General Psychiatry, 28,* 1973, pp. 569–76.
48    Davenport, C. W. and Harrison, S. I., 'Gender identity change in a female adolescent transsexual', *Archives of Sexual Behavior, 6, 4,* 1977, pp. 327–40.
49    Rekers, 'Atypical gender development and psychosocial adjustment'.
50    Bates, *et al.,* 'Intervention with families of gender disturbed boys'.
51    Rekers, 'Atypical gender development and psychosocial adjustment'; Winkler, 'What types of sex-role behavior should behavior modifiers promote?'
52    Rekers, 'Atypical gender development and psychosocial adjustment'; Bates, J. E., Skilbeck, N. W., Smith, K. V. R. and Bentler, P. M., 'Intervention with families of gender-disturbed boys', *American Journal of Orthopsychiatry, 45, 1,* 1975, pp. 150–7.
53    Green, *Sexual Identity Conflict in Children and Adults*; Stoller, 'The transsexual experiment'; Newman, 'Treatment for the parents of feminine boys'.
54    Rekers, 'Behavioral treatment of deviant sex-role behaviors in a male child'; Thompson, S. K. and Bentler, P. M., 'A developmental study of gender constancy and parent preference', *Archives of Sexual Behavior, 2,* 1973, pp. 379–85; Green, *Sexual Identity Conflict in Children and Adults*; Stoller, 'The transsexual experiment'; Zucker, Childhood gender disturbance'; Winkler, 'What types of sex-role behavior should behavior modifiers promote?'
55    Rosen, A. C., Rekers, G. A. and Brigham, S. L., 'Gender stereotype in gender-dysphoric young boys', *Psychological Reports, 51,* 1982, pp. 371–4.
56    Bates *et al.,* 'Intervention with families of gender-disturbed boys'.
57    Green, R., Newman, L. E. and Stoller, R. J., 'Treatment of boyhood "transsexualism"', *Archives of General Psychiatry, 26,* 1972, pp. 213–17.
58    Davenport, C. W. and Harrison, S. I., 'Gender identity change in a female adolescent transsexual', *Archives of Sexual Behavior, 6,* 1977, pp. 327–40.
59    Green, R., *Sexual Identity Conflict in Children and Adults,* Penguin, Baltimore, 1975.
60    Metcalf, S. and Williams, W., 'A case of male childhood transsexualism and its management', *Australian and New Zealand Journal of Psychiatry, 11,* 1977, pp. 53–9.
61    Pruett, K. D. and Dahl, K. E., 'Psychotherapy of gender identity conflict in young boys', *Journal of the American Academy of Child Psychiatry, 21, 1,* 1982, pp. 65–70.
62    Higham, E., 'Case management of the gender incongruity syndrome in childhood and adolescence', *Journal of Homosexuality, 2, 1,* pp. 49–58.

## Chapter 5

1    Stoller, R. J., *Sex and Gender,* Science House, New York, 1968.

2   Hoenig, J. and Kenna, J. A., 'The nosological position of
    transsexualism', *Archives of Sex Behavior*, *3*, 3, 1974, pp. 273–88.
3   Wålinder, J., *Transsexualism: A Study of Forty-three Cases*,
    Akademiforlaget, Goteborg, 1967.
4   Planansky, K. and Johnston, R., 'The incidence and relationship of
    homosexual and paranoid features in schizophrenia', *Journal of Mental
    Science*, *108*, 1962, pp. 604–15.
5   Gittleson, N. L. and Levine, S., 'Subjective ideas of sexual change in
    male schizophrenics', *British Journal of Psychiatry*, *112*, 1966,
    pp. 779–82.
6   Gittleson, N. L. and Dawson-Butterworth, K., 'Subjective ideas of
    sexual change in female schizophrenics', *British Journal of Psychiatry*,
    *113*, 1967, pp. 491–4.
7   Blacker, K. H. and Wong, N., 'Four cases of auto-castration', *Archives
    of General Psychiatry*, *8*, 1963, pp. 169–76.
8   Binder, H., 'Das Verlangen nach Geschlechtsumwandlung', *Zeitschrift
    fur die Gesamte Neurologie und Psychiatrie*, *143*, 1933, pp. 84–174.
9   Baastrupp, P. C., 'Transvestism—a psychiatric symptom', *Excerpta
    Medica*, *117*, 1966, pp. 109–10.
10  Pauly, I. B., 'Adult manifestations of female transsexualism', in R.
    Green and J. Money (eds), *Transsexualism and Sex Reassignment*, Johns
    Hopkins Press, Baltimore, 1969, pp. 59–87.
11  Person, E. and Ovesey, L., 'The transsexual syndrome in males: I.
    Primary Transsexualism', *American Journal of Psychotherapy*, *28*, 1974,
    pp. 4–20.
12  Person, E. and Ovesey, L. 'The transsexual syndrome in males: II.
    Secondary transsexualism', *American Journal of Psychotherapy*, *28*, 1974,
    pp. 174–93.
13  Meyer, J. K., 'Clinical variants among applicants for sex
    reassignment surgery', *Archives of Sexual Behavior*, *3*, 6, 1974,
    pp. 527–58.

## Chapter 6

1   Wålinder, J., 'Transsexualism: Definition, prevalence and sex
    distribution', *Acta Psychiatrica Scandinavica*, *203*, 1968, pp. 255–7.
2   Wålinder, J., 'Incidence and sex ratio of transsexualism in Sweden',
    *British Journal of Psychiatry*, *119*, 1971, pp. 195–6.
3   Hoenig, J. and Kenna, J. C., 'The prevalence of transsexualism in
    England and Wales', *British Journal of Psychiatry*, *124*, 1974,
    pp. 181–90.
4   Ibid.
5   Ross, M. W., Wålinder, J., Lundström, B. and Thuwe, I., 'Cross-
    cultural approaches to transsexualism: A comparison between
    Sweden and Australia', *Acta Psychiatrica Scandinavica*, *63*, 1981,
    pp. 75–82.
6   Heiman, E. M. and Le, C. V., 'Transsexualism in Vietnam', *Archives
    of Sexual Behavior*, *4*, 1975, pp. 89–95.

7    Chia, B. H., 'Male Transsexuals in Singapore', *Singapore Medical Journal*, 22, 1981, pp. 280–3; Tsoi, W. F., Kwok, L. P. and Foo, Y. L., 'Male transsexualism in Singapore: A description of 56 cases', *British Journal of Psychiatry*, 131, 177, pp. 405–9.

8    Wikan, U., 'Man becomes woman: Transsexualism in Oman as a key to gender roles', *Man*, 12, 1977, pp. 304–19.

9    Hellman, R. E., Green, R., Gray, J. L. and Williams, K., 'Childhood sexual identity, childhood religiosity, and "homophobia" as influences in the development of transsexualism, homosexuality and heterosexuality', *Archives of General Psychiatry*, 38, 1981, pp. 910–15.

10   Morgan, A. J., 'Psychotherapy for transsexual candidates screened out of surgery', *Archives of Sexual Behavior*, 7, 1978, pp. 273–83.

11   Roback, H., McKee, E., Vogelfanger, R. and Corney, R., 'Gender identification and the female impersonator', *Southern Medical Journal*, 68, 1975, pp. 459–62.

12   Wålinder, J., Lundström, B. and Thuwe, I., 'Prognostic factors in the assessment of male transsexuals for sex reassignment', *British Journal of Psychiatry*, 132, 1978, pp. 16–20.

13   Stafford-Clark, D., 'Essentials of the clinical approach', in I. Rosen, (ed.), *The Pathology and Treatment of Sexual Deviation*, Oxford University Press, London, 1964, pp. 57–86.

14   McKee, E. A., 'Transsexualism: a selective review', *Southern Medical Journal*, 69, 1976, pp. 185–7.

15   Meyer, J. K., 'Training and accreditation for the treatment of sexual disorders', *American Journal of Psychiatry*, 133, 1976, pp. 389–94.

16   Stoller, R. J., *Sex and Gender*, Science House, New York, 1968.

17   Hoenig, J. and Kenna, J. C., 'The nosological position of transsexualism', *Archives of Sexual Behavior*, 3, 1974, pp. 273–87.

18   Hoenig, J., Kenna, J. and Youd, A., 'Social and economic aspects of transsexualism', *British Journal of Psychiatry*, 117, 1970, pp. 163–72.

19   Wålinder, J., *Transsexualism: A Study of Forty-Three Cases*, Akademiforlaget, Goteborg, 1967.

20   Roback, H. B., Strassberg, D. S., McKee, E. and Cunningham, J., 'Self-concept and psychological adjustment differences between self-identified male transsexuals and male homosexuals', *Journal of Homosexuality*, 3, 1977, pp. 15–20.

21   Meerloo, J. A. M., 'Change of sex and collaboration with the psychosis', *American Journal of Psychiatry*, 124, 1967, pp. 263–4.

22   Stoller, *Sex and Gender*.

23   Pauly, I. B., 'Adult manifestations of male transsexualism', in R. Green and J. Money (eds), *Transsexualism and Sex Reassignment*, Johns Hopkins University Press, Baltimore, 1969, pp. 37–58.

24   Morris, J., *Conundrum*, Faber & Faber, London, 1974.

25   Derogatis, L. R., Meyer, J. K. and Vazquez, N., 'A psychological profile of the transsexual: I. The Male', *Journal of Nervous and Mental Disease*, 166, 1978, pp. 234–54.

26   Person, E. S. and Ovesey, L., 'The psychodynamics of male transsexualism', in R. C. Friedman, R. M. Richart and R. L. Vande

Wiele, (eds), *Sex Differences in Behavior*, Wiley, New York, 1974, pp. 315–25.
27  Althof, S. E., Lothstein, L. M., Jones, P. and Shen, J., 'An MMPI subscale (Gd): To identify males with gender identity conflicts', *Journal of Personality Assessment, 47*, 1983, pp. 42–9.
28  Burnard, D. H., unpublished manuscript.
29  Antill, J. K., Cunningham, J. D., Russell, G. and Thompson, N. L., 'An Australian Sex-Role Scale', *Australian Journal of Psychology, 33*, 1981, pp. 169–83.
30  Derogatis *et al.*, op. cit.
31  Finney, J. C., Brandsma, J. M., Tondow, M. and Lemaistre, G., 'A study of transsexuals seeking gender reassignment', *American Journal of Psychiatry, 132*, 1975, pp. 962–6.
32  Stoller, R. J., *Sex and Gender: The Transsexual Experience*, Vol. 2, Aronson, New York, 1975.
33  Lothstein, L. M., 'The aging gender dysphoria (transsexual) patient', *Archives of Sexual Behavior, 8*, 1979, pp. 431–44.
34  Stoller, *Sex and Gender*; Wålinder, J. and Thuwe, I., *A Social Psychiatric Follow-up Study of 24 Sex-Reassigned Transsexuals*, Akamiforleget, Goteborg, 1975.
35  Tsoi, *et al.*, 'Male transsexualism in Singapore: A description of 56 cases'.
36  Langevin, R., Paitich, D. and Steiner, B., 'The clinical profile of male transsexuals living as females vs. those living as males', *Archives of Sexual Behavior, 6*, 1977, pp. 143–54.
37  Burnard, op. cit.
38  Althof *et al.*, op. cit.
39  Sorenson, T. and Hertoft, P., 'Transsexualism as a nosological unity in men and women', *Acta Psychiatrica Scandinavica, 61*, 1980, pp. 135–51.
40  MacKenzie, K. R., 'Gender dysphoria syndrome: Towards standardized diagnostic criteria', *Archives of Sexual Behavior, 7*, 1978, pp. 251–62.
41  Lindgren, T. W. and Pauly, I. B., 'A body image scale for evaluating transsexuals', *Archives of Sexual Behavior, 4*, 1975, pp. 639–56.
42  Bem, S. L., 'The measurement of psychological androgyny', *Journal of Consulting and Clinical Psychology, 42*, 1974, pp. 155–62.
43  Freund, K., Nagler, E., Langevin, R., Zajac, A. and Steiner, B., 'Measuring feminine gender identity in homosexual males', *Archives of Sexual Behavior, 3*, 1974, pp. 249–60.
44  Althof *et al.*, op. cit.
45  Langevin *et al.*, op. cit.
46  Althof *et al.*, op. cit.
47  Sorensen and Hertoft, op. cit.; Burnard, op. cit.

## Chapter 7

1  Dörner, G., 'Hormone dependent differentiation, maturation and

function of the brain and sexual behavior', in R. Gemme and
C. C. Wheeler (eds), *Progress in Sexology*, Plenum Press, New York, 1977,
pp. 21–42; Dörner, G., *Hormones and Brain Differentiation*, Elsevier,
Amsterdam, 1976.

2   Dörner, 'Hormone dependent differentiation, maturation and function
of the brain and sexual behavior'; Kolodny, R. C., Masters, W. H.,
Hendryx, J. and Toro, J., 'Plasma testosterone and semen analysis in
male homosexuals'. *New England Journal of Medicine*, 285, 1971,
pp. 1170–4.

3   Dörner, 'Hormone dependent differentiation, maturation and function
of the brain and sexual behavior'; Dörner, *Hormones and Brain
Differentiation*.

4   Meyer-Bahlburg, H. F. L., 'Hormones and psychosexual
differentiation: Implications for the management of intersexuality,
homosexuality and transsexuality', *Clinics in Endocrinology and
Metabolism*, 11, 1982, pp. 681–701.

5   Eicher, W., Spoljar, M., Cleve, H., Murken, J. D., Eiermann, W.,
Richter, K. and Stengel-Rutkowske, S., 'H-Y antigen in
transsexuality', cited by H. F. L. Meyer-Bahlburg, in 'Hormones and
psychosexual differentiation: implications for the management of
intersexuality, homosexuality and transsexuality', *Clinics in
Endocrinology and Metabolism*, 11, 1982, pp. 681–701; Wachter, S. S.,
cited by H. F. L. Meyer-Bahlburg, in 'Hormones and psychosexual
differentiation: implications for the management of intersexuality,
homosexuality and transsexuality'.

6   Erhardt, A. A. and Meyer-Bahlburgh, H. F. L., 'Effects of prenatal
sex hormones on gender related behavior', *Science*, 211, 1981,
pp. 1312–18; Money, J. and Erhardt, A. A., *Man and Woman, Boy and
Girl*, Johns Hopkins University Press, Baltimore, 1972.

7   Green, R. and Money J., *Transsexualism and Sex Reassignment*, John
Hopkins, Baltimore, 1969; Hirschfeld, M., *Sexual Anomalies and
Perversions: physical and psychological development, diagnosis and treatment*,
Encyclopedic Press, London, 1952. Also appears in Haire, M. (ed.),
*A Summary of the works of the late Professor Doctor Magnus Hirschfeld*,
Encyclopedic Press; London, 1966; Meyer-Bahlburg, 'Hormones and
psychosexual differentiation: implications for the management of
intersexuality, homosexuality and transsexuality'.

8   Dörner, 'Hormone dependent differentiation, maturation and function
of the brain and sexual behavior'.

9   Steinbeck, A., Egri, S., Gillam, P., Lahoud, H. and Theile, H.,
unpublished data.

10  ibid.

11  ibid.

12  ibid.

13  Dörner, 'Hormone dependent differentiation, maturation and function
of the brain and sexual behaviour'.

14  Steinbeck *et al.*, unpublished data.

15  ibid.

16  ibid.

17   ibid.
18   ibid.
19   ibid.
20   ibid.

## Chapter 8

1   Bralley, R. C., Bull, G. L., Gore, G. H. and Edgerton, M. T., 'Evaluation of vocal pitch in male transsexuals', *Journal of Communication Disorders, 11,* 1978, pp. 443–9.
2   Bralley *et al.*,'Evaluation of vocal pitch in male transsexuals'; Yardley, K. M., 'Training in feminine skills in a male transsexual: A pre-operative procedure', *British Journal of Medical Psychology, 49,* 1976, pp. 329–39.
3   Kalra, M. A., 'Voice therapy with a transsexual', paper presented at the American Speech and Hearing Association Convention, Chicago, 1977.
4   Yardley, 'Training in feminine skills in a male transsexual: A pre-operative procedure'.
5   ibid.; Kalra, 'Voice therapy with a transsexual'.
6   Coleman, R. O., 'A comparison of the contributions of two voice quality characteristics to the perception of maleness and femaleness in the voice', *Journal of Speech and Hearing Research, 19,* 1976, pp. 168–80; Herbst, L., 'Die Umfänge der physiologischen Hauptsprechtonbereiche von Frauen und Männern', *Zeitschrift für Phonetik, 22,* 1969, pp. 426–38; Smith, P. M., 'Sex markers in speech', in K. R. Scherer and H. Giles (eds), *Social Markers in Speech,* Cambridge University Press, Melbourne, 1979.
7   Hollien, H. and Shipp, T., 'Speaking fundamental frequency and chronological age in males', *Journal of Speech and Hearing Research, 15,* 1972, pp. 155–9; Hollien, H. and Jackson, B., 'Normative data on the speaking fundamental frequency measurements of female voices from twenty to ninety years of age', unpublished manuscript, University of North Carolina, Greensboro, 1977; Zemlin, W. R., *Speech and Hearing Science: Anatomy and Physiology,* Prentice-Hall, Englewood Cliffs, New Jersey, 1968.
8   Hollien and Shipp, 'Speaking fundamental frequency and chronological age in males'; Honjo, I. and Isshiki, N., *Laryngoscopic and Vocal Characteristics of Aged Persons,* Kansai Medical University, Osaka, Japan, 1979; Kelley, A., 'Fundamental frequency measurements of female voices from twenty to ninety years of age'.
9   Yanagihara, N., Koike, Y. and Von Leden, H., 'Phonation and respiration — function study in normal subjects', *Folia Phoniatrica, 18,* 1966, pp. 323–40; Markel, N. N., Prebor, L. D. and Brandt, J. F., 'Biosocial factors in dyadic communication: sex and speaking intensity', *Journal of Personality and Social Psychology, 23, 1,* 1972, pp. 11–13.
10   Bennett, S. and Weinberg, B., 'Acoustic correlates of perceived

sexual identity in pre-adolescent children's voices', *Journal of the Acoustical Society of America, 66, 4*, 1979, pp. 989–1000; Fant, C. G. M., 'Vowel perception', in G. Fant and M. A. A. Tatham (eds), *Auditory Analysis and Perception of Speech*, Academic Press, London, 1975; Horii, Y., 'Vocal shimmer in sustained phonations', *Journal of Speech and Hearing Research, 23*, 1980, pp. 202–9; Rubin, D. L. and Nelson, M. W., 'Multiple determinants of a stigmatised speech style: women's language, powerless language, or everyone's language?', *Language and Speech, 26, 3*, 1983, pp. 273–90.

11    McConnell-Ginet, S., 'Intonation in a man's world', paper presented at the American Anthropological Association Annual Meeting, Mexico City, 1974; Pellowe, J. and Jones, V., 'On intonational variability in Tyneside speech', in P. Trudgill (ed.), *Sociolinguistic Patterns in British English*, University Park Press, Baltimore, 1978.

12    Pellowe and Jones, 'On intonational variability in Tyneside speech'.

13    Fischer, J. L., 'Social influences on the choice of a linguistic variant', *Word, 14*, 1958, pp. 47–56; Romaine, S. and Reid, E., 'Glottal sloppiness? A sociolinguistic view of urban speech in Scotland', *CITE Journal 'Teaching English', 9, 3*, 1976, pp. 12–16; Shuy, R. W., Wolfram, W. A. and Riley, W. K., 'Linguistic correlates of social stratification in Detroit speech', Project 6–1347. US Office of Education, Washington, DC., 1967; Trudgill, P., 'Sex, covert prestige, and linguistic change in the urban British English of Norwich', in B. Thorne and N. Henley (eds), *Language and Sex: Differences and Dominance*, Newbury House, Rowley, Massachusetts, 1975.

14    Smith, 'Sex markers in speech'.

15    Bailey, L. A. and Timms, L. A., 'More on women's and men's expletives', *Anthropological Linguistics, 18, 9*, 1976, pp. 438–49.

16    Hartman, M., 'A descriptive study of the language of men and women born in Maine around 1900 as it reflects the Lakoff hypotheses in "Language and Woman's place"', in B. Dubois and I. Crouch (eds), *The Sociology of the Languages of American Women*, Trinity University Press, San Antonio, Texas, 1976.

17    Swacker, M., 'The sex of the speaker as a sociolinguistic variable', in Thorne and Henley (eds), *Language and sex: Difference and Dominance*.

18    Hartman, M., 'A descriptive study of the languages of men and women'.

19    Aries, E. J. and Johnson, F. L., 'Close friendship in adulthood: conversational content between same-sex friends', *Sex Roles, 9, 12*, 1983, pp. 1183–96; Landis, M. H. and Burtt, H. E., 'A study of conversations', *Journal of Comparative Psychology, 4*, 1924, pp. 81–9; Landis, C., 'National differences in conversation', *Journal of Abnormal and Social Psychology, 21*, 1927, pp. 352–7; Moore, H. T., 'Further data concerning sex differences', *Journal of Abnormal and Social Psychology, 4*, 1922, pp. 81–9.

20    Barron, N. 'The production of grammatical cases', *Acta Sociologica, 14*, 1971, pp. 24–72; Haas, A., 'Male and female spoken language

differences: Stereotypes and evidence', *Psychological Bulletin*, *86*, *3*, 1979, pp. 616–26.

21  Eakins, B. W. and Eakins, C., 'Verbal turn-taking and exchanges in faculty dialogue', in Dubois and Crouch (eds), *The Sociology of the Languages of American Women*; 'The influence of female and male communication styles in conflict strategies: Problem areas', paper presented at the International Communication Association Convention, Berlin, West Germany, 1977; Zimmerman, D. H. and West, C. 'Sex roles, interruptions, and silences in conversation', in Thorne and Henley (eds), *Language and Sex: Difference and Dominance*.

22  Yardley, 'Training in feminine skills in a male transsexual: A preoperative procedure'.

23  Exline, R. V., Gray, D. and Schuette, D., 'Visual behavior in a dyad as affected by interview content and sex of respondent', *Journal of Personality and Social Psychology*, *1*, 1965, pp. 201–9; Mehrabian, A. and Friar, J. T., 'Encoding of attitude by a seated communicator via posture and position cues', *Journal of Consulting and Clinical Psychology*, *33*, 1969.

24  Haas, A., 'Male and female spoken language differences: Stereotypes and evidence', *Psychological Bulletin*, *86*, *3*, 1979, pp. 616–26; Smith, 'Sex markers in speech', Oates, J. M. and Dacakis, G., 'Speech pathology considerations in the management of transsexualism: A review', *British Journal of Disorders of Communication*, *18*, *3*, 1983, pp. 139–51.

25  Rubin and Nelson, 'Multiple determinants of a stigmatised speech style: women's language, powerless language, or everyone's language?'.

26  Jesperson, O., *Language*, Macmillan, New York, 1922; Lakoff, R., *Language and Woman's place*, Colophon/Harper & Row, New York, 1975.

27  Kramer, C., 'Perceptions of female and male speech', *Language and Speech*, *20*, *2*, 1977, pp. 151–61.

28  Edelsky, C., 'Subjective reactions to sex-linked language', *Journal of Social Psychology*, *99*, 1976a, pp. 97–104; Edelsky, C. 'The acquisition of communicative competence: Recognition of linguistic correlates of sex roles', *Merrill-Palmer Quarterly*, *22*, *1*, 1976b, pp. 47–59; Siegler, D. M. and Siegler, R. S., 'Stereotypes of males' and females' speech', *Psychological Reports*, *39*, 1976, pp. 167–70.

29  Baumann, M., 'Two features of "Women's Speech?"', in Dubois and Crouch (eds), *The Sociology of the Languages of American Women*.

30  Bralley; 'Evaluation of vocal pitch in male transsexuals', Donald, P. J., 'Voice change surgery in the transsexual', *Head and Neck Surgery*, *4*, *5*, 1982, pp. 433–7; Schapira, K., Davison, K. and Brierley, H., 'The assessment and management of transsexual problems', *British Journal of Hospital Medicine*, *12*, 1979, pp. 63–7.

31  Oates and Dacakis, 'Speech pathology considerations in the management of transsexualism: A review'.

32  Donald, P. J., 'Voice change surgery in the transsexual', *Head and Neck Surgery*, *4*, *5*, 1982, pp. 433–7.

33   Oates and Dacakis, 'Speech pathology considerations in the
     management of transsexualism: A review'.
34   Kalra, M. A., 'Voice therapy with a transsexual', paper presented at
     the American Speech and Hearing Association Convention, Chicago,
     1977; Bralley *et al.*, 'Evaluation of vocal pitch in male transsexuals'.
35   Yardley, 'Training in feminine skills in a male transsexual: A pre-
     operative procedure'.
36   Oates and Dacakis, 'Speech pathology considerations in the
     management of transsexualism: A review'.
37   Moncur, J. P. and Brackett, I. P., *Modifying Vocal Behaviour*, Harper
     and Row, London 1974; Boone, D. R., *The Voice and Voice Therapy*,
     2nd edn, Prentice-Hall, Englewood Cliffs, New Jersey, 1977;
     Aronson, A. E., *Clinical Voice Disorders: An Interdisciplinary Approach*,
     Brian C. Decker, New York, 1980; Bernthal, J. E. and Bankson,
     N. W., *Articulation Disorders*, Prentice-Hall, Englewood Cliffs, New
     Jersey, 1981; Warr-Leeper, G. A. (ed.), *The Language Management
     Library*: Vol. 1, *Therapy Procedures for the Treatment of Pragmatic Disorders*,
     Mariner Graphics and Communications, Ontario, 1982.
38   Yardley, 'Training in feminine skills in a male transsexual: A
     pre-operative procedure'; 'Voice therapy with a transsexual';
     'Evaluation of vocal pitch in male transsexuals'; Oates and Dacakis,
     'Speech pathology considerations in the management of
     transsexualism—empirical base and clinical approach', paper
     presented at the Second Australian and New Zealand Conference on
     Transsexualism, Flinders Medical Centre, Adelaide, 1983.

## Chapter 10

1   Abraham, F., 'Genitalumwandlung an zwei männlichen
    Transvestiten', *Zeitschrift für Sexualwissenschaft*, *18*, 1931, pp. 223–6.
2   Hamburger, C., Sturup, G. and Dahl-Iverson, E., 'Transvestism',
    *Journal of the American Medical Association*, *152*, 1953, pp. 391–6.
3   Benjamin, H., 'Nature and management of transsexualism, with a
    report of thirty-one operated cases', *Western Journal of Surgery,
    Obstetrics and Gynecology*, *72*, 1964, pp. 105–11.
4   Pauly, I. B., 'Male psychosexual inversion: Transsexualism', *Archives
    of General Psychiatry*, *13*, 1965, pp. 172–81.
5   Dupuytren, G., (1817), cited by A. Paunz, in 'Formation of an
    artificial vagina to remedy a congenital defect', *Zentralblatt für
    Gynäkologie*, *47*, 1923, pp. 883–8.
6   Heppner, E. (1872), cited by A. Paunz, in 'Formation of an artificial
    vagina to remedy a congenital defect'.
7   Abbe, R., 'New method of creating a vagina in a case of congenital
    absence', *Medical Record*, *54*, 1898, pp. 835–8.
8   McIndoe, A., 'Treatment of congenital absence and obliterative
    conditions of the vagina', *British Journal of Plastic Surgery*, *2*, 1950,
    pp. 254–67; Counseller, V. S. and Sluder Jr, F. S., 'Treatment for

congenital absence of the vagina', *Surgical Clinics of North America*, 24, 1944, pp. 938–42.

9   Baldwin, J. F., 'Formation of an artificial vagina by intestinal transplantation', *American Journal of Obstetrics and Gynecology*, 56, 1907, pp. 637–40.

10  Graves, W. P., 'Operative treatment of atresia of the vagina', *Boston Medical and Surgical Journal*, 163, 1910, pp. 753–5; Graves, W. P., 'Method of constructing an artificial vagina', *Surgical Clinics of North America*, I, 1921, pp. 611–14; Frank, R. T and Geist, S. H., 'Formation of an artificial vagina by a new plastic technic', *American Journal of Obstetrics and Gynecology*, 14, 1927, pp. 712–18.

11  Kanter, A. E., 'Congenital absence of the vagina: A simplified operation with the report of one case', *American Journal of Surgery*, 30, 1935, pp. 314–6; Wells, W. F., 'A plastic operation for the congenital absence of vagina', *American Journal of Surgery*, 29, 1935, pp. 253–5.

12  Gillies, H. D. and Millard, D. R., *The Principles and Art of Plastic Surgery*, Little Brown & Company, Boston, 1957, p. 387.

13  Jones, H. W., Schirmer, H. K. A. and Hoopes, J. E., 'A sex conversion operation for the males with transsexualism', *American Journal of Obstetrics and Gynecology*, 100, 1968, pp. 101–9.

14  Edgerton, M. T. and Bull, J., 'Surgical construction of the vagina and labia in male transsexuals', *Plastic and Reconstructive Surgery*, 46, 1970, pp. 529–39.

15  Laub, D. R. and Fisk, N., 'A rehabilitation program for gender dysphoria syndrome by surgical sex change', *Plastic and Reconstructive Surgery*, 53, 1974, pp. 388–403.

16  Fogh-Anderson, P., 'Transsexualism: An attempt at surgical management', *Scandinavian Journal of Plastic and Reconstructive Surgery*, 3, 1969, pp. 61–4.

17  Stuteville, O. H., Pandya, N. J. and Arieff, A. J., 'Surgical treatment of the male transsexual', in *Transactions of 5th International Congress of Plastic and Reconstructive Surgery*, Butterworths, Melbourne, 1971, pp. 1279–90.

# Chapter 11

The writer has not used any particular reference material in this chapter. However, the following books and articles may be of interest to the reader:

Dewhurst, C. J., Underhill, R., Goldman S. and Mansfield, M., 'The treatment of hirsutism with cyproterone acetate (an anti-androgen)', *British Journal of Obstetrics and Gynecology*, 84, Feb. 1977, pp. 119–23.

Green, R., *Sexual Identity Conflict*, Penguin, Baltimore, 1974.

Levine, C. O., 'Social work with transsexuals', *Social Casework*, March 1978.

Meyer, J. K. and Reter, D. J., 'Sex reassignment follow-up', *Archives of General Psychiatry*, 36, 1979.

Morgan, J., 'Transsexuals and the criminal justice system', *New Doctor/Legal Service Bulletin*, Feb./March, 1984.
Morris, J., *Conundrum*, Faber & Faber, London, 1974.

## Chapter 12

1   Chambers Twentieth Century Dictionary, W. & R. Chambers, Edinburgh, 1972, p. 448.
2   Waterhouse, E. S., *The Philosophical Approach to Religion*, Epworth, London, 1960, pp. 131–3.
3   Roy, D. J., *Canadian Medical Association Journal*, 125, 1981, p. 689.
4   Lothstein, L. M., 'Sex reassignment surgery: Historical, bioethical and theoretical issues', *American Journal of Psychiatry*, 139, 1982, pp. 417–26.
5   Bourke, V. J., 'Natural law', in J. Macquarie (ed.) *A Dictionary of Christian Ethics*, SCM Press Ltd, London, 1974, pp. 224–5.
6   Lothstein, 'Sex reassignment surgery'.
7   Yezzi, R., *Medical Ethics. Thinking about Unavoidable Questions*, Holt, Rinehart & Winston, New York, 1980, pp. 96–108.
8   Clark, J. F. J. and Guy, R. S., 'Abdominal Pregnancy', *American Journal of Obstetrics and Gynecology*, 96, 1966, pp. 511–20.
9   Hoenig, J., Kenna, J. C. and Yoad, A., 'A follow-up study of transsexualists: Social and economic aspects', *Psychiatric Clinic* (Basle), 3, 1971, pp. 85–100; Wålinder, J. and Thuwe, L., 'A social-psychiatric follow-up study of 24 sex-reassigned transsexuals', *Reports from the Psychiatric Research Centre*, St. Jorgen's Hospital, University of Goteborg, Sweden, 10, 1975.

## Chapter 13

1   Notes and Comments, 'Transsexuals in limbo: The search for a legal definition of sex', *31 Maryland Law Review*, 236, 1971.
2   Green, R. and Money, J. (eds), *Transsexualism and Sex Reassignment*, Johns Hopkins Press, Baltimore, 1969, Glossary, p. 480.
3   ibid., p. 487.
4   Blackstone, W., Commentaries on the Laws of England, Book IV, pp. 205–6.
5   'Transsexualism, sex reassignment surgery and the law', *56 Cornell Law Review*, 963, 1971, pp. 988–9; Sherwin, R. V., 'Legal aspects of male transsexualism', in Green and Money (eds), *Transsexualism and Sex Reassignment*, pp. 420–1; David, E. S., 'The law and transsexualism: A faltering response to a conceptual dilemma', *7 Conneticut Law Review*, 289, pp. 294–5; Belli, M. M., 'Transsexual surgery: A new tort?', *17 Journal of Family Law*, 487, pp. 493–4.
6   James, T. E., 'Legal issues of transsexualism in England', in Green and Money (eds), *Transsexualism and Sex Reassignment*, p. 240.
7   *Corbett* v. *Corbett* (orse, *Ashley*) [1970] 83, at p. 99.
8   Smith, D. K., op. cit., pp. 979–89.

9   *Hannaberry* v. *Crowther* [1945] VLR 158.
10  *Baker* v. *Nelson* [1971] 191 N.W. (2nd) 185; *James* v. *Hallahan* (1973) 501
    S.W. (2nd) 588; *Singer* v. *Hara* (1974) 522 P. (2nd) 1187.
11  *Re North and Matheson* (1974) 52 DLR (3rd) 280.
12  Crimes Act 1958 (Vic.), s. 50 (substituted by the Crimes [Sexual
    Offences] Act 1980 as from 1st March 1981); Crimes Act 1900
    (N.S.W.) s. 81A; Criminal Code (Qld.) s. 211; Criminal Law
    Consolidation Act 1935–1975 (S.A.) s. 58; Criminal Code (W.A.)
    s. 184; Criminal Code (Tas.) s. 123. By virtue of the Crimes
    Ordinance 1974 (A.C.T.) the Crimes Act 1900 (N.S.W.) is in force
    in the A.C.T.
13  Crimes Act 1958 (Vic.) s. 50; Crimes Act 1900 (N.S.W.) s. 81A.
14  *Re X* [1957] Scots LTR 61.
15  *Anonymous* v. *Weiner* (1966) 270 N.Y. Supp. (2nd) 319; *In re Anonymous*
    (1968) 293 N.Y. Supp. (2nd) 834; *Hartin* v. *Director of Bureau of
    Records and Statistics* (1973) 347 N.Y. Supp. (2nd) 515; *K.* v. *Health
    Division, Department of Human Resources* (1976) 552 P. (2nd) 840.
16  Registration of Births Deaths and Marriages Act 1958 (Vic.).
17  Registration of Births Deaths and Marriages Act 1972 (N.S.W.)
    s. 32.
18  Registration of Births Deaths and Marriages Act 1962–1967 (Qld.)
    s. 42.
19  Registration of Births Deaths and Marriages Act 1961 (W.A.) s. 65.
20  Registration of Births and Deaths Act 1895 (Tas.) s. 36.
21  Births Deaths and Marriages Registration Act 1966–1975 (S.A.)
    s. 68.
22  Registration of Births Deaths and Marriages Ordinance 1963
    (A.C.T.) s. 22.
23  Registration of Births Deaths and Marriages Act 1973 (N.S.W.)
    ss. 34 and 45; Registration of Births Deaths and Marriages
    Ordinance 1963 (A.C.T.) s. 22.
24  *D-e* v. *A-g (falsely calling herself D-e)* (1845) 1 Rob. Ecc. 280.
25  Marriage Act 1961 (Cth) s. 46.
26  *Corbett* v. *Corbett (orse. Ashley)* (1970) 83.
27  ibid., p. 104.
28  ibid., p. 106.
29  *M.T.* v. *J.T.* (1976) 355 A (2nd) 204.
30  ibid., p. 209.
31  ibid., p. 211.
32  *Re Marriage of C and D (falsely called C)* (1979) 28 ALR 524.

## Chapter 14

1   Wålinder J. and Thuwe, L., *A Social-Psychiatric Follow-up Study of 24
    Sex-Reassigned Transsexuals*, Akademiforlaget, Goteborg, 1975.
2   Lothstein, L. M., 'Sex reassignment surgery: Historical, bioethical and
    theoretical issues', *American Journal of Psychiatry*, *139*, 1982, pp. 417–26.
3   Hunt, D. D. and Hampson, J. L., 'Follow-up of 17 biologic male

transsexuals after sex-reassignment surgery', *American Journal of Psychiatry*, *137*, 1980, pp. 432–8.

4   Blanchard, R., Clemmensen, L. H. and Steiner, B. W., 'Gender reorientation and psychological adjustment in male-to-female transsexuals', *Archives of Sexual Behavior*, *12*, 1983, pp. 503–09.

5   Meyer, J. D. and Reter, D. J., 'Sex reassignment: Follow-up', *Archives of General Psychiatry*, *36*, 1979, pp. 1010–15.

6   Lundstrom, B., *Gender Dysphoria: A Social-Psychiatric Follow-up Study of 31 Cases not Accepted for Sex Reassignment*, Akademiforlaget, Goteborg, 1981.

7   Roberto, L. G., 'Issues in diagnosis and treatment of transsexualism', *Archives of Sexual Behavior*, *12*, 1983, pp. 445–73.

8   Pauly, I. B., 'The current status of the change of sex operation', *Journal of Nervous and Mental Diseases*, *147*, 1968, pp. 460–7.

9   Walters, W. A. W., unpublished material.

# Glossary

*adductor muscles*  Muscles along the inner aspect of the thigh that move it towards the midline.

*adrenocorticotrophic hormone (ACTH)*  A hormone produced in the pituitary gland that stimulates the adrenal glands to function.

*aetiology*  Science of the investigation of the cause or origin of vital phenomena of disease.

*affect*  Reflection of a mental state in terms of the emotions.

*amenorrhoea*  Absence of menstrual periods.

*anabolic steroid*  Member of the group of chemical substances termed steroids, that has the property of stimulating the building up of new living tissue from nutrient material.

*anamnesis*  Act of recalling to mind.

*androgen*  General name given to the group of chemical substances, both natural and artificial, which promote growth in, and maintain the functions of, the secondary sexual structures in the male, i.e. musculature, body hair, sexual activity, etc.

*androgen metabolites*  Chemical substances resulting from the body's handling of androgens.

*androgyny*  Physical and/or mental state in which characteristics of both male and female sexes are combined.

*androphilic*  A liking for men as opposed to women.

*apocrine glands*  Specialized sweat glands occurring only in hairy skin, that contain gland cells which lose part of their protoplasm when actively secreting.

*areola*  Brownish discolouration of skin immediately surrounding the nipples of the breasts.

*asexual*  Devoid of sexuality.

*A.S.-R.S.*  Australian Sex-Role Scale. A psychological test designed to assist in the diagnosis of gender identity disturbances.

*atrophic*  Pertaining to change characterized by the wasting away of a tissue or organ.

*autoerotic*  Self-stimulation of the body to satisfy sexual drive.

*bilateral mastectomy*  Surgical removal of both breasts.

*bilateral salpingo-oöphorectomy*  Surgical removal of both Fallopian tubes and both ovaries.

*biopsy*  Examination for diagnostic purposes of tissues surgically removed from the living body.

*bisexuality*  Sexually oriented towards both sexes.

*bromocriptine*  Chemical compound that suppresses the production of the hormone prolactin in the pituitary gland, thereby inhibiting lactation.

*Buck's fascia*  Deep connective tissue layer of the penis. Gurdon Buck, born in 1807, was a New York surgeon.

*bulbospongiosus muscle*  Muscle partially or completely encircling that part of the penis closest to the body.

*cannula*  Metal or glass tube used to effect a communication between a body cavity and the exterior.

*carcinoma*  Malignant tumour arising from epithelial cells.

*central nervous system*  Brain and spinal cord.

*chloasma*  Facial pigmentation occurring during pregnancy and during female sex hormone administration.

*chromosomes*  Microscopic, thread-like structures in the cell nucleus: they are comprised of DNA and carry the genetic information of the cell. There are forty-six chromosomes in each body cell and twenty-three in each reproductive cell.

*clitoris*  Female equivalent of the male penis.

*cognition*  Act or process of knowing, including both thinking and perceiving.

*cognitive dissonance theory*  Theory of incongruity in thinking and perceiving.

*colostomy*  A temporary or permanent artificial opening made through the abdominal wall into the colon or large bowel.

*colpocleisis*  Surgical operation to close the vagina.

*computerized tomography*  Production of an image by computer from X-rays of sections of the body.

*conceptus*  Developing products of conception, including the embryo or foetus, amniotic fluid, membranes and placenta.

*congenital adrenal hyperplasia*  Over-development of the adrenal glands, one of which is situated above each kidney, present at birth.

*coronary attack*  Obstruction to the blood supply of the heart muscle giving rise to symptoms and signs of heart attack. The heart muscle is supplied with blood from the coronary arteries.

*corpora cavernosa penis*  Two bodies of erectile tissue, mainly comprising distensible cavernous blood spaces, forming the main part of the body of the penis.

*corpus spongiosum*  Erectile tissue, mainly comprising distensible blood spaces, immediately surrounding the penile urethra (or urinary passage).

*cortisol*  Hormone produced in the adrenal glands situated immediately above the kidneys.

*cross-dressing*  Dressing in clothing appropriate to the opposite sex.

*cyproterone acetate*  Chemical compound that interferes with the action of the male hormone, testosterone. It is used to suppress body hair growth.

*dartos fascia*  Sheet of connective tissue covering the dartos muscle, which is a layer of smooth muscle fibres beneath the skin of the scrotum.

*decompensation*  Failure to meet the normal demands of bodily or mental function.

*dehydroepiandrosterone* (DHA)  Androgenic steroid normally found in the adrenal cortex only and present in excess in cases of overactivity of the adrenal glands.

*Denonvilliers' prerectal fascia* Sheet of connective tissue between the rectum behind and the prostate gland in front in the male. Charles Pierre Denonvilliers, born in 1808, was a Paris anatomist and surgeon.

*depilation* Removal of hair.

*dihydrotestosterone* Androgen with biological properties formed from its inactive precursor, testosterone, within androgen-responsive target cells by means of an intranuclear enzyme, 5 α-reductase.

*diurnal variation* Variation during the daytime; often cyclical variation.

*D.R.O.* Differential reinforcement of other behaviour: a reinforcement procedure in which any behaviour except one particular response is reinforced.

*dyshormonogenesis* Disturbance in the normal production of hormones.

*dysmorphophobia* Intensely held belief that part of the body is deformed, and must be altered at all costs.

*dyspareunia* Painful or difficult sexual intercourse.

*dystrophia adiposo-genitalis* Condition in which excessive amounts of fat are deposited in body tissues associated with under-development of the genital organs.

*egocentric* Self-centred.

*ejaculatory duct* Either of the paired ducts in the human male that deliver semen into the urethra.

*electroencephalogram (EEG)* Record of the electrical activity of the brain.

*electrolysis* Destruction of hair roots with an electric current.

*embolism* Sudden blocking of a blood vessel by blood clot or other subtances carried in the bloodstream.

*encopresis* Involuntary passage of faeces.

*endocrinology* Science of the endocrine glands and their secretions (hormones).

*enema* Introduction of fluid through the anal canal into the rectum, usually for the purpose of cleansing the rectum.

*epidemiology* Study of disease and disease attributes in defined populations.

*epilepsy* Any of various disorders marked by disturbed electrical rhythms of the central nervous system and typically manifested by fits or convulsions, associated with temporary loss of consciousness.

*ethinyl oestradiol* Synthetic female sex hormone of the oestrogen category.

*exogenous* Developed outside the body.

*Fallopian tubes* Two oviducts that carry fertilized or unfertilized eggs from the ovaries to the uterine cavity.

*fetishism* Condition manifested by the association of an object or part of the body with sexual gratification.

*foetus* In the human, this refers to the embryo from the beginning of the ninth week of intrauterine life until birth.

*Foley urinary catheter* Rubber urethral catheter containing a balloon near the eye of the catheter that can be inflated after insertion of the catheter into the urinary bladder, thereby retaining it in the bladder until such time as the balloon is deflated. Foley, born in 1981, was a Minnesota urologist.

*galactorrhoea* Spontaneous secretion and discharge of milk other than during the period of breast-feeding of an infant.

*gender dysphoria*  The condition of feeling ill at ease with one's gender identity in biological terms.

   *primary*  Arising in childhood without any other underlying psychological or physical cause.

   *secondary*  Arising in later life, usually in late adolescence or early adulthood and secondary to some underlying psychological or physical condition.

*gender identity*  One's sense of belonging to the male or female sex.

*generalization*  In psychological parlance, the occurrence of a learned response in the presence of stimulus conditions that differ from those that existed during the establishment of the response.

*genetic*  Pertaining to genes, the hereditary units carried on the chromosomes of every cell.

*genitalia*  Internal and external reproductive organs in both sexes.

*genitals*  Usually refers to the external genitalia only, as opposed to the internal genitalia.

*genotype*  Genetic constitution of an organism as opposed to the phenotype or external appearance of the organism.

*glabrous skin*  Hairless skin.

*goitre*  Swelling of the thyroid gland in the neck.

*gonad*  Reproductive gland whether this be in the female (ovary), in the male (testis), or undifferentiated as ovary or testis.

*gonadectomy*  Surgical removal of the gonads.

*gonadotrophin*  Any substance which regulates the function of the gonads. The pituitary gland produces two gonadotrophins, follicular-stimulating hormone (FSH) and luteinizing hormone (LH). The placenta during pregnancy also produces a gonadotrophin termed chorionic gonadotrophin. FSH controls ovarian follicular development in women and spermatogenesis in men. LH controls development of the corpus luteum of the ovary in women and male sex hormone production in men.

*gynaecomastia*  Condition in the male in which the mammary glands or breasts are over-developed, with or without secretion of milk.

*habitus*  General physical appearance characteristic of those with a constitutional tendency to some particular disease or disorder of bodily function.

*haemostasis*  Arrest of bleeding.

*hallucination*  Perception without objective reality.

*heterosexuality*  Sexual orientation to the opposite sex.

*hiatus hernia*  Upwards displacement of a portion of the stomach through the oesophageal opening in the diaphragm.

*hirsutism*  Excessive hairiness.

*histological*  Pertaining to the minute structure of tissues.

*histrionic*  Deliberately displayed emotion for effect.

*homophobic*  Disliking of males.

*homosexuality*  Sexual orientation to one's own sex.

*hormone*  Chemical substance formed in one part of the body and trans-mitted by the bloodstream to another part of the body where it has an effect on function of that part. Most hormones can also be synthesized in the laboratory and used for medical treatment of various diseases in which the body's production of one or more hormones is abnormal.

*hormonal parameters* Measures of hormone concentrations.

*H-Y antigen* Chemical substance attached to cell membranes in the male but not in the female.

*hypertension* High blood pressure.

*hypertrichosis* Excessive growth of hair on the body.

*hypogonadism* Diminished functioning of the gonads.

*hypoplasia* Reduction in the number of cells in an organ or tissue, often resulting in inadequate function.

*hypospadias* Condition where the urethra opens on to the under-surface of the penile shaft rather than at the tip of the penis.

*hypothalamus* Part of the brain above the pituitary gland.

*hysterectomy* Surgical removal of the uterus (womb).

*hysteria* Neurotic disorder, the symptoms of which may take almost any imaginable form, but have arisen usually by a process of suggestion or autosuggestion and involve some degree of dissociation of consciousness.

*iatrogenic* Pertaining to disorders directly attributable to medical or surgical procedures.

*ideation* Function of the brain which is concerned in the forming of ideas or concepts.

*impotence* Inability to perform the sexual act.

*inferior pubic ramus* Lowermost portion of the pubic bone in the pelvis.

*inguinal* In the region of the groin.

*intrapsychic* Arising or taking place within the mind.

*karyotype* Complement of chromosomes in a cell, usually arranged in an orderly array.

*keloid scars* Cellular overgrowth of fibrous tissue in a scar at the site of injury to or incision in the skin.

*Klinefelter's syndrome* Under-development of the testes in males with an extra X chromosome, or less commonly with an extra two X chromosomes or an extra Y chromosome. Failure of sperm production renders these people infertile, and in those with more than two X chromosomes mental deficiency is often a feature. Harry Fitch Klinefelter, born in 1912, was a Baltimore physician.

*labia majora* Outer lips of the vulva.

*labia minora* Inner lips of the vulva.

*lesbian* Female homosexual.

*levatores ani muscles* Main sheets of muscle forming the floor of the pelvis.

*libido* Sexual drive.

*linea nigra* Longitudinal line of pigmented skin on the anterior abdominal wall.

*Lloyd-Davies stirrups* Special foot and leg supports attached to the operating table to maintain the subject in the lithotomy position. Oswald Vaughan Lloyd-Davies, born in 1905, was a London surgeon.

*mammoplasty* Operation to reduce (reduction) or increase (augmentation) the size of the female breasts.

*masturbation* Production of an orgasm by manual or mechanical friction of the genital organs.

*meatus* Opening or passage.

*median raphe* Middle seam-like union between two anatomical structures.

*medroxyprogesterone acetate* Synthetic steroid compound with actions in the body similar to those caused by the female sex hormone progesterone.

*menarche* Beginning of menstruation.

*methyltestosterone* Synthetic androgen that is active when given by mouth.

*MMPI* Minnesota Multiphasic Personality Inventory. A psychological test that provides an extensive personality profile and indicates the degree of stability or instability in the organization of the subject's personality.

*morphogenesis* production and evolution of form.

*morphology* Branch of biology dealing with the structure and forms of living organisms.

*mosaic* Individual whose cells are genetically different although they have all arisen from the same original fertilized egg.

*myocardial infarction* Death of a part of the heart muscle usually resulting from coronary artery occlusion and causing the symptoms and signs described as a 'heart attack'.

*naevus* Birthmark.

*narcissism* Sexual attraction on the part of an individual to his or her own body.

*nausea* A feeling of wanting to vomit.

*neoplasia* Growth of new tissue; usually applied to tumours of benign or malignant type.

*neovagina* Newly created vagina.

*nodular hyperplasia* Localized overgrowth or increase in the number of cells in a tissue in discrete areas to form nodules.

*oedematus* Swollen.

*oestradiol* Naturally-occurring oestrogen produced in the ovary.

*oestrogen* Any substance having the physiological activity of oestradiol.

*oligospermia* Reduced numbers of sperm.

*orchidectomy* Surgical removal of the testis.

*paranoic* Characteristic of the mental disorder in which delusional ideas are manifested in the presence of a fairly well preserved personality.

*paraphilia* Sexual perversion.

*patency* Openness.

*pathology* Science of disease.

*pectoralis major* Large sheet of muscle extending from the midline across the front wall of the chest beneath the breast on each side.

*pedicle* Stem of a skin flap.

*pelvic peritoneum* Membrane overlying the organs within and the walls of the pelvis.

*penile coronal sulcus* Furrow between the glans and the shaft of the penis.

*perinatal*  Around the time of birth; before, during and after delivery of the foetus.

*perineum*  Area between the medial aspect of the thighs on either side, the scrotum or fourchette of the vulva anteriorly and the anal verge posteriorly.

*periosteum*  Dense membrane of connective tissue covering all but the joint surfaces of the bones.

*phallus*  Penis or male organ of copulation.

*phallic urethra*  Penile urethra.

*phalloplasty*  Plastic or reparative surgery of the penis.

*phenomenological*  Pertaining to the science of phenomena.

*pituitary*  Endocrine gland situated just below the central part of the brain, that has a controlling influence over most of the other endocrine glands.

*polycystic ovary syndrome*  Ovarian hormonal disturbance associated with development of many small cysts within the ovarian tissue.

*post-menopausal*  After menstruation ceases at the menopause.

*prefrontal leucotomy*  Operation for cutting nervous pathways in the anterior parts of the frontal lobes of the brain.

*premarin*  Naturally-occurring conjugated oestrogens; used to produce feminization.

*prenatal*  Before birth.

*prevalence*  Proportion of cases or manifestations in a defined population at a particular point or during a specified period of time.

*progesterone*  Hormone produced in the ovary after ovulation during the second half of the menstrual cycle.

*prognosis*  Considered opinion of the probable course and outcome of an illness based upon all the relevant facts available.

*prolactin*  Hormone produced by the pituitary gland that is responsible for the stimulation of milk production in the breasts.

*prosthesis*  Artificial part or appliance attached to the body to repair or replace that lost, damaged or diseased.

*pseudohermaphroditism*  Condition present at birth in which the gonads are testes or ovaries but the external genital organs are characteristic of those of the opposite sex or are a mixture of both female and male characters.

*psychodynamics*  Science dealing with mental powers and processes.

*psychopathology*  Study of the mechanisms of diseases of the mind.

*psychosurgery*  Treatment of mental disorders by operation on the brain.

*psychotherapy*  Treatment of mental disease by psychological methods.

*pubarche*  First appearance of pubic hair.

*puberty*  Epoch in a person's life during which the sex glands become active.

*pubic symphysis*  Junction between the two pubic bones to form the mid-portion of the anterior wall of the bony pelvis.

*pubic tubercle*  Small elevation of bone on the superior surface of the pubic bone.

*radical mastectomy*  Surgical removal of the breast, underlying pectoral muscles, and lymph nodes of the axilla (armpit).

*radionuclide scanning* Process in which selected radioactive atomic nuclei are introduced into the body, taken up by specific tissues, and their concentrations measured by an appropriate scanning device.

*reassignment* Procedure of gradual transformation from one gender role to the other: it usually takes several years and often culminates in surgical reassignment of the genital organs.

*renin* Enzyme secreted by specialized cells within the kidneys concerned with control of the blood pressure.

*response cost procedure* Procedure in which the eliciting of an undesired response results in the loss of some already obtained reward.

*rhinoplasty* Surgical correction of a deformity of the nose.

*Rorschach Test* Psychological projective test to identify and predict mental disorders of serious nature.

*salpingo-oöphorectomy* Surgical removal of ovaries and Fallopian tubes.

*schizophrenia* Mental disorder characterized by a special type of disintegration of the personality: incongruity between the content of thought and the corresponding emotion, lack of rational thought processes, and lack of contact with reality.

*seborrhoea* Excessive secretion of sebum (oil) from the skin.

*self-monitoring* Systematic recording, charting, and/or display of information relevant to behaviour, which is the target of self-directed change.

*semen* Secretions of the male genital tract containing sperm and other substances produced in the seminal vesicles and prostate gland.

*sex dimorphism* Condition of having characteristics or properties of both sexes.

*somatic delusions* False belief, not susceptible to argument or reason, involving part of the body; usually the result of a mental disorder.

*somatic intersexuality* Condition in which the bodily features of both sexes are present to varying degrees; the affected individual is neither one sex nor the other but somewhere in between.

*sphincter ani externus* External ring of muscle surrounding the anal canal near its opening.

*spider naevi* Localized dilatation of small vessels in the skin giving a spidery appearance.

*spironolactone* Chemical compound used to suppress hair growth and to treat retention of fluid in the body.

*split skin graft* Piece of skin of partial thickness removed surgically from one part of the body to repair a deficiency of skin elsewhere on the body.

*stenosis* Narrowing.

*stilboestrol* Synthetic substance with oestrogenic properties.

*stressors* Any potentially damaging strains, forces or agents, which stimulate physiological defence reactions and are capable of causing disease.

*symbiotic relationship* Intimate association between two organisms to their mutual advantage.

*syndrome* Distinct group of symptoms or signs forming a characteristic clinical picture or entity.

*symptomatology* Study of the symptoms of disease.

*target organ* Organ in which a hormone produces its effect.

*TAT* Thematic Apperception Test. A psychological projective test to identify and predict mental disorders of serious nature.

*temporal lobe* That part of the brain underlying the region of the temple, i.e. the flattened area on either side of the head above the zygomatic arch (cheekbone).

*testicle* Testis.

*testicular feminization* Condition in which a genetic male has the physical form of a female because his body is unable to respond to normal amounts of male sex hormone produced by his testes.

*testis* Sex gland of the male that produces sperm and male sex hormone.

*testosterone* Male sex hormone.

*thromboembolism* Clotting of blood within blood vessels, giving rise to pieces of blood clot becoming detached from the main clot and being carried by the bloodstream to lodge in another vessel, thereby causing partial or complete obstruction to blood supply of the part.

*thrombosis* Clotting of blood within vessels.

*thyroxine* One of the two hormones produced in the thyroid gland situated in the region of the voice-box in the neck.

*thyroxine-binding globulin* Protein circulating in the blood which takes up thyroxine secreted by the thyroid gland.

*token reinforcement* Procedure in which some evaluation or feedback is frequently given regarding behaviour in the form of ratings, points or chips, which are exchangable for some reward.

*transsexogenic* Engendering or creating transsexualism.

*transsexualism* Attempts of an individual to assume the physical characteristics of the opposite sex: the symptom complex of gender dysphoria.

*transvestism* Dressing in clothes of the opposite sex; often associated with sexual excitement.

*Trendelenburg tilt* Position for surgical operations in which the head of the operating table is tilted downwards, the patient being held in place by special supports attached to the table. Friedrich Trendelenburg, born in 1844, was a Leipzig surgeon.

*tri-iodothyronine* One of the two thyroid hormones produced in the thyroid gland situated in the region of the voice-box in the neck.

*Turner's syndrome* A disturbance of gonadal development associated with short stature, webbing of the neck, and infertility. Sometimes other abnormalities occur in affected individuals. The condition is usually due to only one X chromosome, resulting in the karyotype, 45XO. Henry Hubert Turner, born in 1892, was an Oklahoma physician.

*typology* Classification.

*umbilicus* Navel; the central depression in the anterior abdominal wall, where the umbilical cord was attached during foetal life.

*urethra* Urinary passage that conducts urine from the bladder to the exterior.

*urethral bulb* Part of the urethra occupying the bulb of the penis, the deep, posterior part of the penis.

*vagina*   Canal between the urinary passage in front and the anal passage behind in the female: at its upper end it is in continuity with the uterus (womb) and its lower end opens to the exterior at the vulva.

*vaginectomy*   Surgical removal of the vagina.

*virilization*   Change towards masculine features.

*vulva*   Female external genital organs.

*WAIS*   Wechsler Adult Intelligence Scale. A psychological test to measure intellectual capacity, specific cognitive and practical skills and formal thought disorders.

*waxing*   Application of wax in fluid form to hairy skin and its subsequent removal along with hairs after solidifying, thereby acting as a depilatory technique.

# Index